THE CARE OF THE MOTHER GRIEVING A BABY RELINQUISHED FOR ADOPTION

The Care of the Mother Grieving a Baby Relinquished for Adoption

ROSEMARY MANDER
Department of Nursing Studies
University of Edinburgh

Avebury
Aldershot · Brookfield USA · Hong Kong · Singapore · Sydney

Published by
Avebury
Ashgate Publishing Ltd
Gower House
Croft Road
Aldershot
Hants. GU11 3HR
England

Ashgate Publishing Company
Old Post Road
Brookfield
Vermont 05036
USA

British Library Cataloguing in Publication Data

Mander, Rosemary
Care of the Mother Grieving a Baby
Relinquished for Adoption
I. Title
362.734

ISBN 1 85628 597 9

Library of Congress Catalog Card Number: 94-72892

Printed and bound by Athenæum Press Ltd.,
Gateshead, Tyne & Wear.

Contents

Tables

Acknowledgements

I would like to express my gratitude to all those who helped and supported me while I was preparing this book. I am particularly grateful to the mothers and the midwives who shared their experiences and their emotions, their time and their tears. The Iolanthe Trust, administered by the Royal College of Midwives, generously provided the financial support to enable me to undertake the study on which this book is based. I would also like to thank my colleagues, past and present, for being around and for their interest; in particular, Linda Dick's secretarial support has proved to be just what was needed. Iain Abbot, whose presence sustains me, deserves more gratitude than I am able to express.

1 Introduction and background

The research project which is the focus of this book (Mander, 1992a) emerged as the result of the interaction of a number of factors, which I discuss below. Some of these factors serve to establish that, although the relinquishment of small babies may be less common (Triseliotis, 1989), the implications of relinquishment remain with us.

Adoption and power

The observation has been made that, throughout its long and varied history, adoption as an institution has reflected the preoccupations of the society in which it has occurred (Howe et al., 1992; Triseliotis, 1988). The themes which emerge from my recent study suggest that Triseliotis' observation still pertains.

A later observation by Triseliotis (1989) is more closely supported by the findings of my recent study. He noted that 'Adoption work by its nature is seductive because of the amount of power it transfers to its practitioners'. His examples included the decisions about who would get a child and what information would be given to whom. It is possible to reverse Triseliotis' argument by considering that as well as transferring power to certain individuals, adoption has the opposite effect on others. This effect on the relinquishing mother emerges in Chapters 7, 8, 9, 10, 11, 12, 13 and 15. An example of a pre-existing lack of power being associated with poverty is provided by Jaffe (1982) in his account of the large majority of adopted children in Israel who originated in the lowest socio-economic group.

The association between power and adoption, raised by Triseliotis and Jaffe, is clear in my recent study. What fails to emerge, possibly due to the location of the study, is any association between ethnic minority groups and adoption (Fitsell, 1989). In the same way, the implicit association between the pro-life lobby and adoption (Marck, 1994) appeared only tangentially in my recent study. Such associations may need to be borne in mind, particularly when utilising literature originating outside the UK.

Background - Occupational factors

Probably most important among the factors influencing my decision to undertake this study is my occupational experience. As a student midwife in the 1960s, I noticed many similarities between the midwife's care of two vulnerable mothers; these are the bereaved mother and the mother relinquishing her baby for adoption. Both mothers were subjected to the 'rugger pass' approach to care, which involved the baby being removed quickly and often unceremoniously from her presence (Mander, 1994) and no further mention being made of it. Practice as always derived from the current knowledge-base, which at that time leant towards the 'love at first sight' school of thought. So for each mother, we aimed to prevent her loving her baby, in the hope that we could prevent her being upset that she did not have the baby with her.

The dilemma provoked by this approach to care was brought home forcefully and tearfully to me as an experienced midwife. I was asked by a mother contemplating relinquishment whether she could, and should, see her newborn son. Her first question was not difficult. Some staff disapproved, but I knew he was her baby. The second question I found impossible to answer. My understanding was that if she saw her baby she would love him and be unable to part with him. I told her this, little realising that her love for him was already deep and long-lasting. I found myself unable to help her.

We are led to believe that the care of the mother losing her baby through death has moved forward since the days of the rugger pass approach (Mallinson, 1989). This may be attributable to the expansion in midwives' knowledge base about both mother-infant attachment and grief (See Chapter 2). The grief of the mother relinquishing her baby for adoption has, for a long time, been either ignored or unrecognised (See Chapter 6). Such a lack of recognition must inevitably have influenced the care provided by a range of formal and informal carers. My recent research project developed from my concern about whether the care of the mother relinquishing her baby for adoption has developed to a similar extent as that of the bereaved mother.

Background - Personal factors

An almost equally important factor in my decision to undertake this study is my personal experience of friends who have relinquished or been involved with adoption in other ways. I first became aware of the relinquishing mother early in my adolescence. Realisation that babies happen outside marriage dawned with whisperings about the older sister, Kath, of my 'best friend', Cass (all names are pseudonyms). The implications for the family were brought home powerfully to me. My friendship with Cass was frowned on by my mother and my elder sisters, who were at school with Kath. Although I was unclear exactly what Kath had done that was unspoken yet wrong, the feeling of wrongness and the need for censure prevailed. I became very much aware of the long-term reaction of the sisters' parents, which meant that Cass was always collected to go home and never stayed out late. Also, when her peers were regularly and steadily 'going out', Cass remained uninvolved. I was surprised by the way Kath looked when she came back from wherever she'd been sent to to have her baby. Instead of the miserable, guilt-ridden isolate which I'd been allowed to think she ought to be, I met the usual vivacious, pretty comedienne. My adolescent expectations of penitence were shattered, aggravating the question of what she had done that was so wrong and yet apparently went unpunished.

My confusion was compounded by the impact of relinquishment on my relationship with another childhood friend. Pauline, who lived in the terrace house opposite was the same age, and had shared many childish adventures with me. In our early teens, as I became more involved with church activities, we moved in different circles and saw less of each other. When I did see her at school on the last day of term, I realised that she was very pregnant. The next time, in the street, she ignored me and I couldn't understand why. Hindsight tells me that her experience of birth and relinquishment must have carried her into a far more mature world than we had shared and that she had become withdrawn and isolated from her peers.

My perception of adoption as an ideal arrangement came from an older friend Norma and her adoptive parents. Unfortunately, this idealised picture was shattered by Jennifer, a fellow member of the Guides. In a frighteningly hostile outburst she revealed that she had been adopted. Her obvious resentment derived from her perception of herself as a 'second class citizen' (Triseliotis, 1988), due to her debt of gratitude to her adoptive parents. Jennifer, to me, represented the powerlessness of the adopted person, whereas, to me and others, her mother and Norma's mother simply did not exist.

That my personal contact with adoption is not unique was supported by the observations of the midwives I interviewed, who often recounted similar discomforting personal experiences.

Words

Terminology in the context of adoption tends to be overlaid with value judgements. The terms that I use deserve some explanation. The most obvious example is describing the mother as 'relinquishing'. Howe et al. (1992) remind us that the general tendency to ignore the mother who gives birth to the child for adoption, is reflected in the absence of an English word to describe this mother. Terms such as 'unmarried mother' describe nothing more than her marital status, which is of questionable relevance in this context. Additionally, due to social and pharmacological developments, marriage and childbearing are no longer inextricably linked.

Another group of not uncommonly used terms, including birth-mother, natural mother and biological mother, reflect only one (quite physiological) aspect of this woman's motherhood. These words ignore her nurturing responsibility and emotional relationship with her baby during pregnancy. Probably more importantly, they conceal the ongoing emotional effects of her surrender of her child for adoption. Hence, I describe her as relinquishing and her parting from her child as relinquishment.

An assumption often made about the relinquishing mother is her age. There is a tendency to assume that she is young, resulting in the focus of concern and research being on teenagers and adolescent 'girls'. My recent study convinced me that this orientation ignores the situation of certain other mothers who relinquish (See Chapters 3 and 8).

As the title of this book indicates, the focus of this book is on the mother who relinquishes her baby. Some workers in this area believe that the 'birth-father' (Lindsay & Monserrat, 1989) deserves more attention (Breakwell, 1993). I have chosen to focus on the mother for two reasons. First, a mother is invariably involved in a pregnancy and birth, whereas the continuing involvement of a father is less certain. Second, as the mothers in this study told me, the father of the baby plays a relatively insignificant role in the relinquishment (See Chapter 7), even though their relationship is often ongoing.

As mentioned already, there are certain similarities between the care of the mother relinquishing her baby for adoption and the care of the mother who loses her baby through death. I contend in Chapter 6, that the experience of these two mothers has many similarities. In this book I use the term 'bereaved mother' to refer specifically to the mother who has lost her baby through death. In view of the similarities, I use the term 'grieving mother' to include mothers who need to grieve the loss of a baby through either death or relinquishment. Marck and her colleagues (1994) favour the term 'vulnerable mother' when considering women experiencing a range of uncertainties relating to pregnancy, including stillbirth and relinquishment, but I prefer to refer to this group of mothers as 'grieving mothers'.

In presenting this account of my research project, I write in the first person and avoid the third person or passive voice, which may be regarded as a convention in reporting research. This convention is neither necessary nor helpful in reporting a research project in which the researcher interacts so closely with the data (Laws, 1992).

While considering the terminology used in this book, the terms 'Care' and 'Carer' deserve explanation. I use these terms to describe the services and support provided by a range of people. Included are formal carers who are employed to provide this help, as well as less formal carers, such as family and friends, whose help derives from a continuing personal relationship.

One of these more formal carers is the midwife, who featured prominently in the original research. As not uncommonly happens, the mothers in this study frequently failed to recognise the midwife as such. In the data she is often referred to as the 'nurse'. For this reason midwives have been known to refer to themselves as 'invisible'. I have assumed from the context that it is the midwife who is providing care at certain times.

The invisibility of the midwife may be one of the characteristics which she shares with the relinquishing mother. In this book I aim to make the relinquishing mother and her situation more visible and comprehensible, in the hope that her care will be given the attention which it deserves.

2 Grieving, relinquishing and caring

My recent research project (Mander, 1992a) focussed on the care of the mother grieving the relinquishment of her baby for adoption. As with many research projects, my interest in this topic developed out of my own experience of caring for relinquishing mothers (Keen, 1975; See Chapter 1). The need for this project was further related both to the limited research examining the care of the relinquishing mother and to the huge changes which have been implemented in the care of the bereaved mother. Because the experience is common to both mothers it is necessary to consider the literature on grieving, before examining the research relating to the care of these two mothers.

Grieving

An unprecedented study on grieving followed a major fire in the Cocoanut Grove night club (Lindemann, 1944). The sample included traumatised survivors, victims' close relatives and people whose grief was unrelated to the fire. The work produced a description of both physical and psychological symptoms encountered by the bereaved. This prospective study of 101 people led Lindemann to describe first, normal, healthy and, second, abnormal, pathological or disturbed grieving. Unfortunately, though, his data presentation does not clearly define his criteria of normality (Stroebe & Stroebe, 1987). According to Clark (1991) it was Lindemann who first introduced the term 'grief work', thus indicating that grieving is not static, but an active process in which the ability of the person to go through their grief work is one of the factors affecting the duration of their grief.

The model of grieving introduced by Kubler-Ross (1970) featured stages of grieving, based on her work with people facing death. These stages featured (1) denial or isolation (2) confusion or anger (3) bargaining (4) depression (5) acceptance. The concept of stages is valuable in that it builds on Lindemann's work by emphasising the dynamic nature of grieving and the active role of the bereaved person. A serious disadvantage is that this descriptive concept may become prescriptive, potentially limiting individual variability. It is crucial to recognise the variation between individuals in the duration and progress of grieving, as people oscillate and hesitate between stages (Stroebe & Stroebe, 1987). Parkes (1976) summarises the tendency towards a sequential recovery: 'Grief is not a set of symptoms which start after a loss and then gradually fade away. It involves a succession of clinical pictures which blend into and replace one another'.

General pattern of grieving

A general pattern of grieving is common to the various models, although each researcher/author emphasises different aspects. The emphasis is determined by the sample, bereaved or dying people, and the intended audience. Thus, the models which are produced vary in orientation and complexity.

The immediate reaction comprises a temporary defence mechanism consisting essentially of delaying tactics. These protect the bereaved person from the unfathomable reality (Engel, 1961) while they rally their resources in preparation for their ultimate realisation. This delay eventually ends and the bereaved person comes to accept the reality of their loss. Somatic symptoms such as sighing respirations may be evident. This first stage has been described in terms of shock (Jones 1989a), denial (Kubler-Ross, 1970), defence and searching (Parkes, 1976).

Developing awareness (Engel, 1961) gradually manifests itself and with the dawning realisation of the loss come the initial, powerful emotional responses. Bargaining (Kubler-Ross, 1970) permits a gradual, controlled realisation combined with excuse-making. Anger (Jones 1989a; Parkes, 1976) demonstrates a partial awareness of the reality of the loss. The need for searching reflects the preoccupation with the physical absence of the lost person (Stroebe & Stroebe, 1987). Guilt associated with unfinished business features prominently. As each of these emotional responses is found to be inadequate, it gives way to aimlessness and apathy which has been termed 'disorganisation' (Bowlby, 1969) and which heralds the onset of the despair associated with complete recognition of the loss.

Full realisation is typified by the depression mentioned by Jones (1989a), Kubler-Ross (1970) and Parkes (1976). The recognition of the loss may be transferred onto the body of the bereaved one in the form of feelings of bodily mutilation, such as the 'great emptiness' recounted by a widow (Parkes, 1976). Depression brings with it psychological changes, such as poor concentration, as well as somatic problems such as gastro-intestinal symptoms (Stroebe & Stroebe, 1987).

Resolution is usually regarded as the final stage, which is said to have been achieved when the bereaved person is able to remember comfortably and realistically the pleasures and disappointments of their lost relationship (Chaney, 1981). Kubler-Ross (1970) describes this stage in terms of acceptance, whereas Parkes describes recovery, reorganisation and reintegration. The potential for long-term benefits associated with bereavement are suggested in the account of this stage given by Jones. He anticipates the new identity assumed by the bereaved person, incorporating what has been learned from the experience of bereavement. These include personal growth and development as well as the valuing of others' support, both of which permit an increased ability to cope with unknown and unimaginable crises yet to be faced (Jones 1989).

Adoption

In the same way as my recent research project utilises grieving as the theoretical framework, previous research on adoption has tended to focus on a range of issues that reflect the then current concerns of the society in which the research was undertaken (Benet, 1976; Bernstein, 1966; Roberts, 1966; Cole 1984). Although attitudes to adoption may have varied, the adopted child has invariably been seen as the innocent recipient of charity, and adoption as a solution has sometimes been idealised (Dixon, 1988; Howe et al., 1992). The needs of the adopted person have, probably appropriately, been given priority both in terms of care provided and research into that care (Dukette, 1984).

Although adoption was first brought into existence to solve problems of inheritance (Hoggett, 1984), it has in more recent times been viewed as a solution to the twin 'problems' of teenage pregnancy and illegitimacy (Franklin, 1954), a view which still persists in the USA (Simchak, 1990). Because of this association, negative attitudes to such social problems as illegitimacy may have become transferred to the process which seeks to solve them (Barth, 1987).

The relinquishing mother and her care

Research undertaken during the social upheavals of the early post-war period followed up adopted children and adoptive parents to assess the success of the adoption process for these two participants (Richmond, 1957). Later, to help social workers to achieve the most appropriate placement, predictors of relinquishment were sought (Costigan, 1964). These predictors focussed on the personal and other characteristics of the relinquishing mother and particularly, due to some rather disconcerting work (Young, 1954), on her mental health; such attention to her mental state inevitably became confused with her moral health, both in terms of the conception and the relinquishment.

Responding to public pressure Yellowly (1965) examined the timing of the mother's relinquishment decision. This work indicated no reason for delaying her decision and contributed to the changing attitudes which were embodied in the Children Act (HMSO, 1975). Reflecting societal attitudes, the work of Yellowly clearly demonstrated the feeling of failure among the mother's advisers if the adoption was not completed, that is, when the child was not relinquished. The shortage of healthy, white newborns in the UK has led recently to research on other forms of adoption, such as transcultural and older child adoption (Dickinson, 1988b; Triseliotis, 1989).

Open adoption, in which the relinquishing mother plays an active and continuing role in the new family, was the subject of an important study which has led to increasing awareness of the relinquishing mother's long-term reaction (Sorosky, Pannor & Baran, 1984). This study illuminated the prolonged feelings of unresolved guilt, pain and loss encountered by this mother. These findings are reminiscent of an unheeded comparison between relinquishment and bereavement which emerged during an evaluation of adoption practice (Triseliotis, 1970). Winkler and Van Keppel (1984) utilised the similarities between bereavement and relinquishment to study the long-term health of relinquishing mothers. The recent UK study by Bouchier and her colleagues (1991) employs a social work perspective and utilised other countries' moves towards open adoption for its context, to compare the feelings of mothers who do and do not wish to resume contact with the relinquished one. These valuable accounts of the mother's feelings are in general terms, such as degree of stress, changes in feelings, frequency of thought about children, adjustment and effects on health and well-being. Little attention has been given to this mother's care. Recent research on open adoption (Gross, 1993) has been unable to establish whether it affects the grief of the relinquishing mother.

A nursing-oriented study demonstrates both the American interest in this topic and some of the pitfalls encountered when researching it. Burnell and Norfleet (1979) made a valiant but largely unsuccessful attempt to examine this mother's care. The response rate to their postal questionnaire was 26.6% and illustrates the dangers of using an inappropriately hard-edged instrument in such a sensitive area. The problems of tracing this mobile group by using hospital records constitutes a further warning.

A search of the literature suggests that research on the relinquishing mother, her needs and the decisions relating to her care in childbearing, has not been published, and probably not undertaken (MIDIRS, 1988). This lack of research attention also applies to other occupational groups in the UK, such as social workers (Dickinson, 1988b). Such limited research attention may have come to assume more negative features which verge on the judgemental (Dickinson, 1988a). The neglect of the relinquishing mother by researchers has begun to be corrected (Sachdev, 1984). Partly as a result of our increasing knowledge of this mother's feelings, counselling services are being developed in a number of centres (Fitsell, 1988).

The care provided has been criticised by feminist authors (Shawyer, 1979; Inglis, 1984). They argue that the high standard of care for, and interest in, the child and the adoptive parents, which I have mentioned already, may have been at the expense of the care of the relinquishing mother. These authors' work on the relinquishing mother's rights may be a logical, if extreme, progression in knowledge about and her care.

The need to help the relinquishing mother to grieve her loss was observed by a midwife in an opinion piece (Morrin, 1983). She noted the developments in our care of the bereaved mother, with particular reference to the improved support which the midwife is now encouraged to offer. Morrin contrasted the care which, she observed, was provided for the relinquishing mother. She linked the lack of recognition of this mother's grief with the perception by midwives and other carers that her relinquishment is voluntary. The implication being that exercising her choice of keeping or relinquishing her baby, precludes her need to grieve the loss of her child. Morrin went on to discuss some of the areas of difficulty which midwives experience when caring for this mother. These include, first, some uncertainty among midwives concerning what constitutes the most appropriate care, second, interdisciplinary difficulties between carers, third, anxiety about the development and nature of the relationship between the relinquishing mother and her baby and, finally, midwives' need to protect the mother from emotional trauma.

Morrin describes the crucial role of the midwife in assisting grieving in both the bereaved mother and the relinquishing mother, while recognising the emotional upheavals that the midwife herself may experience. Morrin reports her perception of the relative proportions of grieving mothers, suggesting that it is more common for a mother to relinquish her baby than to lose it through perinatal death.

The viewpoint of a nurse working in situations of infant loss is considered by Jolly (1987). Like Sorosky et al., Jolly emphasises the extended duration of grief experienced by the relinquishing mother and recommends that care be continuing and non-judgemental. Although disregarding the mother-fetus relationship, Jolly examines sympathetically the care which may be and which, she states, is offered to the relinquishing mother.

The paper by Morrin (1983), based on personal observation, sought to 'highlight the dilemma' and served to alert midwives to a problematic area of care (Morrin, 1989); the contribution by Jolly (1987), although a milestone in actually including this topic in a text on bereavement, is based on minimal evidence (Jolly, 1989). The danger of these approaches appears in the sensible yet unfounded advice, which is not being questioned, but also in the perpetuation of value-laden assumptions about relinquishing mothers. Jolly states: 'the young girls who, if they have a deprived home, do not have a family to help' (p 44). Such assumptions demonstrate the need for my recent study if only to correct well-intentioned but erroneous advice and oft-repeated yet possibly misleading assertions about who this mother is.

Although other countries' literature does approach the care of the relinquishing mother (Burnell & Norfleet, 1979; Lindsay & Monserrat, 1989), I would question the relevance of such material. In view of the differing cultural bases and societal values, attitudes to adoption reflect somewhat more than just views of a 'social problem'.

In my recent study I envisage relinquishment as a life crisis (Bluford & Peters, 1973; Dohrenwend & Dohrenwend, 1974), which may have certain features in common with the widely recognised crisis encountered by a mother who loses her baby through stillbirth or neonatal death (Dukette, 1979).

The care of the bereaved mother

Although work on the developing relationship between mother and baby was undertaken by Deutsch half a century ago (1945), the main agent to demonstrate the developing mother-baby relationship and to bring about changes in practice has been John Bowlby's work (1969) on the process of attachment. This work was supported by the (perhaps methodologically flawed) work of Kennell et al. (1970) which showed bonds of affection existing well in advance of the mother seeing and holding her child. This knowledge has been integrated with the contribution on bereavement by workers such as Parkes (1986). Midwives and others have examined their care of parents experiencing perinatal loss in research projects (Kenyon, 1985; Lovell, 1983; Lovell et al, 1986; Hughes, 1987; Davis et al. 1988).

The work of Forrest and her co-workers, begun in 1978, focussed on an evaluation of the effectiveness of a programme of support and counselling for parents losing a baby through perinatal death (1983). The study recruited fifty families and followed up their progress for fourteen months. This work clearly showed the anxieties which bereaved families encounter and interventions which they found helpful. The midwifery and other supportive care described by Forrest et al. and the programme of counselling have subsequently become widely accepted.

Of particular significance is the work of Gohlish (1985). This study probed the value of some of the 'nursing' interventions mentioned by Forrest. An important achievement in this study lies in the fact that this midwife was able to complete it, as it involved recruiting mothers of stillborn babies prior to their transfer home and then contacting and visiting the mother one week later. By using a 'Q sort' technique (McKeown, 1988) Gohlish sought to identify the 'nursing behaviours' most and least helpful to the bereaved mother. Many of the statements were concerned with the mother's ability to take decisions which permitted her some degree of control over her situation. Mothers prioritised:

Statement 5 Allow me to stay as long or as short a time in hospital as I wish.

Statement 6 Let me decide if I want a single room or main ward.

This work clearly showed the need for involving the bereaved mother in decision-making about her care and the extent to which she appreciated this involvement when it happened.

A study by Hughes (1987) examined the midwifery care of mothers of stillborn babies, focussing particularly on their physical environment. She used guided conversations with fourteen bereaved mothers, thirty mothers of live-born babies and nineteen midwives. Although her remit was wide-ranging, it was only in the literature review that Hughes mentioned the possibility of the mother making any contribution to her care.

Hughes' examination (1986) of the mothers' perceptions of the advantages and disadvantages of the various ward environments where they were accommodated is couched in terms of 'if given a choice of environment where would they have chosen to be?'; which suggests that the mothers she met were not given a choice. This finding may be partly explained by the fact that the bereaved mothers in Hughes' study had given birth up to twenty years prior to the interview, whereas Gohlish undertook a prospective study. This may be associated with the concept of a partnership between the mother and the midwife in planning and providing care being relatively novel (Mander, 1993b).

A particularly valuable aspect of Hughes' study is her finding of the positive views held by other mothers, alongside whom the bereaved mother may be accommodated.

Hughes identified the difficulties midwives encounter in caring for this mother, focussing on their feelings of inadequacy and unpreparedness. This theme of staff coping is the main point to emerge from a wide-ranging review of the literature on perinatal loss by Davis et al. (1988). The involvement of well-experienced personnel and of other formal and less formal support systems is also recommended.

It may be that midwifery-oriented research such as that by Hughes and by Gohlish, perhaps assisted by ever-present media exposure, has resulted in a marked change in the care provided for the mother who loses her baby through perinatal death.

Conclusion

A search of the literature failed to identify any UK-based material on the care of the relinquishing mother around the time of childbirth. This has not changed since Morrin first made her observation of grieving mothers' care in 1983. The question arose of whether our knowledge of caring for the bereaved mother has been applied to the care of the relinquishing mother; my recent study aimed to illuminate this situation by drawing comparisons with the midwifery care of bereaved mothers. The aim was to correct the deficit in research-based knowledge of perinatal care for the relinquishing mother.

The research questions emerged from this examination of the literature and aimed to develop knowledge relating to the care of the relinquishing mother. The limited literature on this topic indicated the need for a descriptive study; thus, the first research question is:

> What is the experience of the mother relinquishing her baby?

In view of other countries' more extensive literature on the relinquishing mother, comparisons were sought in order to establish whether that literature is relevant to the UK. The second question is:

> To what extent is the experience of the relinquishing mother in the UK similar to that of the relinquishing mother in other countries?

As the focus in this study is on midwifery care, and this could not be studied in isolation, the third research question sought to relate care to that provided for other mothers who may have certain similar characteristics:

> How does the care given to the relinquishing mother differ from that provided for other mothers without babies?

The final three research questions sought to examine the decision-making process which precedes the provision of care, and the knowledge on which these decisions are founded:

> How are decisions made regarding care of the relinquishing mother?
> What knowledge is involved in making these decisions?
> How is this knowledge acquired?

3 Researching the grief of relinquishment

In this chapter I consider the rationale for the research approach and then go on to examine aspects of my recent study (Mander, 1992a) in chronological order. Ethical issues and a critique of the research method complete this chapter.

The research approach

In view of both the lack of previous research in the area of midwives' care of the relinquishing mother and its innately sensitive nature, I chose to use a qualitative research approach incorporating certain quantitative elements. Qualitative research seeks to understand the event from the perspective of the person experiencing it - the 'emic' perspective (Harris, 1968). The term 'verstehen' (to understand) may be used to describe this concept, which involves learning of the subjective viewpoint by direct observation or by explanatory understanding.

Although some may argue that this approach is 'soft' and 'unscientific' (Aamodt, 1982), this is probably a strength in the present context. The reason is that the qualitative orientation is well-suited to the descriptive approach, which was used to come to understand the subjective viewpoint of the mother and her interpretation of the meaning of her relinquishment (Parse, Coyne & Smith, 1985; Van Maanen, 1982). The inclusion of quantitative elements constitute triangulation at the level of the research design, which further increase the rigour of the data (Jick 1983; Denzin, 1970).

According to Leininger (1985) qualitative methods permit a holistic picture of the phenomenon to emerge, which demonstrates the interrelatedness and interdependence of various differing facets of an event. This holistic approach is essential for such a project, as midwives' care may be both perceived and provided through drawing on discrete value systems.

The research design

Throughout this study I have sought help from mothers and midwives, who have acted as informants - people with specialised knowledge to answer the research questions. The verb 'to inform' is used in this context to describe the process of the illumination of the area under study or the enlightenment (by giving information) of the researcher - hence the 'informant'.

I planned the fieldwork in three phases, examining the viewpoints of relevant informants. These were, phase 1, previous relinquishing mothers (those who have relinquished a baby at some time in the past), phase 2, experienced midwives and, phase 3, current relinquishing mothers (those currently planning relinquishment).

This design involved elements of triangulation to provide as complete a picture as possible, by using different methods to obtain each participant's view of one event (Marshall & Rossman, 1989). Focussed interview was the main method for the fieldwork; non-participant observation was planned to learn of the experience of current relinquishing mothers. These methods would allow the themes to emerge inductively rather than having me, the researcher, impose my preconceived ideas on the data. Although the difficulties or 'costs' of interviews are manifold, the spontaneity and richness of the data more than compensate for the problems (Oppenheim, 1992).

It is necessary to consider in detail how I gained access to the informants to learn of their ideas.

Planning and completing the fieldwork

Gaining access to the research site may involve obtaining approval and cooperation from a range of bodies. Whether ethical approval and permission from management are needed depends on whether patients/clients or staff are involved (Wilson-Barnett, 1991).

Phase one

As non-directive interviews with a sample of mothers were being used, I anticipated that about thirty mothers would be appropriate to provide a complete picture of their experiences and observe any pattern which may develop (Nachmias & Nachmias, 1981). This phase of the research sought to assess whether the long-term problems of the relinquishing mother, identified in countries such as USA and Australia, exist in the UK.

This phase involved contacting mothers who have previously relinquished a baby. Recruitment by advertising, described, discussed and used by Sorosky et al. (1984) was found to be ineffective.

I have since learned that local evening papers serve a different function in North America from their equivalents in the UK. In USA these papers are used to advertise very personal services, for which more specialised publications exist in UK. In the locality of this study the paper is used mainly for advertising housing and entertainments.

Advertisements were placed on three consecutive nights. Only four informants made contact using this method. A further four people who contacted me at this time did not keep the appointment. A small number of people seeking counselling and help with locating their birth parents made contact. I gave them details of the agency which exists to help them.

After informal discussion with social workers organising a local birth parents' group I was invited to attend a meeting to speak about this research. The members showed considerable sympathetic interest in this study and were keen to participate. Following this enthusiastic reception I contacted other, national birth parents groups. The organisers agreed to distribute my letters to their members in the northern part of the UK. These letters produced responses from women living from Aberdeen to Hull. One mother was recruited through a university freesheet. Two saw an account of my study in a popular women's magazine and one mother heard and acted on a nationally networked radio interview.

The sample of previous relinquishing mothers

I interviewed twenty three mothers who had previously relinquished a baby for adoption. A minority of mothers were aged below twenty at the time of the relinquishment (Table 3.1.).

Table 3.1.
The mothers' age at relinquishment

Age at relinquishment	Number	Percent
15 and under	3	13%
16-19	8	35%
20-24	8	35%
25-29	3	13%
30-34	0	0
35 and over	1	4%
Total	23	100%

The time lapse between the relinquishment and the interview varied between about thirty years for Anthea, Debra, Gina, Rosa, Vera and Wilma and eight weeks for Ursula (Table 3.2).

Table 3.2.
Years since relinquishment

Years	Number of Mothers	%
1-4	5	21%
5-9	0	0
10-14	3	13%
15-19	4	17%
20-24	4	17%
26-29	2	7%
30-34	4	17%
35-39	1	4%
Total	23	100%

A large majority were living in the family home at the time of the conception. The majority (15/23) of the mothers were unmarried at the time of their relinquishment. One mother was married to the father of her relinquished child. Three were in a stable cohabiting relationship with the father and five were in a stable non-cohabiting relationship, three of which later resulted in marriage to the father.

When the women relinquished their babies for adoption their occupations, for those who were not at school or studying, were largely manual or clerical.

The fieldwork

The interviews with the previous relinquishing mothers were usually in person at a venue chosen by the informant. This was sometimes the mother's home, sometimes at my place of work. A College of Nursing and Midwifery allowed me to use their accommodation for one interview. Two interviews were by 'phone, one with a mother in South Wales and another with a mother in continental Europe.

The duration of the interviews in the pre-arranged venue varied between one hour for Clara, whose children were demanding her attention, and three and a half hours for Francesca. This time does not include information given during preliminary conversations to make arrangements or 'chat' during taxi journeys. Frequently, useful information emerged from conversations while walking to the railway station or in supposedly informal talk over coffee, during which time I tried to help the mother to 'put herself back together' prior to parting. This recuperative time, during which the informant regains her composure, is crucial if a 'single shot' interview format in a sensitive area is being used, as there is no further opportunity for the informant to reconcile herself to her experience of self-disclosure (Clulow & Vincent, 1987; Antle May, 1989).

The instrument

For the interviews I used a semi-structured interview format; this allows the informant to take considerable control over the topics which are discussed. This followed my introduction during which I reiterated my area of interest, which had been explained during the initial contact, regardless of the nature of that contact.

An essential feature of this form of fieldwork is the recognition of the way in which I, the researcher, present and make use of my personality during the interview (Lipson, 1989). This applies to such an extent that my personality may constitute part of the research instrument. As Field and Morse (1987) suggest, it is essential for me to be acutely conscious of any intuitive or personal reactions to the informant or the information she is providing. Examples would be my awareness of my own revulsion when Francesca recounted the group activities of her peers in a (to me) alien youth subculture; or my sorrow at Quelia's pathetically limited outlook on life; or my overwhelming feeling of identification with Barbara and Debra due to our common early post-war working class upbringing. It is essential to take account of such personal reactions in both the fieldwork and the analysis of the data.

Authors who contemplate the discomfort associated with this degree of personal involvement in research are few (Freilich, 1979; Marck, 1994). How I would cope with the emotional effects of such profound involvement and the feelings which were likely to arise was asked by a research ethical committee. Lipson (1989) suggests that the other members of the research team are the ideal peer-support group, but this was not feasible for this relatively small project. The burden of support was borne by my domestic and work relationships. The emotional costs of research are particularly significant in qualitative research, where personal involvement with both the work and the informants is crucial. This aspect of research tends to be given little attention. However, Gans (1982) does focus on the effects of such work on the researcher and recommends that, before beginning, the researcher should identify her emotionally vulnerable areas. Perhaps with the help of a counsellor, she is advised to work out whether her vulnerability is due to research-related factors, informant-related factors or underlying personal difficulties. Knowing the frequency with which such feelings affect researchers may help to put them into perspective, which may in turn be assisted by more open discussion of the 'costs of involvement'.

For the interviews I used a frequently-updated schedule comprising a list of questions. I encouraged the informants to introduce relevant issues. The questions were based on the literature available, my occupational and other experience and (in the later interviews) issues raised by earlier informants. Each interview began by asking for demographic data, such as approximate age and occupational experience. I then asked each previous relinquishing mother to tell me about her life at the time of her relinquishment. This was usually sufficient for the mother to recount her experience. I sometimes needed to ask the mother about her sources of help and information. Questions about the details of care following the birth were usually needed and sometimes the mothers needed to be prompted to describe her contact with the baby. All of the personal interviews were all tape recorded, after the mother had given permission.

Phase two

The aim of this phase was to describe the care provided by the midwife for the relinquishing mother. Focussed interviews with midwives with experience of caring for relinquishing mothers aimed to probe their views of their care of this woman. Each interview aimed to approach the following areas:

The care of a mother experiencing a perinatal death.
The choices are available in the care of this mother.
How these choices are resolved.
The knowledge base used when providing this care.
How this knowledge is acquired.
The aspects of care unique to a relinquishing mother.
The choices available in the care of this mother.
How these choices are resolved.
The knowledge base used when providing this care.
How this knowledge is acquired.
The relevance of knowledge of caring for a bereaved mother to the care of a relinquishing mother.

Because phase two involved no 'patients', approaches for access were made to appropriate midwife managers. It had been necessary to recruit previous relinquishing mothers from a wide area so, in order to contact a sufficient number, it was decided to recruit midwives from a similar area. Approaches were made in eight maternity units (including community) in two cities in Scotland. These approaches elicited enthusiastic, sympathetic and helpful support. The managers gave permission for me to contact midwives to seek their participation. Midwives who agreed to be involved were allowed to be interviewed in their on-duty time in health board premises, if they so wished.

The sample of midwives

Midwifery managers facilitated access to a sample of suitably experienced midwives, from whom interviewees were selected. As had been agreed with the managers when seeking their cooperation, five midwives were chosen 'blind' from each unit in anticipation that approximately thirty to forty interviews would be sufficient and that more midwives could be approached should it prove necessary (Munhall & Oiler, 1986). I sent these midwives a letter detailing the nature of the study in terms of midwives' care of the mother who did not have a baby with her. This letter described the likely duration, the possibility of non-participation, the potential venues, and that contact would be made when the midwife was on duty. In the initial 'phone call the midwife was asked whether she was prepared to be involved in this study.

All the midwives (Table 3.3.) had been qualified for at least two years (range two years to thirty eight years), had worked in various areas of maternity care and had cared for women having a stillborn baby. The midwives were employed in clinical grades.

Table 3.3.
The midwives' age and midwifery experience

Age	Number	Mean midwifery experience
20-29	20	3.6 Yrs
30-39	12	7.6 Yrs
40-49	3	19.3 Yrs
50-59	5	29.2 Yrs

The fieldwork

The informant chose the venue for the interview (at her home, in the maternity unit or in my room: when off duty or on duty: if on duty in daytime or at night). The time taken for the interviews ranged from 45 minutes to two hours. The interview was tape-recorded when the informant gave permission. Six midwives declined to be tape recorded, usually claiming embarrassment; these interviews were recorded in long hand. Although this different method (like the telephone interviews with two of the previous relinquishing mothers) may have affected the reliability of the data and the validity of the study, no obvious variation is apparent (Field & Morse, 1987). The interviews with all informants were transcribed on to disk for analysis. These transcripts generated the quotes used later.

Two midwives refused to be interviewed and a third was unable to keep any of her three appointments. No attempt was made to identify why a midwife might not wish to participate. This was because I soon learned that many midwives have personal experience of, or contact with, perinatal loss and/or adoption. I concluded that, for some, the prospect of an interview may have been too painful. Alternatively, these reactions may be a form of the ambivalence identified by Elbourne (1987), which may be associated with being over-researched.

The instrument

For the midwives' interviews a semi-structured interview format was used, in addition to the essential use of the interviewer's personality (Lipson, 1989). For each interview I used a schedule comprising a list of questions. The interview began by asking for demographic data concerning approximate age and duration of midwifery practice. The midwife was first asked to describe her care of a mother having or having had a stillborn baby (depending on the midwife's area of practice) and I then asked her to recount her care of a relinquishing mother. The care of the bereaved mother is a topic which, personal observation tells me, midwives would be knowledgeable about and comfortable with, largely because of the exposure which has recently been given to this topic in both the lay and midwifery media. This topic was used to lead into the area of the care of the relinquishing mother and to facilitate comparisons.

During the interviews, it was rarely necessary for me to refer to the interview schedule, which served more as an 'aide-memoire'. As new topics were introduced in the series of interviews I added them to the schedule, as it was essential to ensure sufficient understanding of how the midwives viewed them.

An example of such a topic, which was raised at a relatively late stage, was the significance of the presence or absence of the cot in the labour room when the baby was due to be relinquished or when she was expected to be stillborn.

Phase three

The original objective was to describe the ongoing experience of the relinquishing mother. A prospective, longitudinal study was planned. Interviews would focus on her experience of making the decision to relinquish her baby and the extent to which her care helped her through the experiences of birth and relinquishment. Additionally, these interviews would probe any issues raised by the previous relinquishing mothers and the midwives about which any conflict persisted.

The design of phase three

A convenience sample was planned (Burgess, 1982). An interview would be held in the woman's home shortly after the birth and a similar interview would be held a few months later to ascertain whether her impressions of her care had developed in any way. These interviews were to be supported by observation of the care at the time of the birth (Melia, 1981).

Although I realised that such non-participant observation, might be difficult to arrange and time-consuming, it would provide an opportunity for triangulation, which could illuminate certain areas not resolved during the interviews (Jick, 1983). Gaining access to relinquishing mothers, as well as seeking their consent, was planned involving the cooperation of Social Workers in Social Work Departments and Adoption Agencies.

The case-study approach used in phase three

The implementation of the third and final stage of the study presented certain 'challenges' which were not entirely unexpected, but whose inconsistency was quite disconcerting (See Chapter 5.). Difficulties in gaining access to a suitable sample of relinquishing mothers became insurmountable, due to the activities of the 'gatekeepers' (Becker, 1970; Mander, 1992b). Having previously discounted the possibility, as a last resort I by-passed more complex routes and sought the cooperation of midwives in an antenatal clinic.

Within a week I received a response from Aline and realised that she might be the only mother with whom I could make contact. It became apparent that if I was able to recruit only one suitable mother a case-study approach was needed.

Reasons for general non-use: Ignorance about case-study is widespread because it is currently 'unfashionable' (Bromley, 1986); hence, a closer examination of this method may be useful. The unpopularity of case-study may have been aggravated by Campbell's criticisms (Campbell & Stanley, 1963). While discussing experimental research designs, he dismissed case-study as having 'no scientific value', due to the total absence of controls. Campbell emphasised the need for precise, balanced comparison in research, which in the case of experimentation is explicit. Comparison may be implicit in other methods, but he maintained that in case-study there is no possibility of it being either precise or balanced. He accused this method of the 'error of misplaced precision' and recommended ways to facilitate comparison. According to Rosenblatt (1981) Campbell subsequently admitted his own error and modified his extreme views on this research method, acknowledging the 'potential for epistemological discipline'. Campbell presumably realised that comparison does not need to be explicit, indeed it may not even need to exist in more descriptive research. When examining a highly individual area, such as in my recent study, data comparison is neither relevant nor feasible.

The principles of case-study: Case-study utilises in-depth, rather than broad, understanding by drawing on a single incident, individual or setting (Abdellah & Levine, 1986), to study a phenomenon. An attempt is made to seek the 'inner life' (Denzin, 1970) which is not apparent to a casual observer or acquaintance, that is, the material tends to be of a private nature which is not accessible to anyone other than a trusted confidante, which is what the researcher endeavours to become.

In my recent study Aline provided the information which she considered relevant to my topic. There were certain areas, such as the conception, which were too private for her to mention and which I had no reason to probe. This omission is interesting in view of the detail given and the importance attached to this event by the other mothers. Similarly Aline was initially unwilling to discuss how she felt or had felt towards her unborn baby, whereas this mattered very much to each previous relinquishing mother. This difference may be attributable to the retrospective and prospective nature of the data collection in phases one and three respectively.

Case-study method: Case-studies are undertaken in a natural setting (Abdellah & Levine, 1986), rather than in any contrived or manipulated environment. Experimental, rather than descriptive, case-studies are feasible, such as those used in clinical settings to monitor therapeutic interventions (Lobiondo-Wood & Haber, 1986).

Aline agreed that I would be able to visit her and conduct observations and interviews in the settings where midwifery care was being given. Throughout my contact with Aline, as with all parts of this research, the midwives were keen to help with my observations. Their enquiries about the research and unsolicited impressions of their interactions with her provide a useful range of data sources.

Bromley (1986) defines the subject of a single case-study in terms of 'a person in a problematic situation'. The situation is an acute episode, so the time period involved is relatively short. Aline's perception of the short-term nature of her pregnancy and relinquishment became apparent as she talked to me about what she called her 'predicament' when we first met.

Depending on the duration of the study, a single case-study or a life history results; although these two terms may be used interchangeably (Denzin. 1970). The term 'life-event' is useful in this context (Bromley, 1986) as it implies the self-contained nature as well as the situation's formative, critical or culminant features. Childbirth is widely accepted as a 'life event' (Dohrenwend &

Dohrenwend, 1974); relinquishment would seem to be a no less formative experience as suggested by both Dukette (1984) and the previous birth mothers in my recent study.

Bogdan and Biklen (1982) reiterate that the factor which ultimately determines the duration of the data collection is the data themselves, in that 'data saturation' signals the completion of that phase.

The subject must have the relevant experience as well as being an articulate, yet concise, conversationalist with a good memory for relevant detail (Bogdan & Biklen, 1982). The subject's degree of insight may make her more or less valuable as an informant. These authors maintain that a meeting with a suitable subject precedes the decision to undertake the single case-study. Because of the problems encountered in making contact with suitable mothers I did not have the choice of subject which these authors recommend. The strengths and weaknesses of Aline as an informant become apparent in her narrative (See Chapter 12 & Mander, 1992a).

Types of case-study vary according to their duration, the degree of focus, that is whether a wide-ranging or narrowly-defined topic, and the degree of editing (Denzin, 1970). Bogdan and Biklen (1982) recommend that the research design should be envisaged as a funnel, beginning with a wide area of interest which is narrowed to focus on a limited area as the study progresses. These authors go on to warn us of the artificiality of too narrowly defining the subject area and risking separating it from the world into which it is normally integrated. The definition of the topic presented minimal difficulty in this study, as the topics of interest had already been highlighted in the earlier interviews with the previous relinquishing mothers and with the midwives. The risk of distancing this case-study from its context was prevented by Aline, whose accounts of her experience included constant reference to her interaction with a range of formal and informal supporters. The extent to which she defined her experience in terms of what others thought and said is difficult to assess.

Data collection: Typically a multiplicity of methods are used for collecting data, as well as a range of data sources (Abdellah & Levine, 1986). Denzin (1970) distinguishes between private sources, such as research interviews, and public sources such as test results, maps, case records or court hearings. Not surprisingly he recommends the triangulation of data from a number of sources to provide a complete account of the phenomenon. Despite the multiplicity of data sources, selectivity is crucial in the data collection, as the researcher must ignore irrelevant issues (Bromley, 1986). The problem of how much of the subject's life history to describe is not explained and may be a source of bias as it is me, the researcher, who must make the subjective decision about what is relevant.

Prior to analysis, Patton (1980) recommends drawing up a case record, comprising a complete narrative account of the situation, which may employ a chronological or a topical format. Inductive reasoning is an essential element of this method (Lobiondo-Wood & Haber, 1986). Denzin (1970) details the organisation and synthesis of the data, beginning with the formulation of the hypothesis, through selection of subjects and gaining their interpretation of the event to the data analysis. He emphasises the role of internal and external criticism of the emerging theory to ensure validity. This involves the search for negative evidence, drafting and submission to the subject.

Outcome: The final report includes a narrative which is written in the first person, making selective use of anecdotal data (Abdellah & Levine, 1986; Bromley, 1986) to support the interpretation and conclusions.

Advantages: The strengths of case-study lie in the unique opportunities it presents to enter another's world and understand their experience (Denzin, 1970). Although the lack of generaliseability associated with this approach may be regarded as a problem, this is balanced by its facilitation of the exploration of new areas and concepts (Lobiondo-Wood & Haber, 1986). The problem of generaliseability may underpin the selection of a 'typical' subject for more quantitatively-oriented researchers (Bogdan & Biklen, 1982). Any such claims deserve to be challenged and these authors suggest that they are better not made. The question of generaliseability does not feature in a topic which is as individual as relinquishment and in an area which is changing as rapidly as the midwifery care of the grieving mother.

Holm (1983) describes the advantages of case-study more mundanely, in terms of the convenience for clinical workers, as less time and fewer subjects are involved. It must be admitted that in my recent study the lack of suitable subjects, which would have allowed the use of other methods, was the main reason for choosing case-study. Bogdan and Biklen (1982) for similar reasons regard this as the ideal method for the novice researcher. They go on to emphasise the benefits of the flexibility of this method. It may be that excessive flexibility is too much for a new researcher to cope with, while critics may consider that such flexibility constitutes a lack of discipline or academic rigour. As mentioned already the interviews preceding this case-study served to provide natural boundaries and a suitably precise focus.

Potential weaknesses: The main problems associated with case-study relate to the risk of introducing researcher bias (Denzin, 1970; Bromley, 1986; Lobiondo-Wood & Haber, 1986) and the difficulty of defining the boundaries of the area being studied (Denzin, 1970; Bromley, 1986). A discussion of researcher bias leads Diesing (1972) to the question of whether it is possible for the researcher **not** to influence the ideas and actions of the subject by virtue of their presence, indicating that case-study is vulnerable to such inadvertent manipulation. Bogdan and Biklen (1982) admit that the presence of a researcher in a situation 'would change what went on significantly' and recommend increasing the number of subjects.

This was a serious concern in my recent study in two ways. First, in general terms the number of people aware of Aline's situation was limited, making my presence as an observer more likely to influence it, but the outcome of Aline's experience clearly suggests that my involvement did not influence her decision-making. More specifically a knowledgeable observer's presence may have influenced the care provided by the labour ward midwives. I took precautions, such as in my choice of positioning and clothing, to make my presence minimally obtrusive. Any influence on care is unlikely in view of the staff being accustomed to observers in the form of partners and students while their degree of concentration during the labour and birth on the mother and baby excludes other low-priority interference.

It is apparent that the strength of case-study, its flexibility, may develop into its main weakness if the study is allowed to become aimless and too diffuse and that, while it was not the first-choice research method, case-study proved a valuable tool in the completion of the third and final stage of the fieldwork.

Completion of the fieldwork and data analysis of all phases

Field notes were written following each contact. They included immediate impressions of and reactions to the informant and the data she had provided. There was considerable urgency to complete these field notes as the themes were often to be incorporated into the next interview. This involved writing them in trains, hospital cafeterias and motorway service stations.

I listened to the recording of each interview, which was then transcribed on to disk by a typist. One typist found this work demanding due, not only to the highly emotional nature of the material, but also the pronounced accents of some of the mothers. She resorted to converting the speech into standard English. Inevitably much of the feeling and meaning of the mother's words was lost in the hard copy; but the tape-recordings of the interviews were retained. The hard copy produced by the typist was checked with the taped interview; unavoidably certain colloquial and technical terms were incorrectly transcribed.

By the time I had interviewed twenty three previous relinquishing mothers and forty midwives, it was apparent that new conceptual categories were no longer being introduced. I decided that the data had become saturated (Stern, 1980). Thus, it was clear that the data were complete and no more interviews were required.

I began the analysis of the data during the fieldwork using comparative analysis (Stern, 1980). This involves comparing newly-acquired data with that which previous informants have provided, to determine whether the new information supports that which exists already. Thus, theory is constantly developing and being revised. The direction of further fieldwork is determined by developing theory.

In exploring, first, the experience of relinquishment and, second, the experience of providing midwifery care for the relinquishing mother, I was seeking insights to illuminate the essential aspects of that care. This exploration was completed after each phase of the fieldwork by using analytic description. This involves active inspection of the data, in this context the transcripts, in an attempt to identify novel classes or categories to describe the phenomenon. This method of analysis was employed to ensure that all of the essential categories or findings had been explained (Macintyre, 1975; Wilson, 1985).

I corrected and then coded the hard copy provided by the typist using numbered categories which seemed appropriate from my reading of and listening to the interviews. There were about 200 categories for the relinquishing mothers and a similar number for the midwives. Some of the categories were common to both groups, but there were many which were relevant only to one group of informants, such as midwives' accounts of their learning about grieving.

The typist transferred these numerical codes on to disk and this permitted categorised statements to be extracted from the disk copy and reformed into about twenty categories, each of which focussed on one area. Examination of each of these categories, including a count, provided me with a complete impression of the varying aspects, including the salience, of that topic (Fielding & Lee, 1991).

Ethical considerations

Phase one involved a volunteer sample, whose response may have been taken to imply consent, but who were given details of the nature of the study before being asked for informed consent.

In phase two the midwives were given a choice of whether or not to participate, based on an explanation of the study. Information was also provided for midwife managers whose cooperation was essential.

In phase three research ethical committees were approached to approve access to this group of patients. A similar approach was necessary to Social Work Departments and Adoption Agencies for the identification of these women. Each woman eligible to participate in the study would personally be given information about the study before written informed consent to be involved could be sought.

The anonymity and confidentiality of each group of respondents would be maintained throughout by the use of pseudonyms and attention to the security of all records.

The salience of relinquishment in maternity care, or rather its current relative infrequency, may call into question the morality of utilising resources to undertake a research project with limited application. It is necessary to question whether the frequent occurrence of a situation is the only factor which determines the need to understand it. It is possible that the significance of the situation to those involved should also be taken into account. My occupational experience of working with relinquishing mothers made me aware of the difficulties midwives face in this situation and those I interviewed reinforced my impression. The previous relinquishing mothers left me in no doubt of the need to undertake this research.

Conclusion

This chapter has detailed how the research method was developed in view of the questions, which arose out of the literature, and others' research in similar areas. The procedures for handling and analysing the data have been systematically described. The problems encountered by the researcher have been mentioned, together with the solutions.

4 The mothers' experience

This chapter provides a brief description of the background and experience of each of the mothers who took part in my recent research (Mander 1992a). These accounts provide the context for the data discussed in the following chapters. I make no attempt to synthesise or analyse this material, as the data analysis and findings are included in later chapters. The demographic data included in the biographies are also summarised in table form (See Chapter 3).

To protect the confidentiality of those involved the names are pseudonyms. The mothers who relinquished previously have been given names ending with 'a' (Wilma, Vera ... Anthea). The other people involved have been given a fictitious name when the mother mentioned the actual/given name:

Relinquished child	Andrea/Andrew
Father of relinquished child	Billy
Current partner (if not father of relinquished child)	Ben
Other partner	Brian

In a further attempt to maintain confidentiality place-names have been removed when they refer to rural localities or small communities. Having taken these precautions to conceal the identities of those involved, I feel able to give the dates of years/months as they were given to me. These dates are significant as they indicate both the lapse of time between events and the social environment in which these events occurred. When mothers gave me precise dates, for example of the birth, I have amended these dates.

To provide the most complete picture possible of the mother's experience I indicate how contact was initially made, where the interview took place and how long the actual interview lasted. These biographies are in chronological order as the interviews happened, the names having been allocated in alphabetical order. The four mothers who were unable to keep their appointments for interview were not given names.

I have used the mother's own words as far as possible.

Anthea

Contact made through advertisement in local evening paper. Interview at Anthea's flat in an estate on the outskirts of the city. Lasted for 105 minutes.

I'm fifty now. I was 20 or 21 when all this happened. They were born 1958 and 1960, and were adopted in 1964 - he was 2 and she was 1 in 1962.

I don't work now, but at that time I done everything - different kinds of factories, I worked in the telephone exchange, I even went in for nursing - I lasted eight months. I'm a sort of Johnny-all-trades.

I was trapped into marriage, I never drank and he gave me some drinks at hogmanay, and I woke up in bed with blood all over the sheets. When they found I was pregnant my parents forced me into getting married.

We were separated and the children were in care and one particular day I had the children - I used to take them out at weekends - and he came up that night and started his nonsense. Anyway when I took the children back the social work woman said 'We are not having this'. While I was in the hospital recovering the social worker came up and started badgering me to get them adopted, there were people wanting them and all that. And I was always saying I didn't want to get them adopted, I wanted them out, with me, but I couldn't get a house.

I later divorced him, remarried and now I've got a lovely daughter. The two of them got in touch with me and he came over to spend a fortnight with me last October.

Barbara

Contact made through advertisement in local evening paper and a local authority birth parents' group. Interview at her detached house in a modern private housing development in the suburbs. Lasted for 150 minutes

I'm 30 now, 31 this year, and I was 15 when I had the baby. I was 14 when I found out I was pregnant, 15 when I had her - coming up to 15 years ago, the end of May. My Dad was in the navy so we moved around a lot. I wasn't interested in school.

I was 13 or 14 and I rebelled, I was in the first two years of High School. I enjoyed High School there from what I can remember.

It wasn't as if it [sexual intercourse] went on for that long - I mean me being as naive as I was, the actual act couldn't have been longer than about five minutes. I didn't know what was going on. OK I wasn't that stupid, but at the same time you don't. I don't know where he lived, he lived outside the town, but certainly some village.

I went to a nearby mother and baby home. After the birth the nurses must've supported me. I just don't remember. I must have had support by the nurses.

I didn't breastfeed the baby but I fed her. In that hospital then the babies were kept beside your bed - she was taken away at night. I kept her beside the bed and I fed her and changed her.

Afterwards, when I left school I went to work in Princes Street in fact in a shoe shop. Then I went to college. I left school in the May, I just went into hairdressing at college, I got accepted on a full-time course.

I was a hairdresser up until I got married. I'm not working full-time now because the kids are at school. They're only 7 and 9.

Clara

Contact made with the help of a journalist working on a presentation about relinquishment. Interview at Clara's home in a small Scottish town. Lasted for 60 minutes.

I'm now 29 years old. I gave up my baby when I was aged 18 years that was 11 years ago. My mother died when I was 3 years old due to asthma. I have no memory of my mother except for the day she died. The family moved around a lot. I went to 7 different primary schools.

I did not get on well with my father and hated my step mother.

I'd been working in Yorkshire in hotels when I found I was pregnant. I think I must have been searching for love and that's how I got pregnant.

My life was a misery until I went to a nearby mother and baby home. I made friends with one of the girls there, Fiona. I'd cried a lot and there was no-one at home for me to talk to, but I found that I could talk to Fiona.

In labour the nurses were nice but at a very superficial level. They kept me company all through the labour, I was never alone, but this was not the company I wanted. I wanted someone to share the experience with me, someone who would understand my fear.

I've got married and had three children since then and they've helped me a lot. I've worked in hotels but just now I'm a full time housewife and mother.

Debra

Contact made through a local authority birth parents' group. Interview at my place of work. Lasted for 90 minutes.

I'm now aged 44 years. In 1963 at time I gave up my baby for adoption, I'd've been eighteen.

I failed my 11 plus. That was a terrible blow.

I got on well generally with my family. My father was the headmaster of the local special school. Mother was a teacher.

Billy, the father of my baby was my first boyfriend with whom I'd had a sexual relationship.

My nursery nurse course was just starting when I gave up my baby. I was very young at that time, not like today's teenagers, just ordinary.

I went to a mother and baby home. The midwifery care was good, there was good continuity as I'd met both of the midwives before at the antenatal checks and they delivered my baby.

If you could breast feed you were encouraged to do that. So I breast fed. I enjoyed that. It seemed natural to me. It seemed the right thing to do. They did encourage breast feeding, but the tragedy was the breast feeding stopped at one month.

I eventually married Brian, he was not the father of the baby I had adopted, we were divorced.

I now have a very close loving relationship with my second daughter.

Elena

Contact made through a local authority birth parents' group. Interview at my place of work. Lasted for 120 minutes.

I'm 34 years old. I gave up my baby for adoption 15 years ago when I was aged 16, that was in 1974.

I was living in the same house as my Dad, but I wasn't speaking to him, I hated him and he hated me, because I shouted and answered back to him unlike my mother and my sister. As a teenager I was wild. Taking drugs (things like LSD) and I was promiscuous, that was before I got pregnant with the baby. I was staying out all night and sleeping around when I was 15 years old. When I was aged 16 I met the father of my baby. I split with him just after when the conception must have happened. I wrote to him saying that I was pregnant. He refused to marry me, even though I threatened to have a termination.

I was sent to a mother and baby home not very far away.

After the birth the midwife visited me at home. I wanted to open up to her to tell her how I really felt about Andrew, but my mother walked in at just the wrong moment.

My work has been in cleaning jobs and many other similar jobs.

I've got three children although Chrissie here wasn't planned, but my husband does tend to drink a lot.

Francesca

Contact made through advertisement in local evening paper. Interview at her flat in an up-market area of a city. Lasted for 210 minutes.

I'm now 20 years old. I gave up my baby for adoption when I was 16 in 1985. When I was 8 years old I was sent to a convent boarding school and experienced a major culture shock, because before then I'd only been to the UK on holiday. It didn't work at all.

I hated my father, he tried to restrict my activities but to no avail as I resented any pressure. I ignored what he said - totally - although we lived in the same house. I'd already been having sex (with Brian who wasn't my baby's father) for 2 years before getting the pill, as I did not realise the likelihood of pregnancy. It never occurred to me at all, you don't think of that at all. My father didn't approve of the baby's father at all.

I found that, while in the maternity unit, the staff treated me differently from the other women. I think that they were uncomfortable with me and did not know what to say to me as they were used to dealing with happy events. I was not taught how to care for the baby, like when the other women were collected together to be shown a bath I was not invited. I had the baby in my room with me for some of the time, but I was scared to pick him up.

I used to work in a shop then moved on to a restaurant as a chef, where my estranged husband was the head chef.

After giving my baby for adoption another older man tried to date me when I was working in the shop. I married him within a month of meeting him. I left him. I now have a nice, undemanding boyfriend who lives in this flat with me.

Gina

Contact made through a local authority birth parents' group. Interview at my place of work. Lasted for 105 minutes.

At present I'm 52. I was 22 when I had my baby adopted.

At school I got very good reports academically, really. The problem was me. I didn't like being away from my own friends and my own town. I started off as a termly boarder. We were only allowed home mid-term and that was quite a lot for a little girl of 8.

At 18 I was a student nurse at the time. I was engaged, but we'd made up our minds to break off the engagement. Then I was invited to his sister's wedding and that's when I conceived the child. It is the truth - that was the one and only time I had intercourse with him. It was just very unfortunate or fortunate, however one may look upon it, that I became pregnant. In the January I was not recovering from jaundice and my mother said I should go to [another continent] to convalesce. I was sent to [another continent] in March; that was where he was born.

At the birth I never saw my son. But I had to get taken out ... in a wheelchair and I had to hold my baby in my arms and I had a sneaky look at him of course.

I have a son from my subsequent marriage and he has been absolutely wonderful.

I now hold a senior position in a govermental agency.

Hilda

Contact made through a local authority birth parents' group. Interview at my place of work. Lasted for 150 minutes.

I'm 29 years old. I was 15 when I placed my baby for adoption.

I sort of gave up all my friends I went around with I just went around with Billy. I would just come back from school, get ready, go out, go through to the nearby town to see him, come back home and go to school. I had friends but I gave them up because I was always with him. I lived with my mum and dad, but spent more time at my gran's house.

When I was in the mother and baby home, my parents said I was not to have any contact with Billy, the baby's father, but I did.

Andrew, my baby, was in the special nursery so I didn't get to see him. Eventually I thought I'll just have to go and when I seen him. I just broke my heart.

I had to go back to school after the birth, there were one or two nasty remarks like 'Where's the bairn?'

Eventually me and Billy got married. Billy still today swears he did not know anything about the baby, our baby, he had not been told about him. Billy isn't always around now, but I've got the two boys, Dylan and wee Billy.

I worked in the factory, in fact I'm still working in that factory it's an electronic factory. This is the third time I've been back there working as a manual worker.

Iona

Contact made through a local authority birth parents' group. Interview at my place of work. Lasted for 120 minutes.

I'm 45. I was 23 when I placed my baby for adoption. That was 22 years ago, in 1967. She'll be 22 at the end of May.

I wouldn't say my relationship with my mother, who I lived with, was particularly good. I did begin to rebel. I went out on holiday with a friend and I spent most of the two weeks with Billy and I became pregnant through ignorance more than anything else I think. I don't think his family were at all keen on Billy actually marrying me. They had better plans for him. So he didn't come back to Scotland. I went to live with my married sister in [a distant county] while I was pregnant.

My treatment in the hospital was not very good, not very sympathetic, it made me feel even worse. I felt definitely as if I was being punished for what I had done ... it was something I had to put up with. I never saw the baby, apart of the vague memory I have of them holding up this baby and then taking her away.

Ben, who's my husband now, was one of the few people who knew that I'd had a baby and we were married in the October of the following year. I have now got two beautiful children.

Most of my jobs have been in secretarial work and that kind of thing in the past. I have also done some home help work, sort of filling in when the children were small. And I've done a bit of going back into education and I've done one or two courses over the last few years.

Jessica

Contact made through a national birth parents' group. Interview at her flat in a city. Lasted for 120 minutes.

I am 33 years old now and my baby was adopted ten years ago in June when I was 23.

I had been brought up in a small village in the country not far from here, where there was not really very much to do at weekends. I wasn't taking any precautions and neither was he. It was a one off and unfortunately I was caught out. He disowned me, he refused to admit that he was the father of the child which I found hurt me a lot although we were not in love and we were certainly not planning to get married. I was eight months pregnant before I went to tell the GP.

In terms of the care by the nursing staff I felt that I was being ignored. They can't look after you like everybody else, because of your circumstances. They may have felt that they were neglecting somebody when they were with me. I don't think there was anyone that was nice to me.

Just after my baby was born I was in a room with all the other mothers. He was in my arms for about an hour.

My fiance doesn't understand the sadness it causes to me; he can't cope with that.

I work as a secretary. The work is alright, its a secure job which pays the mortgage and the staff are all right. I get on with them.

Kara

Contact made through an article about this research project in the local evening paper. Interview at my place of work. Lasted for 120 minutes.

I'm twenty-eight. It was ten years ago when I had my baby adopted. I was 18 and went out and done the usual things.

I worked as an auxiliary nurse. I was fairly happy. I was going out with this guy who was Italian. He was the person I became pregnant to. He went back for a holiday and never returned.

When I was in the hospital everybody was fine, quite nice quite pleasant, but there was nobody who was exceptionally helpful over and above anybody else.

I saw my baby - the nurse had obviously been feeding him and she had him held in her arms facing towards us and I just knew it was my baby, because they do try to persuade you to go along. I suppose it's quite free and you can go if you want or don't want you don't have to. I could never have handled him or fed him or anything. 'Cos I know I wouldn't have given him up I don't think.

I haven't found the right person to settle down with but for a while I just didn't want to have any more children ever, and I'm good with kids.

I manage a small hotel now.

Lena

Contact made through a national birth parents' group. Interview at her modern house on an estate in a small Scottish town. Lasted for 120 minutes.

I'm 30. I was 14 when I had my baby adopted. My mother was a good doctor but not a very good mother I'm afraid. Another thing is I'm adopted and my family are all white apart from me.

We never really got a good education. My Mum pushed my sister, but she didn't push for any of the rest. When I was 16 I went to do a cadet nursing course, but I had to leave because I couldn't cope with it.

We had to tell them that it happened on the couch. Y'know, in my Mum's house one afternoon. It was really simple, it wasn't a complicated drawn out story. In fact it was more the truth. It was just that we was feared that if I'd've said that I didn't agree to it he would have gone to prison. I didn't agree to it at the time.

They just seemed to leave me to get on with labour and come back when they needed to be there, but they just left you to it. Now I feel that - at the time I probably felt I deserved it - but now I feel that would be a shame. I wouldn't want to do that to someone who was in the same position as me.

One of them did let me see the baby on the last day. But I think they realised that I was desperate and I wanted to say goodbye, so they let me go later on in the night and see her on the last night, and gave me the bottle to give to her and they left me alone with her. I thought that was nice.

When my husband and me got married we wanted to start a family soon. Then we found out we couldn't have children. That was a real blow to me. Its not so bad now. At the time it was heartbreak.

Marcia

Contact made through a national birth parents' group. Interview at my place of work. Lasted for 90 minutes.

I am now 63 and am retired from my work as a waitress.

My first son, Chris, was born in 1960, before I met Billy. I did not go out to work after that because I was looking after Billy's house and my child, Chris. I used to work before as a companion and housekeeper. With Billy being under stress and he was very difficult to live with at times.

I placed Andrea for adoption back in 1964, when I was 36 or I think 37.

Some of the staff were quite nice, some were quite nice and some - perhaps it was natural that ... I don't think it had anything special to do with me because when you go in hospital maybe you always find some are nice, some are not so nice, so I don't know whether it had anything to do with that or not. Some were nice, quite nice. Others were not so nice.

Actually, I breast fed her for some time and then after they came and - because I didn't want to keep it - and then they said 'It's going for adoption. You shouldn't breast feed it.'

I would have liked to take her home but Billy said 'No'. And of course all those other people with influence, you know, some friends of his said 'you're not well' and maybe in some ways it was true. Some way he wasn't well, that's true. But I think we could have managed.

Since I retired and married Billy, I started searching for her. And I've done that all the time. If I went into town or if I see a - if I used to see a child of her age or something I used to think - 'Oh could it be her'. Or even now I keep looking for her.

Nadia

Contact made through a national birth parents' group. Interview at a college of nursing and midwifery in a city. Lasted for 120 minutes.

I'm aged 41 now. I had Andrew when I was aged 19 and he was adopted almost straightaway. That means that he's 22 now.

In the family we were quite comfortably off, I was educated privately. I began nursing in the October, soon afterwards I realised that I was pregnant.

It was all a bit difficult because my parents didn't really approve of Billy, because his family was not very well off. I became pregnant when I was just eighteen. In my pregnancy I stayed with my sister down south.

On the whole I was very happy with the midwifery care. On the other hand on the postnatal ward there was one sister who was older and who seemed to have a thing against unmarried mothers - but she was the only one.

In the single room that I had later, I was nice and private with Andrew and I was able to be unhappy alone as separation was looming. I talked to the vicar. I arranged that I would be churched. I felt that this was necessary to take away the unclean feeling that the experience had left me with. I suppose I felt sort of dirty, but a bit less than that. I was not really a religious person, but it was my upbringing that made me feel like that.

I actually got engaged to Billy in the August and it was in October I signed the final papers and I married Billy a year later. I now work as secretary in Billy's construction business. The sorrow deepens, and the guilt is always present. The years after I placed him for adoption were busy years for me and Billy. I was having the children and he was building up the business. This prevented me from grieving properly Andrew's loss.

Olivia

Contact made through a national birth parents' group. Interview at her house near the centre of a city. Lasted for 105 minutes.

I'm 21 now. She was adopted in November two years ago, when I was 19.

My work's involved with freight forwarding - import and export.

At the time I got pregnant with Andrea I felt I owed the world a child, that's the only way to put it. I didn't purposely go out and have a child, I just didn't go back on the pill.

Billy, who's Andrea's father, provided a shoulder to cry on, but we have parted now, although we still keep in touch by phone.

I told the social worker and Jane, my lodger, and Billy found out. Others guessed.

When I went into labour this nurse who must have been a really junior grade was really helpful to me, she helped a lot. She held my hand, gave me the gas and air. I'm still uncertain who was who, this nurse stayed with me all through the birth and she rubbed my back. She stayed and cleaned the baby up after the birth. She had been popping in half-hourly in the morning and after lunch it was more like every 5 minutes. She stayed with me from two thirty. It was she who brought the phone.

I knew immediately I found I was pregnant that I would care for her while I was in hospital and that if she was fostered I would go and visit her in her foster home.

I'll be getting engaged and married within the next 18 months, and when I have my next pregnancy it'll all be so different.

Pamela

Contact made through a national birth parents' group. Interview at her modern flat in the centre of a city . Lasted for 135 minutes.

I was 19 when I had Andrew adopted, I'm 21 now.

I have no respect for my parents. They were divorced when I was aged 10. My mother left us for another man who she'd been going out with for a year. My father was taking me into gay bars by the time I was fifteen.

My current work is training as an accounts clerk.

My baby's father was not very good. I was reacting badly to him, I was feeling sick of him and the whole thing was turning sour. I left him. At that time I knew subconsciously I was pregnant. I didn't tell my parents because I was frightened of them disowning me and also of them ruining Andrew's life like they'd ruined mine.

I met Ben in April and Andrew was born in November.

Two nurses delivered Andrew; they were wonderful. They reassured me all the time. They did not give me a lot of information about what was happening. I breast fed Andrew.

I'm making a fresh start with my love for Ben, but memories of Andrew will always remain.

There is a need for more understanding. We should not feel left out or that we don't belong. They should treat you as you really are and not assume things. They should not make judgements about us.

Quelia

Contact made through a national birth parents' group. Interview at my place of work after she missed our first appointment. Lasted for 120 minutes.

I was 20 when my baby was born and was adopted. That was 16 years ago. I'm 36 now. I liked school. I got my 'O's and 'Highers'. I enjoy reading. I liked schooling generally, I never had any problem. I started when I was 5 and left when I was 17. Then I went to work beside my father. He worked with the water board in the county at the time.

My baby's father and I knew each other for a very long time. The pregnancy was not planned as these things often aren't. My baby's father was still around and he pleaded with me for the first five months of my pregnancy for us to get married. I just wasn't interested. It was when I was pregnant that I realised that I didn't love him as much as I thought I did.

There was one Sister in the hospital - She were really very good with me. She'd been with me from the Thursday, till the birth. She never even went home that night.

The nurse in the special nursery says 'Come on then, sit down there' and she brought Andrea over to me. I must've sat for about half an hour with her pondering what I would do. There was tears and everything. Then I said 'Take her from me and put her back'. She said 'Are you sure?' and I said 'That's it'.

I know we're not going to have a family of our own now. I feel I've let Ben down an awful lot. We were only married two years when I had to have my hysterectomy done.

Rosa

Contact made through a national birth parents' group. Interview at my place of work. Lasted for 90 minutes.

I'm 61 now. I was 29 when I had my baby adopted. When I was younger I was a librarian, I was a shop assistant, a home help. I also had a cafe in-between times.

Then I discovered I was going to have a baby. I had been going out with the baby's father for quite a while but although he was kind of sympathetic and everything he didn't want to get married at that particular time, unfortunately. I didn't push it.

I remember all the nurses and everyone in the hospital were always nice.

We actually had the babies for the six weeks - we were in complete charge of them. It was actually a very good grounding because the staff were helpful at the mother and baby home from that point of view - you were able to really gen up on everything.

I married the baby's father afterwards anyway, but he never really understood how I felt about it. However, we're divorced now - all water under the bridge. When I got married the second time, my husband never knew anything about it and I certainly wouldn't have told him, because he wouldn't have accepted that anyway.

Yet you hear of these people who get re-united with people they haven't seen for years and years, much longer than this. You think how on earth does it all evolve, how do they start finding people? I know it happens, it is just a lead they get. I seem to have come to a full stop.

Sandra

Contact made through a university freesheet. Interview at my place of work. Lasted for 120 minutes.

I'm 24 just now. The adoption is still actually mid-process, it hasn't been finalised yet. My parents live in [a country town]. I share a flat in this city. I'm working as a secretary.

It happened last June. When I actually had the baby I was 23.

I've had other relationships which I thought were going to work out, but they didn't work out. Basically he was the first steady relationship I had, yes.

My parents didn't want anybody in the town to know. I had to keep it very quiet in the town....

All the staff really were quite considerate towards my feelings really, because of my circumstances being that wee bit different, they were considerate.

The first time when I went to see her, I just sort of looked into the cot. I don't think I did hold her the first time. I just sort of thought she is really lovely and the people who are going to be looking after her are really lucky to have such a lovely little girl. Then I went back with my camera to get the photos taken and held her. That was in the Friday afternoon and then I went back on the Saturday and the Sunday to hold her again.

Billy will be able to come back from his own country and we'll get married and have other children.

Tanya

Contact made through a national birth parents' group. Interview at my place of work. Lasted for 135 minutes.

I'm now 38 years old. My daughter was adopted 20 years ago when I was 18. I was working as a nursery nurse, at the time I was training. I'd left school at 15 and I'd gone into that. Mum and Dad didn't like him because he was Catholic. And they didn't like him because he was unemployed and they just didn't think he was good enough for me in inverted commas. And they just didn't think he was for me. I think they would've felt that was terrible if I'd married a catholic. I think certainly sexually I was very naive, I knew that what I had done, which happened once, was wrong but I honestly didn't know why it was wrong. I think when I found out I was pregnant I was as surprised as anybody! I was sent to a Mother and Baby Home a fair way away.

In labour I cried and cried because I was totally unaware that it was going to be painful. I had no idea what to expect. I was left alone for a lot of the time and was crying out.

There was one nurse who was nice to me, that was the night nurse. She was always cheerful and pleasant with me and actually treated me like I was a human being. I think they didn't approve of me or of what I was doing in giving my baby up for adoption. I was in for over two weeks all together with one thing and another. The baby stayed with me during that time. I fed her and did everything for her while I had her with me.

I met someone else. I can't help wondering if there was a feeling at the back of my mind that I'd better marry him in case it was my last chance. That marriage very sadly broke up.

My second husband knows and two or three close friends.

Ursula

Contact made with the help of a journalist working on a presentation about relinquishment. Interview by 'phone due to distance. Lasted for 150 minutes.

I am aged 29 and I work as a sales receptionist with a television company. My baby, Andrew, is 8 weeks old now.

I split up from my fiance for a few months after an argument and during that time I went with this Arab boy and I caught then while we were split up. When we got back together I told my fiance that I wasn't sure whether he was the father of the baby. And he said that there was no way he could look after it if it wasn't his.

I was particularly upset by the midwife who was with me when I was in labour - she was a cow. She was chilly with me. The midwives who saw me afterwards were lovely, actually they were loving and interested. The midwife came to see me and when my milk came in she was so reassuring.

I went to see Andrew a lot in special care and the bonding was very strong.

I've been fighting my own natural human emotion - my love for my son. My fiance can't really understand how I'm feeling. I'll be sitting there thinking about him and he'll ask me what are you thinking about. As if I'd be thinking about anything else. Some people expect bloody miracles. They expect an immediate recovery from something like that.

Everybody round about keeps advising me to have another child to make me feel better. But no other child will ever be a substitute for Andrew and I'm not going to have a child as a form of therapy.

Vera

Contact made following a nationally networked radio interview about this research. Interview at my place of work. Lasted for 120 minutes.

I remember it all and I'm 57 years old now. My baby was born in 1955, when I was 23 or 24. I worked as a cook to begin with and later joined the MoD to work in the printing department. I had met the father of my baby a year earlier, he was separated from his wife, his wife had actually left him and it was a difficult time because he was missing his son.

When I was in the hospital the staff were all right. There was one grumpy nurse who was with me while I was in labour. She was not very sympathetic.

I did enjoy caring for him and breast feeding him. When he was weaned he would not take the bottle and so I had to keep on breast feeding him for much longer. I was pleased. I was glad to be able to care for him. I had not been given any choice about whether to care for him.

Some time after the birth I met up with the father of my baby again and he was angry that I had given the baby for adoption, but by that time there was nothing that anyone could do about it. We set up home together. He asked me to marry him, but I said only on condition that we didn't have any children because I had made a promise to Andrew that I'd never let anyone replace him. We got married, but when I was 35 he eventually persuaded me that we ought to try for a baby, but by then it was too late. I had my menopause early when I was 38 so we never did have another baby.

I'm not short of money. I can't leave it to my son so I'll have to leave it to my nephew. I'm a lonely and a bitter woman now. I don't know where my child, my son, is.

Wilma

Contact made following an item in a women's magazine about this research. Interview by phone due to distance. Lasted for 50 minutes.

I am 63 years of age now. I am well educated and my daughter was born in 1959. I was about 25-26 when my daughter was adopted, it was two years after she was born that I finally agreed to her being adopted.

After the war ended I had a job as a personal assistant and secretary. I met the father of my daughter. He was my first man, I was a virgin lady. He was not a nice person and the conception occurred after what you might call a seduction, but was more like a rape. My family forced us to become engaged. That was just before I became pregnant. He was the only man I'd had for seven years. He then ran off. He was known as a rotter, but I was very much in love with him.

The people in the home and in the hospital were very helpful, they were very good indeed. This applies both before and after the birth. The staff taught me how to care for my daughter. I arranged to have her christened.

I cared for my daughter in the hospital and in the home when we returned there. I breast fed her, although being my first (my only) child I needed to be told what I had to do.

The man I have lived with for 30 years knows all about this and is one hundred percent supportive. I did have a conversation with Andrea. I spoke to her by pretending to be a wrong number. I had hoped to be able to help financially. But the adoptive parents said 'No contact'. She is half her father's daughter and he was not a nice man. Until I retired I was the personal assistant to a director in an international organisation.

5 Keeping secrets and maintaining confidentiality

It was not surprising that secrecy and confidentiality emerged as important in my recent study (Mander, 1992a), but the serious implications of these concepts could in no way have been anticipated. The findings relating to these twin concepts are significant for the vulnerable mother, for her care as well as for researchers generally.

While the terms 'secrecy' and 'confidentiality' have certain meanings in common, to the extent that we may use them interchangeably. Closer scrutiny, however, reveals fundamental differences. By examining the roles of these twin phenomena in my recent research project, clear similarities in the use and misuse of secrecy and confidentiality emerge.

Meanings

A first glance at these words suggests that their meanings are so similar as to be synonymous, in that they both refer to the withholding of information. Dictionary definitions, though, indicate differences so crucial that each word is hardly mentioned in relation to the other (Simpson & Weiner, 1989). In defining 'secrecy' the focus is on concealment, by being hidden from sight or remaining undivulged. 'Confidentiality', however, features the trust and privacy underlying the confidences which are given or exchanged.

These definitions show that secrecy involves an action on the part of one person or group and that, in the care setting particularly, this term refers to an essentially personal activity. Confidentiality, on the other hand is more involved with the context, situation or framework within which the passage of information is restricted; a framework which is invariably controlled by a more or less explicit code of practice. The relationship between these words may be summarised in terms of the woman telling her secrets to the midwife assuming that the midwife will maintain her confidentiality. In recognition of this distinction Bok (1984:119) graphically states "Confidentiality refers to the boundaries and to the process of guarding these boundaries ... secrets lie at its core".

Maintaining and not maintaining confidentiality

The concept of the binding obligation of medical practitioners to respect the confidences of their patients is derived from the Hippocratic Oath (Jones, 1926; Beauchamp & Childress, 1989). Whereas other components of this Oath have been jettisoned, confidentiality has survived.

Benefits

Harris (1985) suggests utilitarian, even commercial, reasons for adherence to confidentiality, such as encouraging patients to seek qualified medical help and to seek it earlier rather than later. Open, trusting relationships between the patient and the adviser and a healthy community are, thus, assured. Further, a contract requiring privacy between the parties becomes established and the relationship cemented.

Melia (1988) further explores this finely-balanced, professional relationship in terms of its benefits to both the client and, as Shaw observed (1947), the professional. She discusses the difficulty of maintaining confidentiality in the highly specialised and multi-disciplinary team approach characteristic of the current health care system, highlighting the potential for breaching confidentiality.

Gillon (1986) extends Harris' consequentialist argument by suggesting that a further rationale for confidentiality lies in the moral principle of respect for personal autonomy, which is a fundamental moral requirement. The concept of personal autonomy as a form of control over our own lives is related to 'fidelity' by Veatch (1989). He describes how someone who violates our confidentiality is assuming control over 'our lives and our identities'. While perhaps overstating the consequences of a breach of confidence, Veatch indicates the potential for harm in such a breach.

The more questionable benefits of confidentiality are explored by Illich (1977), who builds on Harris' (1985) commercial argument which suggests that this concept also 'keeps doctors in work'. Illich proposes that confidentiality, reinforces medical independence and, hence, dominance. Thus, clients and patients are disempowered and escalating medical control prevents them from regaining control over their own lives.

Breach of confidentiality

Breach attracts as much attention as adherence. Harris (1985) describes this breach in terms of medical respect for confidentiality being 'governed by a sort of schizophrenia'; Harris' supporting evidence, which we all recognise, is the willingness of medical personnel to inform relatives of bad news in preference to telling the patient.

The debate on the extent to which confidentiality constitutes an absolute requirement has been joined by a number of authors, including Kottow (1986) who concludes that if this concept is to be of any value, adherence must be total. Another view has been advanced by Gillon (1986), who argues that exceptions to the concept of confidentiality need justification and not just the usual paternalistic excuses. Gillon's argument in favour of greater flexibility is taken to extremes in a nursing context by Melia (1988) and Moore (1988), who suggest that practitioners must decide for themselves when and to what extent confidentiality is appropriate.

Maintaining confidentiality in practice

Preparing for my recent study, confidentiality emerged as an issue during my search for approval by Research Ethical Committees (RECs). The role of the RECs, like that of other gatekeepers, is to protect vulnerable members of society from those who may take advantage of their vulnerability (Mander, 1992b). RECs ensure that patients and clients are protected from researchers for whom, while intending no harm, the welfare of the patient-respondent is not a priority. RECs traditionally comprise (mainly medical) professional carers who ensure that patients and others are not exposed to excessive or otherwise inappropriate demands or risks in the name of research.

One of the risks from which protection is needed is inappropriate self-exposure. This may relate to either the divulging of unnecessarily personal confidences or the publication of compromising material in which the person is identifiable, resulting in unhappiness for the person and those near her. The possibility of the routine guarantee of confidentiality causing more anxiety than any breach in confidentiality (Levine, 1986) is more of a problem for quantitative researchers.

Munhall (1991) questions whether assurances of confidentiality are realistic for those using qualitative methods, in view of their use of informants' direct quotations in research reports. She concludes that it is impossible to guarantee confidentiality under these circumstances, but that anonymity may be assured. She advocates, in spite of this limitation, that rigorous efforts are made to increase confidentiality by secure storage of data and by omitting identifiable names of people, places and dates in any reports.

The RECs showed appropriate concern that I, as any researcher, should protect the confidentiality of the informant:

> REC One also must take into account the new social circumstances in which these mothers are likely to be and the possibility that individuals close to them, in the social setting, may be totally unaware of their past history.

> REC The ethics committee were concerned with regard to what safeguards there would be in relation to ensuring the confidentiality of women who have previously relinquished a baby and may not wish their present partners to be aware of this.

The RECs' desire for confidentiality was well-founded on established ethical principles. This desire, however, was not always shared by the informants. I found that for many of these mothers openness within the family about the relinquished child is well-established. As far as partners are concerned, of the twenty-three mothers interviewed, Rosa was the only relinquishing mother who had been unable to tell one (the second) of her two husbands.

The *concern of all the midwife-informants* to maintain the confidentiality of the relinquishing mother emerged in my recent study. While the mother is in the maternity unit the midwives consider that other mothers may constitute a threat to her confidentiality:

> Lucy: The hardest thing actually is the other patients - they maybe start to befriend a person who is in this position on the ward and want to find out ... All the normal questions they all ask each other. 'Have you had your baby?' 'Where is your baby' - things like that. I think that is probably the hardest thing - to keep news from the other patients within the ward.

The midwives' difficulty is aggravated by the baby being cared for in the nursery, when all other babies are being 'roomed in' alongside their mothers:

> Marie: [If the baby is in the ward nursery] other mums will be asking who the baby belongs to and you don't really want to go and tell them.

The *relinquishing mothers recounted their anxiety* that their confidentiality may not be safe. Nadia, a GP's daughter, was anxious about the confidentiality of a diagnostic consultation before she had been able to tell her parents of her pregnancy:

> Nadia: In May and June I didn't have my periods, so I went to a strange GP, because our GP was a partner of my Dad's.

Others were concerned about midwives' confidentiality:

> Sandra: In fact my parents didn't want the [community] midwife to know [about my pregnancy] at all, it was the doctor that did all of my after-care ... They didn't want the midwife to know at all. I don't know why. Perhaps 'cos it would get round the Health Centre and then round the town. I s'pose y'know it would tend to [get around] in a small town, it might have slipped out in conversation, just thinking somebody knew and then ... I wouldn't have minded seeing her, but it was my parents who - they are the ones who have to live in the town so ...

Quelia suspects that her confidentiality may not have been maintained by the staff she met:

> Quelia: One of the nurses did say to me 'You're going to regret this for the rest of your life, if you give your baby up'. You do regret it [TEARS] ... She used to ask a lot of really more prying questions than anything else. 'What about the baby's father?' And I said what's that got to do with it? I'm not here to discuss him, I'm here to discuss me and my baby. Quite a few of the women said she was very, very inquisitive. When you're in the hospital you're wanting everything to be kept confidential. I'm not saying that she would go out and blab it, but you just don't know, when it comes to something like that.

Quelia's mention of the inquisitive nurse brought to mind the possibility of her being a gossip in the ancient as well as the modern meaning of the word (Simpson & Weiner, 1981). Gossips were originally the local womenfolk who were present to support and help at a birth. Because these women soon collected a supply of juicy anecdotes, the modern meaning developed.

My own observations suggest that Quelia's concern may be justified. In the series of interviews at one maternity hospital all six midwives mentioned to me the case of one woman who had relinquished her baby under particularly sad circumstances. I am unable to question their telling me (an impartial and confidential researcher), but I was concerned by the way in which all the staff I met were able and prepared to repeat the story - including those who had not cared for her:

> Irene: There was a couple recently who had a baby with [disease]. I had no direct contact with them. I heard about them in here.

I had already become aware of inconsistency in the use of confidentiality during my negotiations for access with a particular group of gatekeepers and practitioners. My request for help with gaining access to a suitable sample of mothers was rejected by a major adoption agency on the grounds that:

> ... to receive an unsolicited letter from us may well intrude on their life since the adoption of the child. It would be different if you were writing to all unmarried mothers giving birth over a certain period at the [maternity unit], as this would not break the confidentiality of our records.

At the same time as I was being denied access, other social workers [SWs] told me heart-rending stories about identifiable clients. An example is the name of the tiny coastal village one mother came from; while in another maternity unit, I was given information including the first name of a relinquishing mother and the (highly significant) occupation of the baby's grandmother.

Although we all accept confidentiality as a crucial aspect of the care of the relinquishing mother, its interpretation and implementation is inconsistent, which may be associated with interdisciplinary difficulties. An example is the sharing of information about the relinquishing mother by SWs, which causes some anxiety among midwives:

> Ottily: The information that we get from SWs varies hugely. Sometimes the reports from social work are far too long. I think that we only really need to know what the girl is prepared to tell us. Sometimes we get far too much information ... The SW reports tend to be either screeds and screeds or else just the name, address and date of birth.

Other midwives were even less satisfied with the information which SWs were prepared to share, in that this may carry implications for their provision of care:

> Annie: Information is lacking. Any information about these mothers would be nice. We get nothing about the woman's circumstances. There was one girl we had in and it was not until after the baby had been born that she told

us the reason that the baby was going for adoption was that she had been raped. We hadn't been told. I'm not saying that it would have made any difference to our care, but I think we should have been told. We would perhaps have given her better psychological care or dealt with her more sensitively. Also if we had more information, it would help us to understand what kind of support she was going to get when she went home.

The extent of interdisciplinary sharing of confidential information, or its lack, may reflect the level of understanding and trust between members of the health care team:

> Queeny: I feel that [SWs] don't tell you enough, its as if they're always keeping something back from you. And when you do have someone admitted you probably get the information about three days after the baby has been born!

> Emily: SWs tend not to report their findings to midwives. So we don't know what she is thinking about and are uncertain what to say to her. It's not awful good.

To summarise the points made so far, the crucial role of confidentiality is emphasised both in the literature and by the gatekeepers. The practice of confidentiality is inconsistent and falls short of the standard recommended by these authorities. Inconsistent maintenance of confidentiality exacerbates interdisciplinary tension and is perceived as adversely affecting care.

Keeping secrets

Not surprisingly, I found studying a topic as sensitive as relinquishment illuminated the ways in which secrecy is used by those involved with the birth and the relinquishment. As mentioned already, secrecy is essentially a phenomenon which has personal implications for those using it. This distinguishes it from confidentiality, which operates within a structured framework.

Bok (1984) further defines secrecy in terms of the intention to conceal. It comprises the probably planned, and certainly deliberate, action or word or inaction or silence. In examining secrecy, we are not considering the casual omission or accidental oversight.

Although we may assume that information is kept secret because its revelation may be discrediting to its keeper, this assumption is not always justified. The words 'guilty' and 'secrets' may be difficult to uncouple, but objective scrutiny requires that, in view of the range of potentially secret material, we must uncouple them. The range of material extends from the sacred secrets known only to the holiest, through the unspoken, to the most shameful and ignominious secrets.

The rationale for employing secrecy may appear to be as wide-ranging as the nature of the secrets themselves. The aim, however, is invariably to provide protection, which is needed for a variety of reasons relating to the present and future, personal as well as objective. As Bok states: 'secrecy serves to protect what we are, what we intend, what we do and what we own' (1984).

Childbearing has been used as a metaphor for secrecy (Brazell, 1973). Although the conception is usually a secret or at least private matter, the pregnancy brings increasing public awareness. The revelation of the pregnancy is initially only to the mother, allowing her to decide with whom she will share her developing realisation. Eventually the existence of the pregnancy becomes manifest to all, but still crucial concerns, the child's sex and other characteristics, traditionally remain unknown until the birth. Even after the birth when much about the child ceases to be secret, lingering doubts may persist concerning, for example, the child's paternity (Strindberg, 1960).

Protecting by secrecy

As I have noted already the role of secrecy is principally to protect something of value. In my recent study the parents of the relinquishing mother played a crucial role in seeking secrecy, supposedly to protect their daughter. For Tanya her parents were trying to protect her from the limited future they anticipated if the pregnancy became public knowledge:

> RM: Why did you have to move to [another city]?
> Tanya: Probably just because my GP chose it and partly because [my parents] wouldn't have wanted me in [this city]. I might have bumped into somebody I knew. So they wanted me out the city, they wanted to keep it quiet, I think they realised that certain neighbours and obviously family were going to know about it but I think it was one thing to know about it and another thing to parade it before their eyes. So they wanted me out the way. I think my father had me so convinced that I had completely ruined my life, that that was it. My life was over, because I had done this.

In the same way as the relinquishing mother needed to be protected, even in a close-knit family, other family members were perceived as being in need of protection from information which would have been hurtful or harmful in other ways:

> Barbara: We didn't tell either set of grandparents. I suspect we felt - I don't really know what we felt. I don't know whether it was to protect me or to protect them, because a lot of things they did to try and protect me I think was there way of trying to do things to make it as easy as possible for me. [After the birth] my Dad's mother was due to come up after a few days and we had to pretend that nothing had happened. I was sitting down gingerly because of having had stitches, so we had to pretend that I had a cold, which we did.

For Tanya and Elena their close loving relationships with their younger brothers were seriously threatened by the secrecy imposed by their parents:

Tanya: Well I know that my younger brother didn't know. 'Cos it was actually years later that he found out. He must only have been 11, because my parents used to come through every second Sunday to see me in [another city] and I remember them saying that George, he was in a terrible state because he hadn't seen me for so long. And he kept saying 'I want to come with you to see her', and they had to keep making up new excuses 'cos they didn't want him to see me pregnant. And they had told him that I was working through in [another city].

Elena: Then my brothers came back and I had to lie to them and say I had been on holiday.
RM: Did they not know?
Elena: One was 17 and he had been to visit me with my Mum in the mother and baby home, but I wasn't allowed to speak about it to anyone ... my little brother - I said I had been on holiday to my aunty's. He said he had had a great time and I said 'So have I'. That was very hard. It was the end of the subject.

Secrecy was used to protect other things held dear, which might have been damaged by knowledge of the pregnancy and relinquishment, such as the newly-rebuilt relationship enjoyed by Olivia and her parents:

Olivia: Now over the two years we have built that [loving trusting relationship] up which is why I had to keep Andrea a secret, I just couldn't risk losing that. I couldn't risk losing what I had built up with my parents. My Dad still doesn't know, my mother may suspect but it is never discussed. I certainly wouldn't raise it because there is a danger of damaging the relationship that we have just managed to build.

Pamela, who endured a long-term, turbulent relationship with her parents, used secrecy to protect her son from the trauma which she had suffered previously:

Pamela: My parents were never told. I'm uncertain whether they know, I acted real well ... I didn't tell my parents because I was frightened of them disowning me and also of them ruining Andrew's life like they'd ruined mine. Protecting Andrew from my parents was the main reason for my not telling them I was pregnant.

Maintaining secrecy

One strategy which was used to maintain secrecy simply involves ensuring that others do not see the woman in her obviously pregnant state. The hope being that those well-placed to observe and report, particularly neighbours, would be unaware of the physical changes. This was to be achieved by using strategies which seem pathetically transparent:

Elena: A couple of nights I went to see [my parents] and then I got told off because the neighbours had seen me pregnant - they didn't want the neighbours to know. I felt really angry then ... I felt really rejected by both of them. I was mostly angry at them. I think [the neighbours] must have known, I remember saying that to them -'I don't care what the neighbours think'.

Clara [Field notes]: My father ... made me keep it a secret from my younger sister who was then 11 years old and from visitors to the house. I had to keep a blanket over my belly and tell them I had a cold when they came into the house.

The parental desire for secrecy frequently resulted in the pregnant woman being 'sent away' in order remove her from the sight of what were considered to be prying eyes. This was invariably to a conveniently distant friend or relative:

Gina: My parents said 'I think ... you should go to [another continent] for a holiday' ... I was sent away to [another continent] in March on my own to friends.

Frequently, secrecy was facilitated by arranging for the pregnant woman to stay in a mother and baby home at a suitable distance from the family home:

Debra: I moved away to the mother and baby home which was in [another city] about fifty miles away. It was a church establishment - the Central Hall. It was nice.

The fact that the relinquishing mothers in this sample had such easy recourse to mother and baby homes is associated with the fact that some of them gave birth during the 1960's and 1970's, when places in these establishments were easily available. In a research project, Nicholson (1968) encountered difficulty in identifying the purpose of these homes. For the mothers in my recent study, mother and baby homes provided care and support; these benefits continue to be provided in countries, such as USA, where this provision still exists (Cushman et al., 1993). A further benefit was that the mother was despatched to a home which was a suitable distance to allow secrecy but not far enough to prevent contact.

It may be argued that societal attitudes have changed since these mothers were pregnant and that what has come to be known as the 'permissive society' has made secrecy less relevant. The data provided by the informants in this study suggest that secrecy is still a significant factor to mothers contemplating relinquishment and to their parents. This is supported by the fact that all of the mothers who relinquished more recently were still concerned about secrecy to a greater or lesser extent.

That secrecy continues to feature prominently among the concerns of relinquishing mothers is evidenced by Aline, the mother who became the subject of the case study. As with other mothers and their parents, Aline was concerned about the possibility of her physical appearance exposing her pregnant state:

Aline [32 weeks]: The bump is not very obvious yet, although the midwife told me that the baby is a good size ... I think people (like my Dad and Ol' Nosey at the office) will not notice. I always wear sloppy sweaters and those can hide a helluva lot.

The premature birth of her baby served to preserve this secrecy:

Aline [Day 7 after the premature birth]: When I said [to you] in the labour room that I was glad it had happened, I think that I was not just glad that the pregnancy was over. I was glad that I was not going to be getting any bigger and having to drag myself around. And probably the secrecy thing as well. If I didn't get any bigger it wouldn't be so obvious. Andrea's coming early really was convenient. It's not a nice thing to say, but its realistic.

Maintenance of secrecy by simply preventing the pregnant woman from being seen was supported by other, similarly simple, forms of deception:

Sandra: Any time any folk came to visit the house I had to disappear upstairs. But [my parents] are usually supportive. I think they probably told the visitors I just wasn't there.

The role of telling lies, as Sandra's parents found necessary, moves secrecy into the realm of even more deliberate, concrete forms of deception, which may not be easily acceptable to those who need to resort to it:

Olivia: I didn't have to lie to anybody [about] where I had been or about anything else. I don't believe in telling lies. I may have had to twist the truth occasionally, like by saying that I had been too busy to call in and see my parents or by saying that the three weeks I had had off [for the birth] was holiday. I had to lie to a friend who had had her baby at the same time as me and her baby was on the critical list, so it might have upset her to know. My parents have always valued honesty, that means that twisting the truth is OK, but it is wrong to lie. I sometimes had to give the minimum of information, too.

The desire for secrecy is supported by those who care for the relinquishing mother. Rosa's example constituted, to her, an amusing anecdote concerning a midwife's attitude to secrecy:

Rosa: I can remember having a letter from one of my friends, addressed to Miss Rosa Smith ... [the midwife] said 'I've put it under the pillow in case anyone should see it'... I used to smile to myself when I thought about that. She wasn't being nasty or anything. She was kind about it. I s'pose she thought 'If someone sees that, they might wonder'. Whoever it was that had written never thought. I suppose that sending it to a maternity hospital, you don't usually put Miss ...

This example from Rosa demonstrates the extent to which midwives feel obliged to respect the mother's need for secrecy, particularly in relation to other mothers in the maternity unit:

> Aline [Day 7 after the birth]: If I'd been in a room with other mothers they may not have been understanding about me having to give my baby for adoption. Other people shouldn't judge about things they don't know about but they do. But what others think about you does get to you. Explaining would be difficult.

The relinquishing mother's ability to cope with the 'others' was a source of anxiety to the midwives. The advice given to the relinquishing mother about how to deal with other mothers' well-meant enquiries caused much concern:

> Kay: I don't think we should give her an explanation to give to other mothers. 'Cos what seems like a good idea at the time she might regret saying in five years time and 'Well that's what the midwife told me to do'. If she wants to lie to the other mothers it should be her decision. I think what you must encourage her to do is deal with the situation as she feels happy. If she feels happy just to say that she's lost her baby or the baby's ill or upstairs - do that. I mean if that helps her deal with the situation that's fine.

Although not explicitly recommending that the relinquishing mother should lie, the midwives, as Kay implied, considered that 'wee white lies' might make the mother's experience in the maternity unit easier. This strategy is assisted by the general practice of caring for a relinquishing mother in a single room, followed by early transfer home - thus reducing the risk of chance encounters with other mothers and having to cope with their questions.

The possibility of the midwife being required to lie in order to maintain the secrecy sought by the relinquishing mother is very real. Midwives, as individuals, are reluctant to tell lies, but they are also clear about the extent to which they are prepared to lie when necessary:

> Bessie: We have had to say she's here because gynae is full, in order to maintain secrecy, although we try not to have to lie. One girl was having a baby and she had told all sorts of lies to her boyfriend. We just could not go along with that.

Despite the current lack of mother and baby homes, the relinquishing mother often chooses to maintain secrecy by arranging to give birth in a maternity unit distant from her home. Secrecy causes midwives some difficulty in dealing with telephone enquires about the progress and welfare of this mother. Midwives described in detail how they deal with such situations:

> Josie: When the woman doesn't want any contact with ... the father of the child, which we do try to keep when they phone up. We don't tell them that she's here, but its very difficult to tell [all the staff] on every phone occasion what to say, it is quite difficult but we do try if they don't want any ... but normally they phone up and as long as we know they don't want any contact then we will quite happily say 'No, she's not here', just in case.

Nellie: There's only ever been one situation where a girl had a baby going for adoption and she had a problem with the father of the baby. She didn't want any information to be given to him. What we always do is if there's a phone call we ask them to hang on while we go and speak to the lady and quite often they come to the phone to speak to them. 'Cos then they can tell if the caller is bogus usually, and there's no information given out. We don't tend to give out information about anybody, we ask the caller to get in touch with the family. You don't usually say anything over the phone. Every case is confidential we don't give any details or anything.

The need for secrecy may become particularly acute after her transfer home, if the relinquishing mother and her parents are concerned that the neighbours should not know about the birth. Midwives' postnatal examinations, which are made daily until at least day ten postnatally, cause definite problems because the majority of these are made in the mother's home. In this situation midwives make special arrangements to maintain secrecy:

Lucy: I have heard of some ladies who actually came up to the hospital for their postnatal examinations, as opposed to having a midwife go out to the home. I don't know whether that was for the benefit of their neighbours ...

Yolandy: A lot of the time its fear as well, what are her neighbours going to think? The last patient I was involved with got taken into hospital and the neighbours thought she was going off on holiday. She was quite adamant that the midwife wouldn't come to her house to see her postnatally. Her mum drove out quite a long distance daily just to get her midwife checks after the baby was born.

Formal carers are able to support the relinquishing mother by providing the degree of secrecy which she feels is appropriate. Midwives recounted how their work is rearranged and how, occasionally, their principles may be compromised.

Using secrecy

So far in this chapter, I have been considering secrecy in terms of being absolute, that is either present or absent. We must consider whether this picture of a blanket ban on any information being given is realistic or whether the situation is actually more complex. The relinquishing mothers indicated that secrecy tends to be applied by and to different people quite selectively and to varying degrees. An example of the selective application of secrecy by the relinquishing mother is found in her willingness to inform her parents of the pregnancy. Although parents tend to assume control of who is 'in on the secret' they themselves are likely to be excluded for as long as the relinquishing mother feels it necessary:

Hilda: When I was having Andrew ... I used to cut myself on my finger and put the blood onto my pants, because [my mother] was always looking for things like that and that was what I would do to make her think I was having periods. I used to take the sanitary towels and flush them away so that she'd think they were being used up.

The selective use of secrecy is also apparent in Aline's reluctance to tell her father, with whom she had a tenuous relationship, despite sharing his house. Aline told her mother at a relatively early stage and, together, they contemplated the problems involved in informing her father of the pregnancy:

Aline [32 weeks]: We've not told him about the pregnancy yet. He certainly won't have realised that I'm pregnant. We may tell him this coming weekend. If he was told he would start drinking in the pub and would tell everybody around ... I have to be careful about what I say to people because my father knows nothing as yet. My mother and I haven't found the right opportunity to tell him yet. I dread to think what his reaction will be. He'll go mad. I think we might be able to tell him this weekend. I'm telling only those people who need to know. I've told the junior I share an office with, because of having to run upstairs for faxes and nearer the birth I'll be asking her to do this for me as it would be too much. I'm not telling Ol' Nosey who tries to find out why I'm having time off my work, by asking about how my sore back is now?

The collusion between mother and daughter appears a wise precaution in view of the anticipated difficulties should Aline's father react badly to the news. Aline's reasons for not telling her work colleague are less clear. This leads to the conclusion that Aline may be assuming control over her situation, at least to the extent of who is and who is not made aware of her pregnancy. This conclusion is confirmed in Aline's account of her father being required to keep the secret of Andrea's birth:

Aline [7 days after the birth]: Dad was asking about whether mother has told anyone. Dad is a bit like a wee kid, he likes to have something to brag about. He wants to tell people about it. But he can't tell anyone outwith the family yet. He goes to a men-only club ... My mother said to him that he could tell the man that he meets there - he's all right. We also said that he could tell Auntie Bella. Dad really is bursting to tell someone. He's not been able to tell anyone yet (LAUGH). We said that he could tell his one friend, but his other friend was there so he couldn't say anything.

Their manipulation of her father's keeping the secret of his new granddaughter was a source of amusement to Aline and her mother. Others were similarly selective or inconsistent in their application of secrecy. The reasons for this inconsistency are not immediately apparent, unlike the hurt which results:

Sandra: Well my parents are usually supportive ... but in this case they didn't want anybody in the town to know. I had to keep it very quiet in the town ...
RM: Is there anybody who you are not telling now?

Sandra: Most of my close friends certainly know. I've got a batch of friends at [town] - and my parents said 'Whatever you do don't tell them because it might get back to [town]'. They are so bothered about it getting back to [town]. I wouldn't have minded telling people, but it was my parents who - they are the ones who have to live in the town so ... The thing is they are starting to tell people now, for example they have told the Minister in the town, after it's all over with. That's another reason why I don't feel I can really go to Church at home because they have told the Minister. I don't really feel I can - I would be ashamed to go to the Church because I know the Minister knows.
RM: Why should you be ashamed?
Sandra: Just because the Minister knows the fact that I've had a baby - a single mother. Personally I wouldn't have wanted the Minister to know but my parents decided that he should know.

The manipulation of secrecy shows the way in which information is being used as a form of control. The relinquishing mother and her parents, having found themselves in this situation, realise that they are powerless. The only asset, strength or bargaining tool available to them is their knowledge of this secret, to which few are privy. Inevitably, knowledge is used as the lever to assume some degree of control over their situation.

The accounts given by Aline and Sandra illustrate this use of secrecy. The interactions within the traditional male-dominated Scottish household which Aline shared with her parents are understandable when viewed in this way. For Sandra's parents, their inability to protect and their failing control over their youngest child were confirmed when she became pregnant. When they welcomed the opportunity to protect her and resume control over her actions by requiring secrecy, the responsibility proved so great that they found they needed extra support from outside the family.

Bok (1984) considers the use of secrets within relationships in similar, clearly relevant, terms. The curiosity which is engendered among those who are not 'in on the secret' lends a respect and admiration for those Bok refers to as the 'insiders'. She goes on to account for the other attractions of secrecy for the insiders. These attractions include, first, a desire to gain control over a situation which, for the relinquishing mother and her parents, may appear uncontrollable. Second, Bok describes the need to feel superior to those not 'in on the secret'. This need is a prevailing characteristic of the relinquishing mother, whose self-esteem is abysmal. The third attraction mentioned by Bok is the longing for the intimacy which sharing secrets brings. This need for intimacy is linked with Bok's final point in its relevance to this mother, which is the need to be an 'insider'. The relinquishing mother, in so many ways stigmatised and isolated, eagerly grasps the opportunity for the closeness of sharing and acceptance which secrets present.

The uses of secrecy listed by Bok have been transposed into a more adversarial context, which may also be relevant when thinking about manipulation of and by the relinquishing mother (Bailey, 1991:33). After considering the extent to which any knowledge about a person constitutes having power over them, Bailey goes on to define a secret as 'a form of ... capital that can be invested in domination or resisting domination by others'. The at least double-edged nature of this weapon becomes more clearly apparent. Secrecy's multiplicity of uses is further clarified when Bailey recounts the not only selective, but quantitatively variable application of secrecy: 'one keeps secrets from people in order to control them, for fear that greater knowledge might diminish the support they give or even make them obstructive. In doing so one limits their options and so diminishes their power'.

To summarise the points which I have been making relating to secrecy, it is primarily and overtly used to protect the relinquishing mother, as well as those close to her and that which she values. It is employed by both formal carers, following the wishes of the mother herself, and also by informal carers. As well as being used to provide protection, secrecy may be manipulated to achieve other, probably personal, goals which are even less tangible. The effects of these goals may be perceived by the relinquishing mother negatively, in that she may consider them harmful to her. Secrecy may be used in more adversarial situations as a powerful form of control.

Conclusion

More generally, in the same way as formal and informal carers employ secrecy to protect the relinquishing mother, the benefits of which may not be experienced solely by the mother (Illich, 1979), the gatekeepers also aim to protect her through using confidentiality. They fervently argue the desirability of confidentiality in maintaining this mother's secrecy.

Confidentiality may be rigorously imposed by the gatekeepers on 'outsiders'. An example already mentioned, given by Ottily, is the occasions when those caring for the mother are told 'just the name, address and date of birth'. Another example is a researcher seeking access for a project which may illuminate and possibly improve this mother's care.

In the same way as I have shown that the practice of secrecy achieves something other than the protection of the relinquishing mother, the practice of confidentiality also tends to be more complicated, if not confused, than its advocates, the theoreticians and gatekeepers, suggest. Confidential material is used, that is shared, by practitioners in the ways and for the reasons which Bok explains that secrecy is being used. The achievement of personal goals is the explanation which Bok suggests for the manipulation of secrecy, its relevance to the manipulation of confidentiality appears comparable.

In my recent study similarities have emerged between the imposition of secrecy by the relinquishing mother and her parents and the imposition of confidentiality by the gatekeepers. These similarities indicate that certain participants exert greater control than others over the balance of power. This control may be of benefit to people other than the person in whose interests secrecy and confidentiality are intended to function - the relinquishing mother.

6 Relinquishing and being bereaved

In this chapter I explore the literature and the data to assess whether and to what extent the concept of bereavement is applicable to the mother relinquishing her baby for adoption.

The relevance of bereavement

The term 'bereavement', carrying its overwhelming connotation of death, may be regarded as inappropriate in the context of a mother relinquishing her live, healthy baby for adoption. Osterweis et al. (1984) appear to hold this view when they define bereavement as: 'the fact of loss through death'. This view was expressed by a Research Ethical Committee (REC) of whom I sought permission to research the comparison of care of a relinquishing mother and care of a bereaved mother (Mander, 1992a). The REC wrote:

> 'there is a voluntary action on the part of this patient ... and that makes the two situations totally different'.

Osterweis' definition may, however, be interpreted differently if taken in context, that is, in a report on caring for those close to people who are terminally ill. These authors' other definitions explain the meaning of grief, mourning and bereavement reactions, suggesting that the emphasis in the definition of bereavement should be on 'the fact of loss ...' rather than on 'loss through death'.

Using the term 'bereavement' in the context of relinquishment is supported by etymological evidence. The active verb 'to bereave' means 'to steal anything of value' (Chambers, 1981). The widely-used adjective 'bereft' is the passive form of the verb 'to bereave' and clearly indicates a loss which may be more or less tangible. Both forms are related to the verb 'to reave' (as in the border rievers) meaning 'to plunder or rob'; feminist writers imply that this term may be highly pertinent to the relinquishing mother, and not only because of its etymological origins (Shawyer, 1979; Inglis, 1984).

In this chapter I suggest that the mother's reaction to the experience of relinquishment is similar to the reaction to loss through death. This suggestion is certainly supported by the mothers I interviewed who had previously relinquished a baby:

> Elena: It's hard to explain, but I felt ... pure grief, how I imagine people would feel if the baby died. I still always feel that sense of loss.
>
> Nadia: Particularly when I left him in the hospital, I felt grief and desperation.

Bereavement and relinquishment

Material relating to the relinquishing mother has mentioned her grief, that is 'the feeling (affect) and certain associated behaviours' (Osterweis et al., 1984). This does not establish the fact of her loss. It is necessary to ascertain whether her feelings and behaviour correlate with those of people bereaved through death in order to assess whether her experience of loss may be regarded as comparable. Through the literature relating to the mother, I sought to discover whether previous workers have been able to describe her feelings following her relinquishment.

The first comparison between relinquishment and loss through death appears in work evaluating adoption policy and practice (Triseliotis, 1970). A proportion of mothers went through a distressing period in the first few weeks after relinquishment and their 'reactions were reminiscent of the reaction of bereaved people'.

Similar observations were made by Dukette in Chicago during early attempts to 'open up' adoption by encouraging participation by relinquishing parents (1979). Her recognition of the 'pain of giving up a child' and the need for healthy grief work was based on her work with self-help groups.

Progress towards open adoption in USA (Richards, 1970) has been facilitated by a perceptive study by Pannor and colleagues (1978). These researchers interviewed thirty eight relinquishing parents who had parted with their children about fifteen years earlier. This study provides background information about the parents at the time of their relinquishment and subsequently (Sorosky et al., 1984). While recognising the role of the adopters, a majority of the parents were concerned that the child might have feelings of having been rejected. Less than a third of the parents were comfortable with their relinquishment decision and half reported that they still experienced feelings of loss or pain associated with their relinquishment. The researchers were, not surprisingly, unprepared for either the depth or duration of the parents' mourning and their research design was insufficiently flexible to probe the nature or symptoms of the parents' grief.

The seminal study by Winkler and Van Keppel in Australia followed and built on that by Sorosky and Pannor, although the major publications appeared simultaneously in 1984. The Australian study drew on the experiences of a sample of 213 relinquishing mothers and utilised a theoretical framework founded on the well-recognised links between grief, maladjustment, stress and ill-health. This study's comparison of relinquishment and perinatal loss concentrates on the **context** of the mother's grief and poor adjustment and its consequences in terms of health. The examination of the **nature** of the grief focusses only on the grief response to perinatal death, without considering whether the experiences of these two mothers are qualitatively comparable. The majority of the data comprise general measurements of health and adjustment using the General Health Questionnaire (Goldberg, 1972). The scantier material on the nature of the grief comprises the data and discussion on the 'sense of loss', which focus on the changes in ill-defined feelings over time, rather than on precise symptoms.

Rynearson (1982), preparing for a large-scale prospective study of relinquishing mothers, interviewed twenty American women who had previously relinquished a baby. His findings correlate powerfully and positively with those of my recent study, detailing the mother's feelings of grief. These findings should be regarded with caution, as Rynearson admits, on the grounds that the sample comprised patients drawn from a population of psychiatric outpatients. He indicates that the unusual sample may have given rise to some degree of 'distortion' by virtue of, first, the nature of the health problem and, second, reliance on recall.

Although not research-based, the argument advanced by Howe (1990) is valuable in this context because it represents a recent, UK-based and midwifery-oriented approach to the grief of the relinquishing mother. He draws on the Winkler and Van Keppel study to establish the significance of relinquishment and its similarity to loss through perinatal death. The similarities which he cites are largely situational, focussing on the care provided for the two mothers. His account of the grieving process summarises the features common to all the models of grieving but fails to advance the present argument because it is not specifically applied to either of these mothers.

The Scottish study by Bouchier and her colleagues (1991) draws on other countries' moves towards open adoption for its context, in an attempt to compare the feelings of mothers who do and those who do not wish to resume contact with the relinquished one. The similarity of relinquishment to bereavement is, again, broadly apparent, but unrelated to any model of grief. The accounts of the mother's feelings are in general terms, such as degree of stress, changes in feelings, frequency of thought about children, adjustment and effects on health and well-being.

On the basis of this brief review of the meagre literature on this topic, it is apparent that any detailed comparison between the grief of bereavement and relinquishment is lacking and the assumption of similarity is based on general observations.

Relinquishment and bereavement

I will now explore the extent to which the data in my recent study support the assumption that relinquishment and bereavement are comparable.

Similarities

Relinquishment and bereavement were, as mentioned above, clearly similar to the mothers:

> Elena: I still have nightmares about the baby, although I am trying very hard not to feel bad about it. The feelings tend to come back and to get worse at night time.
>
> Pamela: I think of him every day and this has not changed at all, but it does vary with what I'm doing.

The typically discontinuous nature of grief is obvious from these comments and reinforces Lindemann's observation of 'sensations of distress occurring in waves lasting from twenty minutes to an hour at a time ... The patient soon learns that these waves of discomfort can be precipitated by visits or by mentioning the deceased'. Similarly, Parkes (1976) discusses 'acute and episodic pangs of grief'. It appears that for all the relinquishing mothers who told me that night time is their time for crying, their day time is too full to allow time for grieving. For some, such as Elena, their days were filled with raising a family; others, such as Pamela, were reconstructing their lives by establishing a career.

Anniversary reactions: In the course of resolution of grief, the 'waves of discomfort' gradually become less frequent as the new identity begins to fit more comfortably (Stroebe & Stroebe, 1987). Symptoms may be 'triggered' (Bouchier et al., 1991) at more or less predictable times, and have become known by the less than satisfactory title of 'anniversary reactions' (Oglethorpe, 1989):

> Tanya: It comes back to me with the birth of each of my babies. Each one makes me remember the separation from her - I know I must come to terms with it.
>
> Vera: Birthdays and Christmas were always particularly bad. Then I'd wonder what he was like and what he was doing. I'd wonder what kinds of presents they were giving to him and what I would have given to him if only I'd been able to. Christmases have got easier, but birthdays are still hard. As [his birthday] approaches it is always a difficult time for me. But I don't know what he is like now, apart from the fact that he is 33, but I don't even know that ...
>
> Olivia: I don't pine for her. There are certain specific times when I think about her, such as when there is something on the TV, or something that I see in the street, or at Christmas.

Denial: The pregnancy of each relinquishing mother featured denial. It tended to reappear as a coping mechanism to assist with her loss through relinquishment. Jones (1989b) discusses the way in which denial was used by a dying man, regarding it as a helpful temporary coping mechanism which acts like a buffer in the face of some overwhelming threat, such as bereavement or death. Used on a more long-term basis, however, Jones maintains that it may hinder communication, invalidate support and render behaviour quite inappropriate.

Despite having mementoes of the birth, such as cot cards, name bands and photographs, the mother still has difficulty working through her denial to accept the reality of the birth and relinquishment.

> Jessica: Sometimes now I think 'Did it actually happen?' I find I can't believe it, even though its happened to you.

During her relinquishment, Hilda experienced a series of unexpected and unwelcome encounters. Her baby was born prematurely and her recollection was, not of her baby's face to facilitate her grieving, but of a mutilated part of the baby, for which she was unprepared and was, not surprisingly, shocked:

> Hilda: ... and I ken he was in my arms but I cannae mind [remember] him, my mind keeps going back to the wee one in the incubator with the wee shaved bit on his head.

Throughout a life swamped with social and emotional difficulties, Lena's denial comprises a long-term protective detachment from the reality of having borne and then relinquished her baby. Raphael suggests that such detachment allows the bereaved person to take some degree of control over the situation in which they find themselves (1984):

> Lena: I can remember that ... as if its somebody else. I feel right sorry for that girl, but its not like it's me 'cos I'm different now from what I was then. Its not like I pretend it's not happened to me 'cos it is me and I look at it from the outside and I think 'God, what a shame for her, she didn't stand a chance really'. But I don't like to think I feel sorry for myself. I feel sorry for that little girl. I used to tell - I told somebody that it had died. That was when I was younger. I think it was at school. I told them that it died. To be honest, I probably felt ashamed of having had it adopted.

As Lena's account shows, denial may also be used at a relatively superficial level to ward off casual enquiries. Examples of 'social denial' are given by mothers who relinquished recently (eighteen months and two months prior to the interview) and who showed no evidence of denial at a deeper level:

> Pamela: I do sometimes deny that I've had a child - its as if he doesn't exist. [Billy] told one of his friends who then asked me about it. I just said 'I lost him'.

> Ursula: Sometimes customers ask questions about how I got on, but I just say there were some problems at the birth, implying that he had died. Then there is no more said.

Whether this form of denial has any significance, other than its social function of discouraging unwelcome curiosity, is difficult to assess. It may be that, in spite of their relatively recent relinquishment, Pamela and Ursula have been able to make good progress with their grief work, although it is more likely that, because of their tough experience of life, both were adept at coping with taxing social situations.

Denial by others: With only a few notable exceptions, the family of the relinquishing mother experienced major difficulties in recognising either the pregnancy, the relinquishment or the implications:

> Quelia: I don't know if it's because my mother's put this big social barrier up, like this child never existed I don't know.
>
> Lena: It wasn't that people were unhelpful, but they just weren't helpful either. They were just - it was just like they were pretending it didn't happen really. As if it wasn't real.

It is difficult to judge whether the fact that both of these relinquishing mothers had themselves been adopted as babies influenced their (adoptive) mothers' difficulty in accepting the pregnancy. This is unlikely to be the case, as many other mothers reacted equally adversely, but Quelia and Lena were better able to articulate their dissatisfaction.

Jones (1989b) links denial with closed awareness, although in the situation he describes it was controlled by the dying man. Closed awareness is considered a deceptive manoeuvre imposed on the dying patient by the caring staff in order to facilitate the smooth functioning of the unit (Glaser & Strauss, 1968); but it has been used similarly in maternity (Morrin, 1983; Mallinson, 1989).

Those mothers who avoid closed awareness and are able to enjoy some degree of openness with their partner and their other children value such honesty. They remain concerned, however, at their continuing inability to open the subject up with significant others:

> Nadia: Later, I returned home after the birth, [Mum and Dad] came down to pick me up. I'd left Andrew in the hospital at eight days old and from that moment when they saw me the whole episode was never ever mentioned. Never. The fact that the fostering fees had been returned was the only mention ever made of it by my father. No no, you're not allowed to grieve you're not allowed to take on! Its only now that I'm starting to come to terms with that and he's twenty two now. I don't feel any bitterness, I can't blame them, they did what they thought was right for me at the time.

Nadia extends her account of this aspect of her relationship with her parents to show how the pattern of closed awareness has reappeared at another time of crisis - to her sorrow:

> Nadia: At the time my husband was ill, I found that again I was quite unable to communicate with my parents about how worried I was about him. It was a bit like it had been at the time of my baby's birth.

It may be that this pattern of non-communication had become established in her family prior to her pregnancy, but these data show that it has been perpetuated well beyond her relinquishment.

Searching: Bowlby (1980) interprets searching behaviour during grieving as a form of the separation anxiety which is a feature of childhood/infantile attachment in a wide range of animals. It is, however, more generally regarded as a possibly irrational, but nonetheless powerful reflection of the prevalent obsession with the physical need for the one who is lost (Parkes, 1976; Stroebe & Stroebe, 1987); although Jones (1989a) argues for its rationality, stating that searching constitutes a form of denial (See Chapter 9). In my recent study mothers reported physically searching for their relinquished child:

> Elena: Quite often I'm at the shops and I see children and babies about the same age as he might be - it gets me thinking that I haven't got that.

> Francesca: After giving him up I found myself looking at babies and wondering is that him? It was merely curiosity. No way was I searching for him.

The duration of physically searching for the relinquished one is variable:

> Anthea: I used to run after children in the street ... That lasted for three or four years.

> Tanya: I still look at other people's babies and those who are the same age as she would be now - twenty years old - and I sometimes wonder ...

> Ursula: I look for him all the time. When I see a tiny baby in a pram I think that it might be him being taken out by his foster mother. I'll always be searching for him up until the day I die.

The mother may extend her searching behaviour to involve her subsequent children, which has the potential to adversely affect her relationship with them (Oglethorpe, 1989).

> Anthea: It was sad actually, you know. I kept comparing my new baby with the other... I was looking for the similarities.

Searching for the one who was relinquished in subsequent babies may represent some sort of 'magical thinking' (Raphael-Leff, 1991) as described by Lewis in terms of reincarnation (1979).

Searching behaviour in the context of the relinquishing mother assumes an added significance, because it reflects not only a relatively early stage in the grieving process, but also the long-term possibility, even hope, of resuming contact with the relinquished one:

> Kara: Another six years and it could be all coming back into your life again - which doesn't bother me at all.

Incompleteness: Parkes (1976) explains the feelings of incompleteness reported by widows in terms of their difficulty in adjusting to the array of new roles which face them due to the death of the spouse. The extent to which this explanation applies to the relinquishing mother is uncertain. It may be that she is very much aware of her bodily changes and the physical and psychological preparations for the baby, but in conflict with these is the absence of any baby to care for:

> Kara: I just felt really empty, I felt there was nothing. I was on the verge of tears constantly but I was really quite unhappy. ... I think I've lost - when I gave the baby away, I think I gave a piece of me away as well because I'm not the same person as I was. At this particular point in time and for a long time I think I feel really insecure and I don't know whether that's anything to do with my experience of the birth.

> Anthea: Y'see, you feel the ... you feel as if part of you has left as well.

> Pamela: I felt that a piece of me has gone with him. I was ready for a fresh start. But giving him away really split me apart. I felt lost as if part of me was missing. All my love had gone with him, that is all my mother love. I am making a fresh start with my new love, but memories of him will always remain.

> Gina: Yes, I'm still very sad. It's part of me that's missing. We came through so much ... conception and going to [a distant country] and being very young and not knowing what was happening.

The incompleteness clearly demonstrated in these comments may also reflect the depth of the relationship which each mother had formed a with her baby during pregnancy. This is supported by Kennell et al. (1970) who state in the context of perinatal death: 'the length and intensity of mourning after a loss is proportionate to the closeness of the relationship prior to death'. The duration of the pregnancy has been shown to have a similar influence (Kirkley-Best & Kellner, 1982). For many of the mothers I interviewed pregnancy had featured emotional trauma involving those who might have been expected to provide support; the result was that prior to the birth each mother developed a sense of 'oneness' with her baby, in that she identified with her fetus against a wide range of potential and real threats (See Chapter 12.). This applies particularly to Gina (above), who was despatched to an alien culture where her isolation took her to the Salvation Army when labour began, as well as others:

> Francesca: It was a case of me and my baby versus the rest of them - my family and all.

> Jessica: During the pregnancy I felt very close to my baby. I had a strong feeling that it was him and me against all the rest.

Having given birth only eight weeks prior to her interview, Ursula was clearly experiencing much pain and anger while the legal process of her relinquishment was still continuing and possibly impeding her grieving.

Ursula: Its really like a battle when you don't have any support. Its a case of me and the baby versus all the rest of them. At least while I was pregnant I still had my son on my side, now I just have an emptiness, a hollowness, a hollow feeling. It must be a bit like losing an arm. And it hurts, like the woman always suffers if there is any hurting. And I'm angry, its a bit like hurting, angry with everyone. If only I'd had more support it might all have been different. Its a bloody trauma, giving your baby up. People don't understand how bad it is when you do it.

Future childbearing: The effect of grieving on 'bonding' is well-recognised. The difficulty for the mother in establishing a 'bond' with a new baby while still grieving the loss of a previous relationship was demonstrated by Caplan (1957), which has helped dispense with traditional advice to a mother suffering perinatal loss to 'Have another'. The adverse effect of pregnancy on grieving is similarly clear (Lewis, 1979; Scott, 1989), raising the question of the time lapse between pregnancies (Morris, 1976). Ursula recounted how she endured bad advice and reached her own decision:

Ursula: Everybody round about keeps advising me to have another child to make me feel better. But no other child will ever be a substitute for him and I'm not going to have a child as a form of therapy. I did want to have anther baby fast, but now I'm planning to delay having another baby for at least two years.

Thus, Ursula envisages the problem of the 'replacement child syndrome' (Oglethorpe, 1989) as does Kara:

Kara: I don't know, sometimes you think if you had a baby you'd be saying you wanted it to be the same as the one that you gave away and it won't be.

As Oglethorpe identified in the context of perinatal death, Ursula recognises the risk of 'idealising' the one who was relinquished, with the potential for trauma to children who are present:

Ursula: Another problem is that he is the perfect child. He has no bad points and will always be quite unique to me. Because when I first saw him he was perfect at his birth and every time I saw him after that he was being good. I s'pose that its like meeting anybody for the first time, you don't get to know any of their bad points until you've met them a few times.

For a few mothers, the pain of their subsequent infertility was intensified by having previously relinquished:

Lena: Even my Mom felt a twinge of guilt about it all. Because I couldn't have any more and I've always wanted more family. Its not so bad now. At the time it was heartbreak.

Staff reactions: The similarities between relinquishment and bereavement which I have mentioned so far relate mainly to the experience of the grieving mother. The reaction of staff to the mother's experience of loss further endorses the similarities. Based on a combination of personal and occupational experience, Janowski (1987) recounts how mothers contemplating relinquishment may encounter avoidance by nursing staff, which confirms their lack of mothering skills and tips the balance in favour of relinquishment. The midwives I interviewed, especially those who were mothers, articulated difficulty in understanding how a mother could place her baby for adoption. It may be that this problem in understanding may manifest itself in the mother's care. When caring for a bereaved mother, a similar avoidance may be present, but for different reasons. One of the midwives I interviewed told me:

> Queeny: I can't help feeling that sometimes the staff have difficulty caring for this woman and this may be part of the reason for her getting home so soon.

Queeny's comment reminds us that our difficulties in caring for the grieving mother may be associated with our sense of failure and may lead to avoidance of further potentially painful encounters (Stack, 1982). The possibility that we use transfer home as a coping mechanism is also suggested by Kellner and Lake (1986); although the midwives I interviewed, with only the exception of Queeny, believed that it is the mother who decides when she returns home. It may be that, although the reasons for the staff reaction may be different, its manifestation, avoidance, is the same.

Summary: This detailed examination of the data on grief in my recent study endorses the widespread assumption that the experience of bereavement and at least one aspect of care are similar in the relinquishing mother and the mother bereaved through death.

Differences between relinquishment and bereavement

The data further suggest that, as in any grieving, there is a capacity for deviation from the general pattern described above. Certain deviations appeared regularly among the mothers I interviewed, leading me to conclude that there is scope for midwifery intervention to benefit this mother.

Unshared grief: In emphasising the 'shared' nature of grief, Clark raises the inevitability of death for all of us and thus the community experience in which the bereaved person is nurtured and sustained by those around (1991).

It may be argued that relinquishment is perceived as a deviant form of behaviour in a society such as in the UK where the prevailing pattern is for each mother to care for her own baby. This perception of being deviant and being stigmatised, described by Lena (above) as 'shame', was strongly felt by some mothers:

> Ursula: I think that a hospital is there to give care to people. It is not a courtroom where you are judged for what you have or have not done. This midwife did this, because when she read my notes her attitude to me changed. She had been kind and welcoming when I came into the labour ward, but after she read them she was chilly. I asked her 'Have you read my notes now?' She said 'Yes'.

This perception was also reported by some midwives:

> Gay: I think secrecy's quite important for certain people, yes. If it was a concealed pregnancy and then they want to go back and - because for some people unmarried mothers are still - especially out in the country it seems to be very much frowned upon. Yeah. I don't really think we are as permissive as all that. I think people like to think that we are, but I don't think that we are.

Jones (1989a) discusses grief in the context of a different group who may be stigmatised or considered deviant, though he prefers to discuss the 'absence of recognition' of their relationship. Because homosexual love is not sanctioned by society the bereaved partner may not be offered the support which, according to Clark, is invariably available to the bereaved person. Jones maintains that this inhibits their grief work. If the relationship of the relinquishing mother with her baby is similarly unrecognised, she may find herself not only being isolated from this essential community support but possibly additionally being stigmatised for her deviant behaviour in parting from her baby. This silent isolation was clearly felt:

> Kara: I found it really hard to adjust myself back into a normal ... it was like mourning a bereavement. It is like somebody's died but when somebody dies it is different because it is talked about.

To Clark (1991) the significance of the funeral is fundamental:

> 'While we have been robbed of relatedness and are threatened with brokenness, through coming together to remember and to honour the person who has died, we affirm the vitality of our bonds with others'.

Although a funeral is now accepted and expected in the event of perinatal death (Borg & Lasker, 1982), the mother who relinquishes has no equivalent rite of passage:

> Debra: On the day when I gave her up I dressed her ready for the adoptive parents. My parents and me were sitting in a bare room and I had planned what I would do when I handed her over, adjusting her shawl and everything. Then the social worker came and said 'I'll take your baby now' and she did. I was unable to do any of the things I'd planned - no ceremony, no kiss or anything. It's the hardest thing I've ever done, I'll never get over it. (TEARS) The family were hungry so we had to go and have a meal and I was unable to cry there in the restaurant. But when we got into the back of the car I dissolved in tears.

A mother who relinquished her baby recently organised a suitable ceremony:

> Olivia: I arranged for our church leader to come in and bless her. I felt that this was appropriate. We had to go into the utility room to do it ... It was not really a goodbye ceremony it was more a way of recognising her as my

child that is a part of me to go to Christian parents. The blessing was my way of establishing the baby's rights as an individual, a way of recognising the break from being mine. The blessing was the right thing to do ...

Delayed grieving: Bowlby (1980) includes delay in grieving as one of the pathological forms of grief and associates it with an apparently voluntary avoidance of the pain of loss. For a small number of the relinquishing mothers the voluntariness was apparent:

Iona: OK, so I grieved when I was in hospital. I cried nearly all week ... But I think you can't just shut off something like that completely, which is what I tried to do.

Rosa: At the time, the feelings were bad when it actually happened - up to a couple of years afterwards - you kind of push it to the back of your mind in a way, although it is always there. It was just that my life sort of filled up afterwards so I didn't have time on my hands.

The extent to which the delay in grieving experienced by the relinquishing mother is voluntary must be questioned as many appear to have had some external pressure applied to 'conform' in the interests of secrecy for the benefit of the family:

Barbara: Because I had had to go from the hospital home, the circumstances of my dad's mother staying, having to pretend that nothing had happened and in effect not being allowed to mourn ... I hadn't been allowed to do any of this and this was it coming out ten years later.

As mentioned above the occurrence of the relinquishment while the mother is relatively young means that her life soon becomes filled with events that may impede or delay her grieving. These events often involve family responsibilities:

Hilda: Its getting worse now. Because I had the boys to think of, that kept it in the background. Now the boys are grown up I think more now, I was busy with them and its hurting worse now.

Work-related factors also serve to impede grieving:

Marcia: Since I retired I used to work after - later on you know I was working as a waitress and it's a very busy job and you have no time to think of anything, which was probably very good and it was quite a happy time for me.

Nadia: I find that the sorrow deepens, and that the guilt is always present. The years after I placed him for adoption were busy years for me and my husband. I was having the children and he was building up the business. This prevented me from grieving properly for the loss of my baby.

Occasionally, as for Marcia, work was regarded by the mother, with help from others, as therapeutic in resolving her overt grief. Some, like Jessica, came to realise that the therapy recommended to her was only papering over the cracks:

> Jessica: There was no outlet and so there are lots of feelings which have never been let out. The main thing was to get back to work.
>
> Barbara: I had to go for counselling - not counselling but appointment at the [Psychiatric] Hospital. I just needed the one appointment, I didn't have to go back because it had all come out. Hours of crying turned out to be what I hadn't been allowed to do then. I'm sure if I hadn't seen that TV programme it would still be inside and something somewhere along the line would have unlocked it, you know? So I think a lot of feelings then weren't allowed to come out - at the time and after - perhaps at the time of the birth.

It is clear that for the relinquishing mother, her grieving is suspended while she, with the connivance of others, gets on with her life. The reactivation of her grief when her life is less busy is a shock, although there is another factor which exacerbates the grief when it does manifest itself.

'Letting go': Clark suggests that even in normal, healthy grieving it may never actually be possible to 'let go' of the one who died (1991). He suggests that the terms 'integration' or 'consolidation' may be a better description of the final stage of the grieving process. If this is so, on the basis of the findings of my recent study and the work of Marck et al., (1994), we have to question whether there is any possibility of the relinquishing mother ever completing this stage of grieving in view of her profound awareness the possibility of the physical reappearance of the relinquished one?

The work of Bouchier and her colleagues (1991) establishes the widespread prevalence of the desire to resume contact with the relinquished one and touches on the effect of this desire on the mother's grieving. The mothers in my recent study were acutely and optimistically aware of the possibility of future contact:

> Jessica: I often think about the possibility of my child trying to trace me and make contact ...
>
> Pamela: As soon as I left hospital, I started looking forward to when he was eighteen and he would be able to start looking for me.
>
> Ursula: I'll always be searching for him up until the day I die. And I know that if he wants to he can come looking for me. I know that he may come knocking on my door when he is eighteen.
>
> Rosa: If it was me, I'd be [delighted] if he would turn up on the doorstep.
>
> Lena: I'd be pleased to see her if she ever came.

It is clearly apparent that for the mother who relinquished her baby, the possibility, even hope, of future contact is genuine. Some mothers demonstrated real awareness that the lack of a conclusion to the relationship impedes grieving:

> Ursula: They always say that adoption is like a bereavement, but it's not it's worse than that. This is because when someone dies you know that that is it, but when you place a baby for adoption they are still around and so you keep on searching for them.
>
> Lena: But sometimes I think when you're young and you have them adopted it's like a death - its a bereavement when you lose it, y'know. But if you lose somebody through death, you know that that's them gone. When you give up your baby you know that he is somewhere else. Sometimes I think I wish she had died then I would know that I might see her again.

These comments would appear to reinforce the observation by Bouchier et al., (1991) 'The balance between loss and hope is a difficult one for all human beings to maintain'.

Conclusion

The data given here show that the relinquishing mother is experiencing a loss similar, in terms of the grief response, to bereavement through death. Her care, therefore, deserves the attention given in both the general and midwifery media to any grieving mother.

The factors which delay or otherwise impede grieving have been shown to be the responsibility of all involved, but the midwife is ideally situated to educate both the relinquishing mother and those close to her about grieving and the interventions which may facilitate the resolution of her grief.

Although we may believe that our society may be becoming more 'open' and honest in sensitive matters, this research has shown that secrecy may still be imposed on the relinquishing mother (See Chapter 5) which may limit her ability to share her grief and cause her to be deprived of the support which this sharing carries with it.

Despite having established definite similarities between relinquishment and loss through death, which indicate that relinquishment is a form of bereavement, the differences between the two experiences may impede the resolution of grief due to relinquishment. The problem of the inconclusive nature of the relinquishing mother's bereavement is not easily amenable to action on an individual basis, but requires procedural and legislative changes which need to be engendered by political action resulting from increasing openness and awareness of this mother's situation.

Although relinquishment is unavoidably stressful, it does not need to be a totally negative experience. At a personal level midwives are in an ideal position to help relinquishing mothers achieve a less negatively stressful experience (Osterweis et al., 1984):

> Annie: I think in a way it is similar to the lady who is losing her baby through death in that she still isn't going to have this child ... at the end of the day and she has obviously made a very, very hard decision to carry on the pregnancy and give up her baby for adoption. I think it is equally important that we help her to have as good an experience of childbirth as possible.

In the same way as a stressor provides an opportunity to learn new adaptive techniques (Selye, 1956) and a crisis is a situation for personal development (Caplan 1961) so, as Clarke (1991) suggests, bereavement, such as by relinquishment, may facilitate a greater ability to appreciate life and a deeper self-knowledge.

7 Family implications of relinquishment

In this chapter I consider how relinquishment affects a family and how a family responds to relinquishment. To do this, it is useful to remember the variability of the groups of people which we know as 'families'. Obvious examples of variation are the extent of the family, in terms of its lateral spread as well as vertical spread through generations, and the interdependence of the family members. Family interdependence may not always be apparent, but it is a feature of the systems approach to the family that each individual member is affected in some way by any critical event impinging on it (Skynner, 1976). Whether the underlying cause of these effects is recognised depends on the nature of communication within the family.

The term 'family' is open to a variety of interpretations, determined largely by the cultural and socioeconomic context. All too often in the UK the term is used synonymously with 'nuclear family', but I am using it in its widest sense to include not only those related through blood, marriage or cohabitation, but also foster, adoptive and step-relations. I include too those less formal adult relatives who in the past have been (and sometimes still are) honoured with the title 'uncle' or 'aunt' (Baggaley, 1993), as Aline told me when explaining her relationship with a young friend:

> Aline: I got on really well with her dad, my Uncle Keith. Well, he wasn't really my uncle, but that's what we called him.

Family system response to crisis

Systems theory is useful in facilitating understanding of how a stressor event, such as relinquishment, contributes to a family crisis (Cook & Oltjenbruns, 1989; von Bertalanffy, 1969; Whyte, 1989 & 1994). This approach defines the family in terms of being a unit whose interacting parts, first, operate within certain defined boundaries, second, adhere to mutually accepted rules and, third, communicate with a characteristic degree of openness.

Communication within the family

Interaction within each family system is characterised by its own level of openness or closedness. The nature of communication typically reflects the family's flexibility; for example, a family system which adopts a more closed communicative style is less equipped to adapt to changes in the external environment, as well as being less sensitive to the needs of its own individual members.

There is a tendency for more responsible or more powerful members of the family to 'protect' others from the effects of a stressful event by limiting communication (Rando, 1986), perhaps by demanding secrecy. This practice endangers, first, the protectors, who may not allow themselves to react appropriately to the event. Second, the protected are endangered by being prevented through ignorance from reacting directly in any way at all, although they may react, albeit unknowingly, to the tensions in those around them aroused by the event.

Stephenson (1986) maintains that the degree of openness of communication within the family system is a family characteristic which influences their ability to cope with a crisis. Denial of the crisis may feature prominently. He suggests that the closed family behaves in 'bizarre' ways which have been learned from earlier, but not necessarily similar, experiences. Thus, the limited ability of the closed family to accept and share new influences and experiences severely limits its coping ability.

The 'conspiracy of silence' which may develop in families following a crisis, such as relinquishment, may be attributed to family guilt (McNeil, 1986). Guilt-ridden, unfounded and unrealistic beliefs about individual personal responsibility for stressor events and the crisis may be experienced by all family members. Thus they find themselves individually isolated and united only in their inability to share their pain.

Glaser and Strauss' account (1965) of open and closed awareness among dying people and those close to them, was utilised by Lugton (1989) who researched communication between a person who was dying and their relatives. Glaser and Strauss' original research showed the ease of communication when all involved understood the terminal nature of the illness; this situation was termed 'open awareness'. On the other hand, when closed awareness operated, the relatives were unable to admit the significance of either the illness or the anticipated loss. Lugton identified varying degrees of communication between the extremes of open and closed awareness. Although all of her informants were able to demonstrate to her an appropriate understanding of the prognosis, the extent to which this understanding was shared within the family varied hugely. In those families in which awareness was open, family members were able to prepare themselves and each other for their forthcoming loss. In contrast, Lugton showed the disquiet which prevailed within families where closed awareness operated.

Maintaining equilibrium

Clearly, the balance or homeostasis of the family system is seriously jeopardised by the experience of relinquishment, as it is by any stressor event with the potential for crisis. The degree of jeopardy varies according to features of both the family and the circumstances surrounding the relinquishment (Herz, 1980). The stressor event which precipitates the family crisis has been defined as one which is of sufficient severity to generate change within the family system (Cook & Oltjenbruns, 1989). The crisis itself is characterised by disruption, disorganisation and incapacity. The recovery and resumption of homeostasis of the family system depends on the family regenerative power (McCubbin & Patterson, 1983); this is determined by family resources, the interpretation of the severity of the stressor event and the existence of concurrent stressors. The extent of family recovery ranges on a continuum of adaptation between the extremes of maladaptation and bonadaptation.

Concurrent or coincidental stressors, such as unemployment, illness or the other phenomena in the well-known scale (Holmes & Rahe, 1967), may exert impossible demands on the family's usual coping resources and render them less useful. The cumulative effects of a multiplicity of stressors lead to 'pile-up' which, again, is associated with dysfunctional coping. The temporal discrepancy in coping mechanisms between individuals is identified as dissynchrony and asymmetry; through engendering resentment between crisis-ridden family members these discrepancies give rise to secondary losses, such as deteriorating relationships (Rando, 1984).

Family resources

The resources utilised during a crisis may be located either within or outwith the family system. The internal resources include social, emotional and psychological strengths. The external resources, however, range from the informal social support of friends and neighbours, through the more formal support offered by organisations such as churches and voluntary groups, to the statutory provision through agencies such as social work departments. McCubbin (1979) reminds us of the need for the family to muster sufficient strength to be in a position to take advantage of the resources available to it.

Realignment of roles

As well as physical and communicative boundaries, the family system operates within its own framework of rules, be they implicit or explicit. This framework determines the roles of the family members within the family system and to maintain, through constant fine-tuning and occasional major readjustment, the homeostasis of the family system in the event of threat. The re-establishment of family equilibrium will follow the realignment of roles and responsibilities. This realignment itself constitutes a threat, first, to family stability and, second, to those most closely involved in the stressor event because at this time they are vulnerable and in a comparatively weak negotiating position.

Perception of the stressor event

Family coping may be further facilitated or inhibited by the family's interpretation of the event, in that if a meaning is identified it becomes more manageable (Marris, 1986). An example of the varying perception of an event may be found in the religious beliefs of the family members. In the case of a stressor event such as relinquishment, moral judgements may aggravate the family perception of crisis; for some the event may be interpreted as a test of faith or as a challenge to strengthen their religious faith. Thus, in the search for a meaning to the event, identifying positive meaning facilitates coping, and secondary gains, such as increased family cohesion, may ensue. On the other hand a totally negative meaning or an absence of meaning of the event may only serve to damage the family system.

Family reaction to relinquishment

In my recent study most of the relinquishing mothers were still in close contact with their family of birth at the time of the relinquishment. For each of these mothers the family was perceived as a powerfully important, often instrumental, influence on the events surrounding the birth and relinquishment. The mothers who had been adopted as children reported similarly strong family influences from their adoptive family. For only a small number who were older and who were geographically more mobile, there was little contact with the family. Because the systems approach emphasises the significance of the family situation and the background to the stressor event, I consider the family prior to the pregnancy and then move on to examine the effects of the pregnancy and relinquishment on the family.

The family before the conception

In their study of relinquishing mothers' seeking contact, Bouchier et al. (1991) found that a large proportion of the mothers in their sample had experienced major life-events during their childhood and, because for many childhood was incomplete, near the time of the conception. In my recent study, the mothers reported similar largely negative events disturbing their childhood. For these reasons I draw on the framework introduced by Bouchier et al. to describe the mothers' family background. An insecure childhood manifested itself in my recent study in the organisation of family life as well as in the relationships between family members.

The geographical mobility of the family, a common feature, was perceived as limiting the young woman's opportunities and ability to form enduring peer relationships, as well as destabilising her family background:

> Barbara: My Dad was in the Navy so we moved around every couple of years. We didn't really stay anywhere more than two or three years. We lived abroad in [country] up until I was ten, then back to Scotland and [town]. I enjoyed high school there from what I can remember. Then we moved down to [town] because my Dad had got a move down there, that was in 1972/73. As soon as we got moved down there my Dad got shifted back up. He had bought a house - the first he had ever bought because we had always lived in Navy houses - the one in [town] had actually been a council house, God forbid!

Francesca: I had been in a boarding school in [country] and in [land]. The family moved around a lot in association with my Father's work, through Africa and Asia. When I was 8 years old I was sent to a convent boarding school in [Scotland] and experienced a major culture shock, having only been to this country on holiday. It didn't work at all. I was not happy there, far from my parents. The teachers were nuns. I was alright until I got into form one and then I went crazy. I hated boarding school and became very rebellious and naughty. I badly wanted to be at home, that is wherever Mum and Dad were. I swore at the nuns and [yet] did not get expelled like others had.

Whether being sent away to school contributed to or resulted from these young women's poor relationships with their parents is difficult to judge, but these two factors appear together repeatedly among those who had been expensively educated.

Gina: We were brought up by a succession of nannies and shunted off to boarding school. We weren't a family unit as such. I was always a rebel. I was only at boarding school for a wee while. I was there from eight until I was eleven. I was too much of a rebel. By the time it came for me to go to secondary school I couldn't take the discipline. Then the writing was on the wall and they said there was no point in my being even a day pupil so 'Take her away'.

Poor relationships with her parents predating the conception featured among the mothers in both Bouchier's sample and in my recent study, not necessarily associated with a particular form of education:

Clara: I did not get on well with my Father and hated my stepmother. My relationship with my stepmother's mother is now good, we are united in our dislike of my Father and stepmother.

Elena: I was living in the same house as my Dad, but I wasn't speaking to him. I hated him and he hated me, because I shouted and answered back to him, unlike my Mother and my sister.

Strict moral or religious codes: Even prior to the conception many of the relinquishing mothers found themselves in conflict with parental value systems. The mothers almost invariably regarded their parents as being unnecessarily authoritarian (Gross, 1989). The conflict may have been associated with parental attitudes based loosely on religion or may have been more broadly based:

Olivia: My Mum and Dad are Mormons and they were very strict in the sense that up to the age of 15 we came in from school, we did our homework, we watched TV, we were in bed by 8 o'clock.

Tanya: I think my Dad was one of these people who thinks that he's not biased or bigoted in any way ... So he didn't like Billy because Billy was Catholic. And they didn't like him because he was unemployed and they just didn't think he was good enough for me in inverted commas. He was very much a Glaswegian, very broad Glasgow, y'know.
But I think my Dad felt that it was dreadful that I got pregnant - that was terrible. But I think he would have felt that too if I'd married a catholic. It wasn't done in our family. And all the aunties and uncles would twitter y'know. Or so he thought. Perhaps they wouldn't've done, but so he thought and that influenced him, I think. My Mum has since told us that she feels that my Father was far too strict with us, he was a very strict disciplinarian.

Gina: I couldn't marry a Roman Catholic. I couldn't have done that to my parents because they were very much an influence in my life at that point, very well known in the community ... of course when I contravened the family rules about religion, then it was apparent that our marriage would never work.
... [After the conception] How could I possibly go to my parents? As I say, they were very well respected in the community and there was no way me having a child out of marriage would have been tolerated. I would definitely not have been accepted back into the family if I had had a child outwith marriage. I suppose it was with their standing in the community.

Iona: I think one of the reasons why [Mother] had such a bad reaction was the fact that my brother had got married because his girlfriend was pregnant years beforehand, when I was 13, and that had caused a terrible uproar in the family. We had been so strictly brought up. I don't blame my Mother for any of this. She had had, in her turn, a very strict upbringing and so had my Father.

Domestic violence: Violent and abusive relationships featured in the families of many of the relinquishing mothers. For some this happened in childhood, for others violence continued through into adult relationships and beyond the relinquishment:

Elena: My Father had sexually abused me.

Lena: And also our family life wasn't very good. ... and I was very frightened of Billy [teenage boyfriend]. He used to knock me about a bit. Y'see my Mother, she was never there - she had her own career. She was a good doctor, but not a very good mother, I'm afraid. None of us was supervised, perhaps if we had been it would never have happened.

Anthea: I was being beaten up systematically [by my husband] ... I was getting knives used on me and a red hot poker.

Marcia: I would have liked to keep her but everything seemed to be sort of against me and with Billy [my partner] being under stress. It was very difficult to live with him at times.

Adoption: Although Bouchier et al. provide examples of various aspects of family life which rendered the relinquishing mother's childhood insecure, including social deprivation and alcoholism, they do not include adoption in this category. It is possible that no relinquishing mothers in their sample had themselves been adopted. If this is so, it is more surprising that two mothers in my recent study considered this aspect of their background sufficiently important to mention, although their experiences of being adopted appear quite different:

> Lena: My Dad's one of the nicest people you could meet and I mean I'm his daughter and I say that and another thing is I'm adopted and my family are all white apart from me. So when I was in a children's home [my adoptive mother] came one day and she said to me that she was giving up custody of me. So literally it meant that I was no longer her daughter anyway and that the church of England would be my guardian. And that hurt a lot. 'Cos then I felt totally chucked out. Like I had nobody then.
> ... they believed everything she said and not only because of that but they talked to me as if because I was adopted I ought to be grateful. And y'know I've brought shame on the family and I'm adopted and what do you expect from adopted children?
> Y'see my own Mother had me when she was 14 and my adopted Mother brought this up and said you're just doing what your own Mother did. And that worried me.

> Quelia: [The social worker] did mention adoption to me but I thought 'I've been adopted, I know what its like being adopted' ... I came to the decision that I would have Andrea adopted. She would obviously go to a good home.

Death and loss For a surprisingly large proportion of the relinquishing mothers, the loss of a parent was a prominent feature of their young lives. For many of the mothers the parental loss was through death:

> Clara: My Mother died when I was three years old due to asthma. I have no recollections of my Mother except for the day she died.

> Francesca: My Mother died when I was 9 years old, after I started the boarding school in Scotland. I first learned of her death by a nun telling me that as a special treat I was going to be allowed to go home to Edinburgh to have a holiday with my family for the week end 'because your Father has come back'. My aunt and uncle met me off the train and they were stony faced. I felt that I really wanted a holiday and was keen to enjoy my week end. It didn't click at all, I thought it was a holiday. I went to my Father's house with my sister and we were taken upstairs and sat on the bed with our Father who told us that our Mother had died ... I only realised a few months later that I would never see my Mother again. I returned to school a week after the funeral.

Rosa: My Father wasn't living when all this [relinquishment] happened. He had already died so that's really why my Mother and my auntie were in business. They both sold their respective houses and bought this wee place in [town].
RM: How old were you when your Father died?
Rosa: I was seventeen. He was always there, I always got on all right with him and everything. Obviously when he died I was pretty devastated ...

Iona: It wasn't a terribly close relationship [with my Mother] and it went through a particularly difficult patch after my Father died ... I always felt - not rejected - but of little consequence, whatever I had to say was of little consequence. I was the youngest by a good bit. I was a very insecure child. I think I resented being left with what I felt was the responsibility of my Mother - when my Father died. I was going through quite a rebellious streak - it sounds a bit late in life, I was twenty two when I became pregnant, but I was very much under the influence of my parents. I had a very strict upbringing. I think I was still quite frightened of [my Mother] to a certain extent, but another part of me was trying to rebel against a lot of things ... I didn't particularly enjoy living with my Mother just myself - I felt all the attention was then focussed on me.
RM: Do you mean that all your Mother's attention was focussed on you?
Iona: Yes. Shortly after my Father died ... my Mother had nursed him at home and I was sent away when he was going downhill very fast ... I had never been close to my Father at all. I felt I didn't know him - I regret that now. My Mother was the strong person in the household and my Father interfered only when there was any discipline to be meted out. I felt that I personally didn't really grieve - I feel really selfish about this - but I didn't grieve for his death, I was grieving for me. I was also going through a very difficult patch with a relationship at that time. I was more concerned about this relationship than I was about the fact that my Father was about to die.

Although for some of the mothers their loss of a parent was through death, for others it took other forms:

Pamela: I have no respect for my parents. They were divorced when I was aged ten. My Mother left us for another man who she'd been going out with for a year. When the divorce case came up in court and she was offered custody as the Mother usually is she rejected us saying 'I don't want to have to look after them'. There were the three girls, I'm the eldest. I, from the age of ten, have had to bring up and look after my two sisters and my Father who is an alcoholic. This is no way for a young girl to grow up. I didn't have an adolescence. I was grown up at age eleven. My Father was taking me into gay bars when I was aged fifteen.

It is clear that for a number of reasons the mothers who relinquished their babies considered that the family environment and relationships within which they had grown up were less than secure. For other mothers, such as Anthea and Marcia, their adult relationships featured domestic violence.

Menfolk

The mothers' experience of relinquishment was influenced, though in differing ways and to differing extents, by their menfolk.

The father of the baby: Although not part of the family in the usual sense, the father of the baby merits some attention. This is because for a few mothers the baby's father was, at the time of the birth and relinquishment, effectively part of her family. For a larger proportion of the mothers, however, the father of the relinquished baby was of relatively minor significance in her experience. This applied to such an extent that he may not even have been mentioned. For a small number of mothers their relationship with him was brief and almost totally sexual:

> Barbara: I didn't know what was going on. OK I wasn't that stupid, but at the same time you don't. I don't know where he lived, he lived outside [city], but certainly some village ...

For a larger proportion of mothers, a previously established relationship was seriously damaged to the extent of being ended by the pregnancy. The conception and relinquishment engendered differing and unequal levels of antagonism between the parents. There was some variation in which partner seemed to be more 'wronged'.

> Wilma: He was not a nice person and the conception occurred after what you might call a seduction, but was more like a rape ... I had known him for seven years. He was known as a rotter, but I was very much in love with him.

> Gina: I had no more contact with the father of the child. But I never told him either, so it is something that I have kept under the surface all these years.

> Jessica: I wasn't taking any precautions and neither was he. [Sexual intercourse] was a one off and unfortunately I was caught out. He disowned me, he refused to admit that he was the father of the child, which I found hurt me a lot, although we were not in love and we were certainly not planning to get married.

> Quelia: The baby's father and I knew each other for a very long time. He was still around and he pleaded with me for the first five months of my pregnancy for us to get married. I just wasn't interested. It was when I was pregnant that I realised that I didn't love him as much as I thought I did.

For some of the mothers, the conception and relinquishment did not dampen her developing affection for the baby's father in spite, or possibly because, of parental attempts to control and terminate their daughter's relationship with him:

Nadia: I became pregnant when I was at college. I met the one who's now my husband when I was 17, he became my stable boy friend. I became pregnant when I was just eighteen. Billy was forbidden to see me, but while I was [away] I wrote to him every day. I actually got engaged to Billy in the August and it was in October I signed the [adoption] papers and I married Billy a year later.

For some of the mothers the conception comprised one episode in a long-lasting, albeit turbulent, yet for some ongoing relationship.

Hilda: Billy still today swears he did not know anything about the baby, he had not been told about him ... My Mum and Dad did not want him to have anything to do with me they just wanted him to leave me and let me hae the bairn and sort o' get on wi' it. Eventually me and Billy got married.

Rosa: I had been going out with the baby's father for quite a while. It was all rather stupid because I married the baby's father afterwards anyway,

Vera: When I found out that I was pregnant I felt that I had to part from the father of my baby. Some time later after I gave my baby away I met his father again and we were still in love. He was angry with me for giving his baby away but I had had no choice. The baby had been conceived in love and we still loved each other. He asked me to marry him.

The findings of my recent study correspond closely with those of Marck (1994) in her research into women experiencing unexpected pregnancy. Thus, the baby's father appears to be 'extraneous'.

The mother's father: A generally far more significant contributor in the mother's experience was her father, that is, the relinquished baby's grandfather. The mother's relationship with her father was typically that he loved and admired her (Bronfenbrenner, 1961), to the extent that her father tended to idealise or 'pedestalise' his daughter:

Tanya: He called me 'princess' all his life and I was his little princess.

It is hardly surprising in view of the father's doting on his daughter that news of the conception shocked him beyond anything the mother had expected. The father's expression of shock took differing forms:

Quelia: My Dad, I think he was stunned into silence with the shock - his daughter could actually let this happen to her, he's kind of had me up on a pedestal to this day, but that time I kind of knocked myself off it.

Tanya: Frightened. That was the only feeling [when my Mum told my Dad] I can remember. I'm surprised you didn't hear him in Edinburgh. He went berserk. He came through [to my room] and he started calling me all these really horrible names, I remember he called me a slut ... it was just the way he said it. He was absolutely horrified, absolutely disgusted with me.

Y'know for being in that condition. It was terrible, y'know he was not going to let up, he was going on and on and on. 'Cos my Mother was in tears and it was she who eventually said 'That is it, enough'.

With time for quiet reflection each mother was able to come to understand the reason for her father's powerful and painfully negative reaction to the news. For some fathers, the realisation of their daughter's maturity and forthcoming independence had been impressed on him in an unexpectedly blatant and abrupt way:

Quelia: I think he realised that he'd lost his wee girl. She's now a woman, she's pregnant herself and all of a sudden this wee girl is not a wee girl any more - she's a young woman now, with responsibilities of her own. We never actually discussed it properly, my Dad and I.

For other fathers, the difficulty lay in the stark contrast between their idealisation of the daughter and the reality, which may be described as 'depedestalisation':

Tanya: [he reacted so badly] probably because [he couldn't understand] how could I have done that, let him down like that. I think he felt so badly let down by me.

The father's adverse reaction to his daughter's pregnancy is reflected in the instrumental role which he played in decision-making concerning the future of the pregnancy and child. The initial decision concerning the continuation of the pregnancy comprised a knee-jerk reaction by some of the fathers that a termination of pregnancy was indicated. For various reasons (See Chapter 8) the mother did not recognise the pregnancy until it was well-advanced, which meant that termination was not a possibility even for those mothers who conceived after the enactment of the 1967 legislation:

Francesca: The scan confirmed that I was 6 months pregnant so I knew I would have to go through with it. Dad was ill with worry. I was away with it. We spoke to an obstetrician and Dad asked for me to have an abortion. The obstetrician refused. Dad said he would get it done privately, and the obstetrician said that was impossible 'cos it was illegal.

Tanya My Father had obviously ... phoned his sister. They were very close - my Father and his sister. I think it was her doctor we went to see actually. I think she must've phoned her doctor - it was a lady doctor and we went along and she confirmed the pregnancy. And I can remember [him] asking her if there wasn't any way I could have an abortion? ... And she said 'no' because there wasn't really any reason for it. ... So it was decided that I would just have to carry on with the pregnancy and have the baby adopted. This was all decided for me; by the way, nobody asked me.

The crucial decision-making role of the father became fully apparent when, after termination of pregnancy had been excluded, the mother was presented, like Tanya (above), with adoption as the only feasible alternative:

> Debra: It was not my decision - it was suggested, it was always suggested. It probably started with my Father.

> Francesca: When Dad found out I couldn't have an abortion, he said 'Adoption adoption' and I said 'Yes yes'. Me being so small and young, I went along with the plans for the baby to be adopted in order to avoid further hassle my Father.

> Clara: I was forced into [adoption] by my Father.

After the birth of the baby the new grandfather's behaviour continued in the same established pattern:

> Debra: My Father was uncomfortable looking at the baby. He came with my Mother to visit but he wouldn't look at her or hold her.

> Sandra: [My Mother is interested in newborn baby] but my Father just says 'How are things going?' 'Are they finalised?' He just wants to see the adoption finalised.

For some of the mothers the father's consistency was more positive, helpful and appreciated:

> Kara: I went home (after the birth and relinquishment) and my Mother and everybody was really fine ... My Dad came in from work and he gave me a big hug.
> RM: Does he do that often?
> Kara: Seldom. This was unusual. Because he was really upset about me. I knew because for the whole of the time that I was pregnant he hardly spoke.

> Lena: I love my Dad. He made me feel as if it wasn't the end of the world, 'cos my Mom always made me feel I was the only one in the world that had had a kid at fourteen.

In the same way as signs of emotion were repressed by most of the fathers, verbal communication relating to the baby tends to continue to be restricted. Although this may be more a reflection of the openness of the family system, mentioned above, than a personality characteristic of the father:

> Quelia: I've never really discussed her. My Father is about the only one that ever really talks about her at any time. My Dad says she's still his grandchild. It was coming up to her first birthday before my Dad and me got round to talking about her in the house, my Dad was wondering how I was feeling and I was wondering how he was feeling ...

When a closed pattern of communication becomes established within the family, the family members face great difficulty in overcoming it. Nadia was concerned that this form of 'unfinished business' should be dealt with while there was still an opportunity, that is, while her father was alive:

> Nadia: He has **never** spoken to me about [my relinquishment]. The whole episode was **never ever** mentioned. Never. The fact that the fostering fees had been returned was the only mention ever made of it by my Father. About 12 years ago I raised it with him and he seemed quite relieved at that. I think my Dad is still upset about it though.

In the same way as the father's helpful and supportive behaviour, as well as non-communicative behaviour, tended to continue beyond the birth and relinquishment, his desire to help by protecting his daughter persisted. This was usually viewed by the daughter as misplaced and unhelpful protection, which served mainly to prevent her from continuing her life as she wished, building the relationships she preferred and maintaining her options for contact:

> Francesca: My Father warned the others in the family not to help me to keep the baby by giving me somewhere to live. He wanted to prevent me from 'ruining my life any more'.

> Tanya: I told my first husband, it was just after he had proposed to me. When we told Dad that we wanted to get married he said that he was surprised that anyone would want to marry me after they knew I had had a baby adopted. I can't help wondering if there was a feeling at the back of my mind that I'd better marry him in case it was my last chance.

> Barbara: ... you have to register a birth within so many days ... I registered her Andrea. ... the Registrar said 'What's the surname?' And I can remember to this day just going to say Jones-Donald. My Dad said 'No, it's Donald'. I know, and I knew then, that he was doing that to protect me in future. But sometimes it bugs me because I think, you are making the path - if she wants to come and find me - you are making the path a bit harder. I think that is what he was thinking of at the time.

The father's initial reaction to the news of his daughter's pregnancy was invariably negative, to differing degrees. The duration of his negative response was variable. The reasons for this powerfully negative response may be attributed to a variety of factors. The first, mentioned by Martin (1985), relates to the father's need to be a successful parent. In the success-oriented world of men, a daughter's apparently unwanted pregnancy may constitute the ultimate evidence of failure as a parent. The second reason is associated with the father's increasingly obvious failure to control his daughter's behaviour. Martin considers that fathers' fears focus most strongly on those activities in which errors are least easily solved. Her examples include sex, drugs and alcohol. The father's inability to control his daughter's sexual behaviour, perhaps indicating slipping control in other areas of his life, may be partly responsible for the overwhelmingly adverse reaction which the mothers in this sample encountered.

It is clear that her father features prominently in the mother's experience of relinquishment. Occasionally he was able to provide much-needed and appreciated support, but more often he assumed a decision-taking and decision-imposing role. This both reflected the ongoing relationships within the family, had serious implications for the future of those relationships and affected the mother's potential for relationships with any partners as well as her child.

The mother's mother

As with many aspects, the relationship of the relinquishing mother with her Mother was variable. The variability depended on the underlying bond between the two women as well as the stage in the cycle of pregnancy and relinquishment. For some of the relinquishing mothers the relationship was ordinarily open and affectionate:

> Tanya: I've always been really close to my Mum. Probably because I'm one of these people that if I've got a problem or something bothering me ... I like to talk about it, to have somebody that I can sit down and say 'This is what I'm thinking and feeling, what do you think?' ... And my Mum's the type of person you can go and you can talk to. And you can tell her.

> Rosa: I was more of a mother's daughter. I know a lot of times daughters seem to go more to their father's, but it didn't work that way with me.

For other relinquishing mothers the experience of a mother-daughter relationship appears to be totally negative:

> Pamela: My Mother left us for another man who she'd been going out with for a year. When the divorce case came up in court and she was offered custody ... She rejected us saying 'I don't want to have to look after them'.

For a large majority of the relinquishing mothers, the relationship with her Mother was mixed:

> Vera: I was closer to my Mother, as I was one of the eldest in a large family of ten, and I had to help her to bring up the other younger ones.

> Ursula: I have always been close-ish to my family. But very early in the pregnancy I had some arguments with my Mum and then I stopped seeing her.

> Iona: I was living at home with my Mother. I think it wasn't a terribly close relationship and I think it went through a particularly difficult patch after my Father died ... I always felt - not rejected - but of little consequence, whatever I had to say was of little consequence.

> Gina: She certainly wasn't a Mother ... when I was very small, she would never let me kiss her on the mouth, she always turned her face. I always remember my Father cuddling me, never my Mum.

Barbara: My Dad was away so we had always been used to Mum. As far as I remember it was good with my Mum and then my Dad would come home and it would be hell. Because my Mother had to be mum and dad when my Dad was away at sea, but when he came home obviously her loyalties were divided in that she had to go back to being a wife and mother ...

Olivia: One of my Mum's favourite sayings [about me] as I grew up was 'I love her, I've got to, she's my daughter. But I don't particularly like her as a person'. That used to upset me. I never showed it. At first I took it as a joke. Now it's got to a point where Mum actually likes me as well.

Rosa: Although I was close to my Mother, I never was able to talk openly with her about things, not like my daughter and I talk. So maybe if I had been able to talk to her more maybe we could have solved something.

The mother's reaction when informed of her daughter's pregnancy appears to be more variable than the emotions shown by the father. This may be because the relinquishing mothers had better insight into the feelings and attitudes of their own mothers:

Quelia: My Mum used to say 'Come on, what's wrong with you?' I think she was hoping I would say that I was pregnant. I had to tell them eventually. In fact ... After scraping my Mum off the sofa, my Mum - furious - that is the only way I can describe it. [She] totally didn't want to know.

Rosa: I was actually a bit frightened to tell my Mother although I wasn't exactly a teenager. I didn't know how to tell her at all. In fact I left her a note, really rather awful and she nearly went mad ... more upset really, not really knowing what to do.

Good support was found by some of the mothers in their mothers during the pregnancy and preceding the relinquishment:

Kara: My Mother was probably the best one of all of them. She chummed me to the AN Clinic and anything I had to go to. ... They probably go through quite a lot of feelings about it as well because my Mother in particular ... my Mum, she actually came with me to the hospital, she was with me during my labour and she stayed .... She must feel quite a lot as well.

After the birth and relinquishment the reaction of the mother to her daughter was a source of some surprise and was initially perceived as inconsistent:

Quelia; My Mum funnily enough was the one who went more 'Goo goo gaa gaa' over this baby than my Dad did or even a typical woman. I think my Mum was the one who was kind of torn more than my Dad, but she never actually showed anything. Just certain wee things ... I suppose that someone had to be the harder one and it was my Mum that had to be that pillar.

Sandra: My Mother is the one that, out of the family, tends to ask 'How is the wee one?' She is the one that asks how she is doing and everything.

Ursula: My Mother promises that she will be a bit more supportive to me in my next pregnancy. I suspect that she feels a bit guilty.

Limited control: Many of the relinquishing mothers reported how her mother was less able to help than she would have liked. Often this was because her mother had limited control over her life. Francesca's mother had found herself living an unsatisfactory lifestyle in an alien country:

Francesca: My Mother had had high aspirations for herself and was very frustrated by being a 'coffee morning' wife in an ex-patriate community with nothing to do. It was a mining community. There was no television and there were no phones.

Similarly, Barbara's mother was required to adopt a lifestyle which did not meet her expectations or abilities:

Barbara: My Mum was working. I think she must have resented my Dad in a way because ... she had been at College in Dunfermline doing teacher training and she had not much option but to go south before she took her final exams. So she must have resented it. She went to work in a chemists and in a pub at weekends.

Tanya: My Mother's a very quiet ... We tell her she's a doormat and always has been. The sort of person who's very obliging, we used to feel she shouldn't be like that. So my Father had the say in everything going on in the house. My Mother should have known better [than to allow relinquishment], but she was influenced far too much by my Dad. I did have a discussion with my Mum 6 weeks after [Andrea] was born. I wanted my Mum to want the baby, 'cos I thought it was like her. Mum refused to help me keep her. She said it was because my Dad would never accept her, also because she had to go out to work.

For Elena, her mother's inability to control her life was a source of dissatisfaction and even anger:

Elena: I felt angry at my Mum mostly rather than my Dad, because I was used to not thinking much about him. And because she came to see me once at the Mother and Baby Home. She said she had got back too late so my Dad had said she couldn't come any more at a night-time because she had my little brother - he was always the one big excuse like. I was very lonely because the others went home at weekends. She said she would see me on Saturday. I saw her the once on Saturday and then I got a letter to say she couldn't see me on a Saturday because she had got back too late on a Saturday as well. I felt really rejected. She wasn't coming to visit me because it was too far away and she got back home too late. She couldn't see me on a Saturday because my Dad said she was too late getting tea.

In the case of Rosa's widowed mother, her reliance was on a more streetwise elder sister rather than a male partner:

> Rosa: I never really discussed it with [my Mother]. I think she accepted the fact that this was what it was going to be, you know. She never tried to talk me out of it. I don't think she really knew how we would cope if I did keep the baby. She wasn't an outgoing person really, she was a gentle sort of person. I don't think she would have known what to do. My aunt did though. She had, so I found out afterwards, been a social worker before she went into business ...

It is clear that, on the whole, the relinquishing mothers sympathise with their own mothers' inability to take control of their lives. It is necessary to question whether the relinquishing mother is identifying with her own mother, in that she has had to relinquish her baby and that this is seen as demonstrating her own lack of control over her life. This may equate, in the eyes of the relinquishing mother, with the way in which her own mother was prevented from intervening to help her and prevent relinquishment being necessary.

Mothers who are not natural mothers feature prominently and numerically in this study. That is, they are mothers to the relinquishing mothers through adoption or through remarriage (Collins, 1988). This group are reported as having consistently poor relationships with their daughters:

> Clara: I did not get on well with my Father and hated my stepmother.

> Quelia: My [adoptive] Mother - I could gladly strangle sometimes. Even to this day she's very domineering ... I love my Mum, I would never do anything basically to hurt her as such, but there are times when I could gladly see her far enough.

> Lena: I was in a children's home she came one day and she said to me that she was giving up custody of me. So literally it meant that I was no longer her daughter ... And that hurt a lot. 'Cos then I felt totally chucked out. [Now] We talk on the telephone occasionally but we don't really have a very good relationship. We've talked over the past but she still sees things - she believes her own stories. She tells you things and you know its a lie and I tell her, but she really believes what she's telling you.

> Anthea: I asked my stepmother if I could bring the children back for three months to her house until I could get a house. She said they were no relation to her so 'No you can't'. I never spoke to her for twelve years.

The possibility of the relinquishing mother herself being adopted also emerges in Marck (1994). It is difficult to assess whether these early, formative experiences may have had any effect on the relinquishing mother in terms of her experience of childbearing and relinquishment.

Siblings

As mentioned above, closed systems of communication may be utilised within families, supposedly to protect the more vulnerable members. Non-communication was required by the parents of the relinquishing mother in a number of situations. The most poignant of these is when the mother who has just relinquished her child is made to conceal the truth from her loving and potentially supportive siblings. For Elena the pain lay in the initial concealment:

> Elena: I got on really well with my kid brother. When my brothers came back and I had to lie to them and say I had been on holiday or something. One was 17 and he had been to visit me with my Mum in the Mother and Baby Home, but I wasn't allowed to speak about it to anyone, specially my little brother. I said I had been on holiday to my aunty's. He said he had had a great time and I said 'So have I'.

For Tanya, though, the concealment by which she was required to deceive her younger brother, presumably to protect him, caused more long-lasting pain:

> Tanya: And my younger [brother] is only six years younger than I am and you can imagine that at six years old with a baby appearing I just thought it was a doll - a big doll - I just loved him on sight, and I used to take him out in his pram and I think he thought I was his mother. I don't know when he discovered I wasn't! So we've always been really close up until he was fifteen [then] I got married ... he never quite forgave me for that because he's so possessive of me, that he thought I was his and how dare some man come along and take me away from him. 'Cos he used to tell me everything and we were really close. And then I got married and that closeness - he felt almost as if I'd been unfaithful to him. Very strange.
> I know that the younger one didn't know [the truth of the situation]. 'Cos it was actually years later that he found out. He must only have been eleven because my parents used to come through every second sunday to see me in [city] and I remember them saying that Jamie, he was in a terrible state because he hadn't seen me for so long. And he kept saying I want to come with you to see her, and they had to keep making up new excuses, 'cos they didn't want him to see me pregnant. And they had told him that I was working through in [city]. And that where I worked they came to visit me but children weren't allowed in. So he couldn't come. So in fact he just didn't see me for those months and I think it was actually years later that he discovered. I think he must have been about seventeen before he discovered that was why I had disappeared all those years ago.

The pain encountered by this adoring and vulnerable youngster is not easy to imagine. But her perception of it remains very much alive with Tanya. The family relationships, for Tanya, were sufficiently secure for contact to be maintained. In Lena's more friable family, comprising adopted children and separated parents, the sibling relationships were sorely tested:

Lena: [It was] very hurtful 'cos [my Mother] cut the rest of the family off from me as well. Y'know she wouldn't let them come and visit me and stuff like this. They wasn't allowed to mention my name at home - it was pretty rotten.

In spite of parental sanctions, Lena's brother was able to give her loving support when she most needed it:

Lena: The only thing that really sticks out in my mind was my oldest brother, he wouldn't speak to me. And I was sitting on the bed and I was just lying having a good cry and my brother put his arm round me and said 'It doesn't matter - I'll still love you'. I thought that was nice. And - if you knew Geoff - for him to have done it of all people was quite shocking, it was quite 'stand back in amazement'.

Acceptance by siblings, some relinquishing mothers recounted, was both surprising and welcome:

Barbara: [After the birth] there was a card from my brother saying 'From Uncle'.

Nadia: My eldest brother (he'd got three small children) ... tends to be a bit selfish, but he came to the hospital to collect me and take me back to their house. He was absolutely wonderful to me after the birth and that was the first time I'd actually seen him be human, y'know outwardly emotional.

For Sandra acceptance was variable among her siblings, while Vera encountered a quite negative response:

Sandra: They were a bit taken aback, but there's one of my sisters is training to be a doctor and she was a bit more understanding about it. The other sister is a nurse and she was a bit ... totally resentful of [Billy]. My brother hasn't really said much about it.

Vera: [My shame] was particularly bad when I told my sister. She reacted badly when I eventually told her that I had had a baby and had given it up. She said that it was 'distasteful'.

Informing their siblings of the pregnancy caused the mothers much difficulty which, in In view of the potential for such negative responses, is hardly surprising:

Iona: [My Mother] felt it was my responsibility to tell my brother and my sister about what had happened to me and that of course was very painful to me. I had to sit and write a very painful letter to my sister who was the only stable member of our family (LAUGH). She did everything the right way - my brother and I seemed to do everything the wrong way.

Grandparents

In the UK the contribution of the grandparents to the family system tends to be underestimated and undervalued (Hurme, 1991; McHaffie, 1991). The importance of the grandparent role became abundantly clear through the relinquishing mothers' accounts. Their importance took two forms.

Support provided by grandparents for the young woman, was first. This tended to be cut off by the parents in order to 'protect' the older generation in the same way as young siblings were protected:

> Hilda: My Gran used to spoil me, as if to make up for anything that I was not getting at home, particularly attention. I was ruined by her. I would sleep in my gran's bedroom and got in by the side of her when Jimmy got up [to] go to the pit. Gran was never told. She must have known. She said I was getting fat and I was ta'en away from her. That was the worst bit, rather than facing anybody else, having to go back and face her. Cos the thing she'd have done is put her arms round me. I mind that if she knew I would not have had to go there. If anybody could've helped me and kept me, she would've.

> Jessica: But I know that it would have been too much for my gran and it would have hurt my parents [for her to be told]. It was also difficult when I had to neglect my grandmother.

The concept or ideal of grandparenthood also featured significantly, of which the relinquishing mother was depriving her parents, more especially her mother:

> Quelia: I do feel deprived. I've also deprived my Mother and Father of their one and only grandchild. They'll never have any now.

> Barbara: She made soft toys to go. Because I suppose her attitude was it was her grandchild. It's true of my Mother. It must've broke her heart to lose a grandchild, but she never ever put any of those feelings on to me, she never let me see what she was going through.

> Tanya: My Mother would now very much like to see Andrea, she says that she feels upset for me and guilty because of what she made me do in giving my baby away. I find now that I am able to talk to the family about Andrea. And my Mother actually counts Andrea in when she is counting her grand-children.

Conclusion

The implications of relinquishment for family relationships appear immense. These implications are largely in spite of attempts at concealment by the parents of the relinquishing mother. These attempts usually involve hiding the pregnancy, birth and relinquishment from family members who are perceived as being vulnerable. In this way a source of support is removed from the relinquishing mother; also painful emotions are engendered with either hindsight or revelation. The role of the father of the relinquishing mother has been shown to predominate in both its direct effect on his daughter and through an indirect effect via her mother. The power of the family emerges clearly, especially when contrasted with the vulnerable position of the relinquishing mother.

8 Recognising being pregnant

Reading the words of the relinquishing mothers as a woman in her forties, with over twenty years experience as a midwife towards the end of the twentieth century, I register surprise that some mothers in my recent study (Mander, 1992a) failed to recognise their pregnancy. In this chapter I explore the circumstances and reasoning which prevented these mothers from drawing what may seem to be an all-too-obvious conclusion.

The more sceptical reader may question how I could be sufficiently naive to accept the word of women whose accounts are so incredible. My answer would be that these mothers had no reason to embellish their experiences, so I work from the initial premise that each of the relinquishing mothers who were my informants told me the truth as she saw it. According to Cunningham (1977) the researcher has no choice but to trust the informants and accept their statements 'at face value'; but she warns us to be wary of the effects which bias may introduce. The concept of trust in research is examined in three dimensions by Lee (1993) in his account of research into sensitive topics. Lee, first, effectively demolishes the argument that the researcher should invariably assume an attitude of distrust to what the informant says, because there is no reason why powerful informants particularly should tell the truth. Second, Lee reminds us of the reciprocal bond of trust between the researcher and the informant. Third, Lee shows that trust needs to be fostered and allowed to develop by the researcher, rather than taken for granted.

By recounting the conception, birth and relinquishment each mother in my recent study felt that she had so debased herself that she was unable to sink any lower. Far from being powerful and being motivated to conceal and fabricate, not one mother had any reason to mislead me during the interview. Thus, the accounts of the relinquishment are being accepted as they were reported to me and show that diagnosing pregnancy is less easy than it seems.

Significance of recognition

The mother's recognition of her pregnancy is significant here for three reasons: first, as with every mother, she must realise that she is pregnant before she is able to seek care to promote her own and her baby's health.

Second, recognising the pregnancy allows the mother to begin the developmental tasks of pregnancy and which constitute the foundation for the psychological adjustment to motherhood (Rubin, 1970): (1) seeking a safe passage for herself and her baby through pregnancy, labour and birth (2) ensuring acceptance of her baby by her significant others (3) forming a loving relationship with her unknown baby and (4) learning to give of herself. In the relinquishing mother, these tasks constitute the foundation for her grief.

Third, for the less well-supported mother, recognition of the pregnancy is necessary before seeking help in making decisions about its future. In the context of the adolescent pregnancy Corbett and Meyer (1987) consider the mother's recognition of the pregnancy alongside her choice of a supportive confidante. These authors indicate that the confidante may be instrumental in helping the mother to recognise her pregnancy; this certainly applied in the experience of Francesca in my recent study:

> Francesca: My friend Caroline came round to visit me with a complete stranger named Ann. We got to talking about my periods having stopped. Caroline asked about pregnancy directly, but I denied it. I wore big floppy clothes. Ann asked to see my abdomen to see if I was pregnant. Ann, who was only 16, and me went out the next day and we went round the shops. Ann asked me to 'chum' her to the family planning clinic as she had an appointment there. I agreed to walk down with her. When we got to the door Ann admitted that she had made the appointment for me, not herself, and had tricked me into going to help me to find out once and for all. Ann said she would stay with me. We both went in anyway and I had an internal examination which confirmed that I was pregnant.

Although the sequence of events varies according to the individual mother's circumstances, parents feature prominently in her concerns about who and how to tell. The daughter-parent relationship is not uniquely problematical to adolescent mothers (Corbett & Meyer, 1987), as the situation of a slightly older mother illustrates:

> Olivia: During my first pregnancy I was taken into social care after a blazing row with my parents. I miscarried and it has never been mentioned between us since then. My parents wanted to make it up to me for their lack of support and lack of contact with me at the time of the miscarriage as there was a lot of bitterness between us at the time. We have now managed to build up a new relationship. We went through a lot of bitterness in a lot of ways. We still saw each other, we were still parents and daughter, but there were too many subjects that couldn't be broached to be really close. Now, over the two years we have built that up, which is why I had to keep Andrea a secret. I just couldn't risk losing that. I couldn't risk losing what I had built up with my parents.

Despite being fused into one for some mothers, like Francesca, the recognition or diagnosis of pregnancy in western society is ordinarily a two-stage process. As with Francesca, a number of the mothers in my recent study encountered difficulty with the first stage, that is the identification by the mother of bodily changes or symptoms (Sweet, 1992). They were, thus, unable to move on to the next stage, in which other bodily changes or signs, are sought by an attendant, usually the GP but for Francesca the family planning staff.

Textbooks all too often create the impression that the recognition of symptoms of pregnancy is easy for the mother, the only uncertainty relating to whether she experiences breast changes and sickness before or after she misses a menstrual period (Myles, 1989). This impression contrasts with Oakley's research (1979) which explored the first-time mother's experience of pregnancy, including her identification of her early symptoms. The accounts are written in the mothers' words, and make us less and less surprised that young mothers have difficulty recognising the significance of symptoms such as amenorrhoea, breast tenderness and sickness. What never ceases to surprise is the failure of GPs to diagnose pregnancy in healthy young women; regularly, Oakley found women being fobbed off with a convenient diagnosis such as gastroenteritis or urinary infection. Oakley suggests that difficulty in making the diagnosis is compounded by excessively sensitive pregnancy tests, which become misleading if their timing is not precise. This applied to Clara who, realising the possibility of pregnancy, undertook a pregnancy test. The negative result was later proved false:

> Clara: I became concerned when I was two months pregnant that I might be, but my pregnancy test was negative. I was relieved and believed it. The next time I had a pregnancy test it was positive and I was told I was six months pregnant by that time.

Oakley summarises the variability in the symptoms which help women to recognise pregnancy (See Table 8.1.). Her data emphasise the limited significance of a missed period, as this was noticed first by less than two-thirds of the women in her sample.

Table 8.1.
First pregnancy symptoms

Missed period	62%
Nausea and/or vomiting	12%
Sore breasts	9%
Light period	5%
'Felt pregnant'	3%
Urinary frequency	2%
Other	6%
Total	100%

(Oakley, 1979)

Oakley shows the value for some of the woman's self-knowledge. Her examples include a woman with a very predictable menstrual cycle and another who experienced breast changes which were previously unknown to her.

Intuitive feelings may be helpful to those women for whom pregnancy is either a likely or a desirable possibility, making us realise the effects of planning or hoping for a pregnancy.

On the basis of her data, Oakley questions the need for a medical diagnosis of pregnancy when, despite some difficulty, the women in her sample were no less effective in making the diagnosis than their medical advisers. She goes on to link this medical 'proclamation' to the more general medicalisation of child-bearing by emphasising the apparent conflict between the woman trusting her own bodily symptoms and her need to defer to all-powerful medical authority.

Being ignorant

The mothers in my recent study appeared to adhere to the view that the diagnosis of pregnancy is straightforward. Their assumption that their inability to recognise something so glaringly obvious was due to their own ignorance is an example of the generally low esteem in which they held themselves. Their claim to have been ignorant about sex as well as reproduction is supported by a research report which was published near the time when some of the mothers in my recent study were becoming pregnant (Schofield, 1972):

> Barbara: I mean me being as naive as I was, the actual act couldn't have been longer than about five minutes. I didn't know what was going on. OK I wasn't that stupid, but at the same time you don't.

It is apparent that the significance and consequences of a hasty act of sexual intercourse may be wasted on a fourteen year-old with a relatively sheltered up-bringing.

Although Iona was twenty-two when she conceived, her circumstances led to her inability to realise the implications of her sexual relationship. This conception happened in the 1960s when a young lady brought up in the refined middle-class suburbs of a Scottish city may have been less street-wise than her modern sister.

> Iona: I was twenty-two when I became pregnant, but I was very much under the influence of my parents. That summer I went on holiday with a friend and I spent most of the two weeks with Billy and I became pregnant through ignorance more than anything else, I think. I was so ignorant about sex. My mother had never spoken to me about sex. All I had learned was from school and things people said at school.

The lack of openness between mothers and daughters is a theme which recurs throughout these interviews. The relinquishing mother seems to blame her mother for not providing information which would have prevented the need for relinquishment. This becomes clearly apparent in the words of Tanya (See below). Alternatively, the relinquishing mother may be unfavourably comparing the limited relationship which she had with her mother with the more complete understanding she now has with her children who are with her.

For Lena, who was aged fourteen at the time of the conception, the pregnancy resulted from an unequal, perhaps abusive, relationship in which she hoped to find some security in what had been, even at that early stage, a turbulent life:

> RM: What were you like at the time?
> Lena: Och aye, naive, stupid. I was young, very young and naive, I would say. I didn't have a clue. I didn't know I was pregnant. It was my Mum that noticed. It never occurred to me. She just came, she asked me. I didn't know what she was talking about.

Tanya was a similar age to Lena when she conceived and, like other informants, considers that she was going through a rebellious stage, presumably testing her parents to find out what behaviour was permissable. This involved embarking on a long-term relationship with a young man whose religion, age and social class would be unacceptable to her parents. Tanya spells out very clearly how the absence of accurate sex education compounded her difficulty in deciding how her sexual relationship should develop.

> Tanya: I think I was going through that probably rebellious time with my parents from I think when I was about fourteen when you think they're just trying to stop you from having a good time, when actually they're trying to protect you. I think certainly sexually I was very naive, I knew that what I had done which happened once, was wrong but I honestly didn't know why it was wrong. I really didn't know the consequences. I think when I found out I was pregnant I was as surprised as anybody else was! I just didn't realise. My parents, I suppose, and a lot of people in their age-group were the same. Their idea of sex education was that when you started menstruating 'Now you just watch yourself, just you be careful'. And you sort of thought 'Yeah, right'. Although you really didn't know what they were talking about. They never ever went into things, and in fact my mother to this day still doesn't believe that I honestly didn't know. And when I ask her where she thought I was going to get this information she doesn't really have any answer. I suppose she just thinks, and I suppose its true, she thinks that you just picked it up at school or in conversation at street corners with your friends. And you weren't able to see that a lot of it was inaccurate, which is why these things happen to you I think. Not that I'm blaming my mother at all, 'cos I still knew that what I did was wrong, but I honestly did not know why. That sounds ridiculous doesn't it? But when I think of seventeen year-olds now, they just seem to be so grown up. Fourteen year-olds now seem to know the score don't they? And I just didn't.

Young people's sources of sexual knowledge were examined by Schofield (1972), who found that, unlike Tanya, twenty-seven percent of their sample gained their knowledge from their mothers. This is a small number in comparison with the fifty-three percent who learned about sex from their friends, usually by way of jokes. Those young people who learned about sex from their parents, invariably their mother, tended to be from more middle-class backgrounds in contrast to widespread assumptions of working-class openness.

Tanya's assertion that her pregnancy resulted from a single act of sexual intercourse exemplifies another frequently recurring theme among this group of informants. This may serve to emphasise both their innocence in sexual matters and also their feeling that they in no way 'deserved' what they saw as the punishment of becoming pregnant and having to relinquish the baby:

> Gina: It is the truth - that was the one and only time I had intercourse with him. It was just very unfortunate or fortunate, however one may look upon it, that I became pregnant.

While it is clear from the work of Oakley that self-diagnosis of pregnancy is less than easy, for those women who are not planning or hoping to conceive the self-diagnosis is even more complex. This complexity is further aggravated in the mother for whom the pregnancy is unwanted. The concept of 'wantedness' is 'vague, elusive and beset with operational difficulties' (David et al., 1988), but David and Baldwin (1979) attempt to differentiate between intended and unintended conceptions, wanted and unwanted pregnancies and kept and relinquished babies. David et al. (1988) conclude that a mother's decision about whether to continue her pregnancy and whether to relinquish her baby results from the balance between unwantedness on the one hand and the tolerability, or even attraction, of the pregnancy and motherhood on the other hand. Making such distinctions would have been neither possible nor helpful in my recent study, partly because of my general reliance on retrospective data and partly because my focus is on the fact of relinquishment and the associated care.

A prospective study by Macintyre (1975 & 1977) focussed on the decision-making process by seventeen single mothers, a crucial element of which was the mother's identification of and reaction to her pregnancy. Like Oakley (1979), Macintyre emphasises the imprecision of pregnancy diagnosis due to the likelihood of the symptoms being caused by a range of conditions unrelated to pregnancy. Macintyre then discusses the knowledge-base which a woman needs in order to self-diagnose pregnancy or at least refer herself to someone who will make that diagnosis. Unfortunately, this knowledge-base may allow her to exclude pregnancy as a possible cause of her symptoms, as Aline did:

> Aline: With my back trouble and not being able to move I thought that my increasing tummy was due to lack of exercise, and that my swollen ankles were because I was sitting the whole time. My mother did not notice my changing size, probably because she'd never had either of those things. I did not recognise the fetal movements for what they were. I thought that the tummy feelings were nothing more than the usual rumblings and that the cramps were due to restarting exercise when I did start walking to work and things.

Macintyre questions the relevance of the compatibility of the mother's knowledge-base with that of the scientific or medical community. Inevitably and eventually the mother will find that her self-diagnosis is confirmed or refuted by events and perhaps by a medical practitioner. The possibility which some may warn against lies in the lack of congruence between the mother's own ideas and those of the medical fraternity, which determines the timing of the mother presenting for advice or confirmation of her pregnancy. This lack of congruence resulted in Aline having her pregnancy confirmed by ultrasound at thirty-one weeks gestation.

As well as the existence of a relevant knowledge-base, Macintyre argues that the self-diagnosis of pregnancy is facilitated or impeded by the salience of pregnancy to the woman, which may be comparable with the extremes of 'tolerability' of pregnancy and motherhood (David et al., 1988) mentioned already. On the basis of her knowledge/salience framework, Macintyre categorised her sample into four groups and suggested that this determined the timing of their self-diagnosis of their pregnancies. She maintains that Type One women recognise the pregnancy earliest and Type Four women latest.

Type one women were highly knowledgeable and very concerned about becoming pregnant. For these women pregnancy constituted a crisis.

Type two women possessed knowledge congruent with medical knowledge but for whom pregnancy was less salient. These women required more evidence to persuade them to take the possibility of pregnancy seriously.

Type three women were those in whom pregnancy was highly salient, but who could give no knowledge-based reason for their belief that they were pregnant. Their absolute conviction of their pregnancy was founded on intuition. Macintyre interviewed women only after the pregnancy had been medically confirmed; these mothers had, therefore, been proved right.

Type four were those women in whom both knowledge and salience were low. For a variety of reasons pregnancy was not a central concern for these mothers. It is this group of mothers who approximate most closely to those interviewed in my recent study. Some of these mothers, such as Lena and Tanya, decided that it was ignorance that prevented them from linking physiological and behavioural information. For others more complex mechanisms were operating.

The women in Macintyre's sample reacted to the realisation of pregnancy much more variably than the mothers in my recent study. Macintyre categorised the women's responses as ranging between pleased to be pregnant, problematic, wrong time and outright crisis. For the mothers in my recent study only the last of these is appropriate, as evidenced by their eventual relinquishment. This crisis response may have been partly responsible for the mothers' difficulty in recognising the pregnancy, that is, it featured the psychological defence mechanism of denial.

Denying the pregnancy

Although used in a non-technical everyday sense, we are considering denial here, along with rationalisation and repression, as one of the unconscious processes which we may use to cope with emotions which are too unbearably painful to contemplate (Altschul & Sinclair, 1981). In the context of my recent study denial extends to the physiological development, the pregnancy, which was giving rise to such powerful emotions and the prospect of such awful consequences (Leigh et al., 1977).

Defence mechanisms are used to help us to maintain our equilibrium in the face of powerful emotional onslaughts. A valuable example is the denial which manifests itself in the early stages of grieving as shock and disbelief (Kubler-Ross, 1970), allowing us some time to begin our adjustment before accepting the reality of our loss (See Chapter 2.). Defence mechanisms such as denial only become counterproductive when used on a continuing basis, beyond their initial protective value.

As mentioned already, the acceptance of the pregnancy is one of the fundamental tasks which the mother must complete for the sake of her own health and possibly that of her baby (Rubin, 1970). Accepting the pregnancy may be difficult for some, such as the mother who is recently bereaved, has previously lost a baby or who is unable to cope with her feminine identity (Raphael-Leff, 1980). Raphael-Leff emphasises the likelihood of the unsupported mother facing difficulty accepting the fact of her pregnancy. Jones and Jones (1991) consider the buffering effects of social support in helping the mother to adjust to the emotional changes as well as the provision of that support by members of the health care team.

The relinquishing mother uses a number of strategies to protect herself from the realisation of the increasingly obvious developing pregnancy. The extent to which the mother's denial is conscious is difficult to assess, as shown by Hilda who was able to identify the strategies which she used to convince herself and her mother:

> Hilda: I kept on denying it, but I knew I was but I would not sort of let on. So I kept from going home. I thought if I stayed at my Gran's they'll not notice. I denied that I was pregnant, but I used cut myself on my finger and put the blood onto my pants, because [my Mother] was always looking for things like that and that was what I would do to make her think I was having periods. I used to take the sanitary towels and flush them away so that she'd think they were being used up.

> Francesca: I realised I was pregnant when I was 6 months pregnant. I had just assumed that it would go away, that it was not really there. 'Couldn't accept it.

The relinquishing mother was sometimes assisted by others, for whom the recognition of the pregnancy would be only marginally less painful, to deny the reality of the situation. Again the mother of the pregnant woman features prominently:

> Iona: I became pregnant but I think [Mother] had suspected for some weeks and, like me, tried to bury her head in the sand.

> Hilda: I knew when my period didn't come, but you ignore it. Mum said you're getting fat, I said she was washing [my jeans] wrongly, I'd have used a shoe horn.

The relinquishing mother was invariably eventually forced by incontrovertible evidence to accept the reality of her pregnancy:

Jessica: I basically did not know what to expect, I was 8 months pregnant before I went to tell the GP. I think I did not want to accept the fact that it had actually happened to me. But my ankles were swelling up so I eventually had to go. He told me that I had to accept it then.

Denying with medical help

As mentioned already, there is a widespread assumption that the recognition of pregnancy is easy for the mother. Similarly the diagnosis by medical personnel may be assumed to be, if anything, easier. Research by Oakley (1979) serves to refute both of these assumptions. Medical diagnosis and prognosis was not invariably helpful to the relinquishing mother in my recent study. The relationship between self-diagnosis and medical diagnosis deserves attention before examining the issues which the previous relinquishing mothers raised; although it is necessary to bear in mind that the work on self-diagnosis has, not surprisingly, focussed on illness rather than the 'altered state of health' which constitutes pregnancy.

Our attention has been drawn to the differing theoretical frameworks on which mothers and medical practitioners base their diagnosis of, in this context, pregnancy (Helman, 1985:65; Macintyre, 1977; Schofield, 1972). The medical perspective claims to be based on scientific rationality, objective measurement, physico-chemical data, mind-body dualism and disease entities. Helman maintains that this perspective derives from a consensus among medical practitioners about the acceptability of 'facts' relating to health and illness. These facts are based on objective technological and numerical measures of physiological and pathological phenomena. Unfortunately, if a phenomenon cannot be measured it cannot be regarded as a fact and it thus becomes less than real. In this way biological factors have assumed greater significance in medicine than psycho-socio-cultural issues, and have engendered the medical model. Dingwall (1977) takes issue with the argument propounded by Freidson (1971) that medical knowledge is inherently more prestigious than lay or folk knowledge. The sharp distinction between medical or scientific knowledge claimed by some authorities is an artefact of the community which values such knowledge. Dingwall continues by asserting that the lack of theoretical conceptualisation by 'most doctors' increases the likelihood that medical knowledge is commonsensical, concluding that there is no reason to suppose that scientific thought is superior to lay and folk ideas.

As mentioned already, the principles of medical diagnosis are founded on consensus among medical observers (Helman, 1985). While this consensus may be regarded as immutable, in reality its acceptance and durability is variable, giving rise to heterogeneity among practitioners in their diagnosis of the same set of symptoms. The lack of homogeneity observed among medical practitioners is more widely recognised among those for whom they care. The person's social and cultural background as well as their individual personal characteristics profoundly affect their self-diagnosis of and response to ill-health (Fox, 1968).

Although for Jessica (above) the role of the GP was to confirm her self-diagnosis, there was limited scope for interpretation because her pregnancy was so far advanced. However, the contribution of medical evidence and medical people to diagnosing pregnancy was less straightforward for some mothers. Several of the relinquishing mothers were assisted in the denial of the pregnancy by medical evidence which served to convince them, at least temporarily, that they were not pregnant.

Infertility

For Francesca and Iona previous long-term infertile sexual relationships fostered the belief that they could not become pregnant:

> Francesca: But I'd already been having sex with Brian for two years before getting the pills, 'cos I didn't realise the possibility of pregnancy. It never occurred to me at all, you don't think of that at all.

> Iona: I often wonder in fact, when Brian found out I was pregnant - because we still kept in touch, he was absolutely horrified ... because we had had a relationship over the years and had taken very little precaution and how I never became pregnant I'll never know.

Admission to hospital

For two mothers hospitalisation supported their denial. Early in their pregnancies Gina and Jessica were admitted to hospital for conditions apparently unrelated to pregnancy. They, not unreasonably, assumed that if they had been pregnant their medical attendants would have noticed. They concluded that as no one mentioned it they could not actually be pregnant:

> Jessica: I didn't know I was pregnant and had to have an operation when I must have been 3 months. I carried on with my work and didn't accept it. I felt it was strange that they said nothing and I thought 'I can't be in here and pregnant without them noticing, so I can't be pregnant.'

> Gina: I was admitted into hospital in December. The hospital never even said anything about pregnancy to me. They said I had severe jaundice.

Gina was a well-brought up young lady, who had been privately educated and whose parents were not short of funds to provide her with her own horse. Her experience of jaundice of pregnancy suggests the existence of assumptions and value judgements influencing diagnosis and care. These contrast with the claims of objectivity in diagnosis and the use of only factual data mentioned already.

A previous diagnosis

For Sandra a comment following a childhood investigation served to convince her of the impossibility of pregnancy, encouraging her denial of the reality:

> Sandra: At one point I actually had to have a brain scan because I had a special sort of epilepsy when I was younger and apparently the result of that was supposed to mean I couldn't have children. So they were a bit puzzled by this.

A complex picture

The problem of recognising a pregnancy is not unique to ill-informed teenagers in relatively inhibited environments or to women whose medical attendants' advice may seem to confirm their fervent hopes. Aline, the subject of the case study, was unable to recognise her pregnancy, mainly because of her infrequent periods, about which she had previously sought medical advice and been reassured. Thus, to a certain extent her non-recognition of her pregnancy was encouraged by medical advice. Her disappointment with herself was aggravated when she failed to recognise the onset of premature labour:

> Aline: They must've thought I was stupid - not realising I was pregnant and then I must have been daft not to recognise that I was in labour. I've always had a very long menstrual cycle - only two periods a year. So I'm never surprised when I have no period for months on end.
> I went to see my GP about my swollen ankles. She was reassuring until I mentioned not having had my periods. I'd consulted my GP about this before and had been told not to worry about it. Now the GP asked me to climb up on the couch to examine my tummy, did an internal and sent me straight to the gynae clinic.

Conclusion

The relinquishing mother's non-recognition of her pregnancy does not derive from her refusal to accept a fact which is blatantly obvious to those around her. Inadequate sex education has traditionally been a factor and may continue to apply. Other factors assume greater importance in convincing this mother that she is not pregnant. These include the connivance of members of the family in a form of group denial, using or making assumptions based on medical information and inaccurate or incorrectly-used pregnancy tests.

On the basis of the findings of my recent study, it is apparent that if a woman is to be able to self-diagnose her pregnancy the following criteria must be satisfied:

knowledge that sexual intercourse has happened,
knowledge of the possible effects of intercourse,
knowledge of the symptoms of pregnancy,
recognition of the symptoms of pregnancy
the ability to accept that symptoms are not caused by anything else
the ability to accept that there is nothing to prevent pregnancy
the absence of confounding (that is, medical) information.

9 Searching

In my recent study searching emerged as an overwhelmingly important concept. This was not only because their search for the relinquished one was of such immense significance to the previous relinquishing mothers, but also because it was indirectly because of their search that I was able to recruit them (See Chapter 3.).

In this chapter, because there is no suitable single word for the 'one who was relinquished', I refer to this person as the 'child'. While the word 'adoptee' may indicate who the person is, it is not a term which in any way reflects the views of the relinquishing mothers. I realise that many of these people had grown to become mature adults and that their mothers recognised this, but I use the term 'child', as Bouchier et al. (1991) did, for the sake of brevity.

Searching and grieving

Searching for the one who is lost is a well-recognised component of the grieving process. Bowlby (1961) compares the loss through death of a loved one with the loss among lower animals of the mate. In animals the location and recovery of the mate aims to resume the previous interdependent relationship. The behaviour of the grieving human being shows many features in common with the single, undefended and therefore vulnerable animal. An example of a common feature is the tendency to call out, in the vain hope of eliciting a response from the one who is lost (Littlewood, 1992). While the utility of searching for a lost animal-mate is clearly apparent, the irrationality and futility of searching for a human loved-one who is lost may be similarly obvious. The need to search for evidence of the one who is lost reflects the preoccupation with their physical absence (Stroebe & Stroebe, 1987). This search may be aggravated by feelings or perceptions involving various senses, which may be dismissed as hallucinations, indicating the presence of the person who is lost. As well as the search for the person, grief features a search for meaning. If we are able to help the grieving person to find meaning in a seemingly meaningless tragedy, they may be better able to comprehend the value of what is otherwise a totally negative experience (Marris, 1986; Craig, 1977; Mander, 1994).

In his account of searching, Parkes (1976) emphasises the need of the bereaved person to protect themselves from the awful reality of their loss and suggests the tentative movement towards the acceptance of that reality. Searching may constitute the latter stages of denial (Connor, 1994). Parkes goes on to vividly describe how, despite the futility of the search, a profound compulsion drives the bereaved person to continue searching. He conjures up a forlorn picture of the grief-stricken person, describing characteristics which show them to be in a state of:

Alarm and tension
Perpetual restlessness
Preoccupation
Concentration on the lost person
Disinterest in themselves and their environment
Concern with locations where the person might be

Their precisely-focussed searching activities may be contrasted with the aimlessness and apathy which the bereaved person demonstrates increasingly at this stage of their grief. These behaviours derive from their realisation of the futility of their unremitting search, together with the more general meaninglessness of life itself. These behaviours feature prominently in the account of the stages of grieving given by Bowlby (1980), being preceded by numbness and followed by reorganisation.

Searching following relinquishment

Searching assumes new dimensions of meaning in the context of the relinquishing mother (Roll et al., 1986), as it reflects both the grief of the mother and the unequal nature of her desire for contact (Fitsell, 1989; Howe et al., 1992).

The almost universal intention of the mothers in this sample to resume contact with their child reflects how I recruited them. Birth parents' groups were the primary route by which I reached the relinquishing mothers and the main reason for the existence of these groups is to provide support for birth parents, as well as more practical help, while they are seeking to make contact with the child. This aspect of the sampling may warrant criticism, demonstrating the unrepresentative nature of the sample and the limited generaliseability of the findings. That these criticisms are hardly relevant is apparent from the reluctance to claim generaliseability in qualitative research. In spite of this, it is interesting to observe that the relinquishing mothers who were recruited from other sources, such as advertisements and articles in newspapers and women's magazines, shared the need to search for the child to only a marginally lesser extent.

A research project by Bouchier and her colleagues (1991) attempted to examine the views of relinquishing mothers in relation to their wish for contact with the child. Although these researchers attempted to recruit equal groups of relinquishing mothers who did and who did not wish for contact with their child, they were unable to locate sufficient numbers of mothers who did no want contact. The final sample comprised a 'Contact Group' of forty-one mothers who were seeking contact and a 'No Contact Group' of five mothers who were not seeking contact. We may surmise the reasons for difficulty in recruiting 'No Contact' mothers. Data collection was by structured interview.

Despite the research project being undertaken in Scotland, Bouchier found that a large majority of the mothers (thirty-three = 72%) reported that they had not been told at the time of their relinquishment of the possibility of their child eventually seeking them. The reasons for this information being withheld are not discussed. The need for other changes in adoption practice are also raised, such as the desire among a majority (thirty = 65%) for birth parents to be able to obtain information to help them to seek their child as well.

Searching for the child

In my recent study the form which the searching took varies between the enthusiastic, almost dogged, persistence of mothers such as Marcia and Tanya and the quiet, inactive confidence of being reunited eventually, shown by Sandra.

Actively searching

As well as differing in the degree of activity, the search varies in its formality or organisation. For Anthea, as she told me through her tears, her search began in a haphazard way:

> Anthea: I used to run after children in the street, blond-haired ones, just to see - I used to turn them round - it's a wonder I never got arrested! Some of the mothers cried 'What are you doing?' 'I'm looking for my daughter'. I think I was really searching for them, y'know.

Anthea's words remind us of the point emphasised by Parkes (1976), that the bereaved person is seeking someone who they picture with intense clarity as they were known to them. Thus, Anthea sought blond children, perhaps forgetting that a child's hair may darken as she grows older. For the mother who saw her baby only briefly, or worse, did not see her baby at all, the searching phase is made even more difficult by the absence of any clear picture of the child. Although, the mother's search is likely to be based on her own physical appearance combined with that of the child's father (Roll et al., 1986).

A far more systematic approach was employed by Gina, who was able to make good use of her financial and intellectual resources. Her account shows very clearly the switchback of failure and success encountered during her search:

> Gina: I went back to [another continent] six years ago, I went back to the city where he was born and I tried to do some research myself, but of course I was only there for two weeks ... I didn't have enough time to do the research. So many years had elapsed and the building where the records were kept was no longer there. I just didn't know how to pursue it on my own. It was a dead end.

For Marcia and the father of her relinquished daughter, the search verged on the conspiratorial, as I learned while walking with her to the railway station and recorded in field notes:

> Marcia was told by the social worker that Andrea had been adopted by a professional couple and the nature of their profession. On the day of the adoption Billy identified the couple by surreptitiously observing the childrens' home and took the registration number of their car. He was thus able to trace them to [town]. Billy and Marcia then found their name through their professional register.

Similarly, it was necessary for Wilma to resort to some degree of subterfuge in her search to make contact with her daughter:

> Wilma: I probably shouldn't tell you this, but I had a conversation with Andrea. I spoke to her for quite a while, secretly, by pretending to be a wrong number. She sounded very nice ...

Not searching

The two mothers who denied any attempts to search for their child were quite adamant in their decision, but for different reasons. Although she freely admitted her interest in babies following her relinquishment, Francesca refused to contemplate that she might be anything more than curious:

> Francesca: After placing him for adoption I found myself looking at babies and wondering 'Is that him?' This was merely curiosity, nothing more.

On the other hand, Vera made a sincere vow to herself and her son that she would not actively seek him. She has, however, taken every opportunity to facilitate any attempts which he might make to locate her.

> Vera: I loved him when he was born, I kissed him goodbye and gave him away. I promised him that I would never try to contact him or to play any part in his life at all, so I have never tried to trace him. There was no thought in my mind of ever seeing him again, as I was never told anything about it, but I've laid all the trails for him.

In their small sample of mothers not wishing contact with the child, Bouchier and her colleagues (1991) sought the reason for their decision. The mothers gave as their reason their concern that the disruption caused by this new and unexpected arrival in the midst of their own current families would be unbearable.

Yearning

According to Worden (1992) yearning is a common experience of survivors of bereavement; whereas the word 'pining' which is more clearly and closely related to separation anxiety is preferred by Parkes (1976). Such feelings, for many of the relinquishing mothers, stimulated their search to be reunited with their child:

> Clara: I fervently hope that I'll see my child again sometime. I will get to see her again, won't I?

> Anthea: There is also the hope that the kids will come and see you. That is one very burning desire that a mother has.

Those mothers whose relinquishment was far more recent, such as Pamela, Sandra and Olivia, showed me that the yearning began at a very early stage:

> Pamela: As soon as I left hospital, I started looking forward to when he was 18 and he would be able to start looking for me.

Anticipating contact

The possibility of the child making contact was very real to each mother. Although many recounted this anticipation in wishful terms, other mothers were more anxious about contact being made. Each mother was wary of the effect that this might have on others who had subsequently become significant parts of her life. This observation is reminiscent of the findings of Bouchier and her colleagues, mentioned above:

> Kara: ...and I suppose when he possibly returns, that's the only time you're ever going to know any more about it. So for, say, sixteen years you've got to just have an open mind about it - wonder but not know. It's hard. Hard. Another six years and it could be all coming back into your life again which doesn't bother me at all, it's certainly one thing that doesn't frighten me, that sort of thing. If I was planning on marrying or anything like that, they would know that this person could appear on my doorstep which is my son. To me that's quite important. If he wants to find me then I won't hide from him at all.

The findings of Bouchier are further congruent in terms of the mother's anticipation of contact. Bouchier found that the mothers wanted facts about the child which would prepare her and those close to her for when her child resumed contact. Bouchier further found that because wariness was the main emotion felt by the mother at the prospect of reunion with her child, most of those she interviewed needed an intermediary in their search for contact. The intermediary was also perceived as a buffer to moderate the pain should the child not want contact. When Bouchier's contact group were asked how they would react to this situation equal numbers gave one of three responses: first, some would accept it, second, some would be really hurt and, third, the others would not give up, hoping the child would change her mind.

Facilitating contact by leaving markers

In my recent study, as in the work by Bouchier et al. (1991), each mother had planned and implemented certain strategies which would help her child to trace her. Interestingly, Bouchier found that such strategies were used by the non-contact as well as the contact group. The strategies which the mother used varied; for Clara and Marcia, the child was given a rarely-heard first name:

> Clara: A new first name was given by the adoptive parents but this distinctive name was kept by them as her middle name, which I really did appreciate.

> Marcia: I named her for Billy's mother and my own name, and also I thought if she ever wanted to search for me it would be easy. It's quite an unusual name. If she wanted to search she could have found me long ago I think. I must be the only one in Great Britain.

Anthea and Vera, who both led relatively mobile lives, ensured that they always gave their addresses to 'official agencies'. For Anthea this strategy proved successful when her children happily re-established contact:

> Anthea: It didn't matter what name I was under ... I reverted back to my maiden name. But when I changed my address, which was quite often, I left it with the [adoption] agency just in case. That's what happened. They were able to write a letter to the Church of Scotland in [main] Street and by me leaving my name and address and my telephone number, they were able to get in touch with me saying that they had this letter from my kids looking for me.

> Vera: I've always registered on the electoral roll wherever I have lived, so that if he tried to look for me it should not be too difficult. Like Tanya who was on the radio with you, she had left markers for her daughter and I have done the same things.

The opposite was achieved when, in order to protect his teenage daughter from further trauma, Barbara's father subtly changed the name on her child's birth certificate. Barbara clearly regrets this attempt to confound any attempts by the child to locate her relinquishing mother:

> Barbara: My dad took me down to [district] where the baby was born, to the Registrar's there. My maiden name was a double-barrelled name and when we went to register I registered her Andrea, but rather than Jones-Donald - the Registrar said what's the surname? And I can remember to this day just going to say Jones-Donald, my dad said 'No, it's Donald'. I know, and I knew then, that he was doing that to protect me in future. But sometimes it bugs me because I think, you are making the path - if she wants to come and find me - you are making the path a bit harder.

Thwarting the search

As mentioned already, Anthea had been successful in re-establishing a mutually satisfying relationship with her relinquished children. For others, like Barbara, the search was proving far from successful. The re-establishment of contact was impeded by a variety of factors:

The adoptive parents

It is not surprising that the approaches of the relinquishing mother are not welcomed by the adoptive parents (Hubbard, 1947). Triseliotis (1985) notes that the adoptive parents are officially supported in their stance by giving them 'the maximum autonomy' over their adopted child. Despite this situation the hurt to the relinquishing mother is clearly apparent:

> Hilda: On saturday I got a letter frae [the social worker] saying that they'd got in touch wi' his parents. I never even got a photo or anything of him - never. She said they had nae answered the first letter, so she wrote again and his adopted father wrote to say that they'd discussed it wi' him and that for the moment they don't want nothing tae dae wi' me. Things are piling up on top o' me.

At a particularly distressing point in Marcia's interview, when her crying prevented further recording. I switched off the tape-recorder and have to rely on field notes made immediately afterwards:

> Marcia wrote a letter to the adoptive mother in the hope that some contact would be possible. Marcia found that the act of writing that letter did actually help her. The adoptive mother replied in an unfortunate letter which Marcia tearfully showed me. The adoptive mother recommended that Marcia should 'Forget about her'.

The child

The child may prove reluctant to establish any form of contact with the relinquishing mother:

> Gina: But the response was that he's very bitter, doesn't want to know me, and I am finding that very hard to cope with.

Such rejection has been informally observed to be more common among males who were relinquished (Buckland, 1989). Informal observation is supported by a study of the experience of adoptees, which found that only 12.1% of his volunteer sample was male (Sachdev, 1992). This reflects the usual membership in adoptee search-support groups as well as the finding of earlier researchers. It is necessary to consider how the views of male adoptees may prevent them from seeking their mothers. In my recent study the mothers blamed the lack of contact from their child on the adoptive parents having turned the child against them. The antipathy perceived by the relinquishing mother from the adoptive parents was clear in Wilma's words:

Wilma: I was able to delay the [adoption] by putting my child in the care of adoptive parents, but the mother was particularly spiteful against me and I was constantly battened upon to give my child up by these people and by the agency in London. The most unhelpful thing was the visits that I made to her when she was being fostered [by the adoptive parents]. The foster mother accused me of having given her blackberries from the roadside, I would never have thought of doing such a thing - she was really just trying to tell me what a bad mother I was. I wrote to them after the adoption and all I got back was a nasty letter from a magistrate.

The adoption agency

During the time span between the relinquishment and the mother being in a position to organise her search for her child, the administration of the adoption agency and the responsibility for the maintenance of records may have changed out of all recognition, thus impeding the search:

Debra: My attempts to trace Andrea have not gone well, I have not had any help from the [adoption] agency, I think its an old people's home now.

Bouchier et al. (1991) found that information to help with tracing the child was similarly lacking. While twenty-six of the forty-one mothers in her contact group had sought information to help locate the child, only one mother had been given information with which she was happy. As also reported by Howe et al. (1992), many of the remaining mothers were not at all satisfied with their information.

Searching for information

Closely linked with issues relating to searching is the prevalent anxiety among relinquishing mothers about the well-being of the child. This anxiety tends to focus on the absence of information provided by the adoption agency (Inglis, 1984; Fitsell, 1989; Silverman, 1980):

Iona: All she would tell me was that the name had been changed and that one of the baby's names was Andrea. And that is all the information I have about her. I don't know whether she will still be in this country even, because if he was in the Navy and they may well have moved, abroad or wherever. That is all the information I was ever given.

Vera: Also I have never been able to get any information about how he's getting on or anything. About six months after I gave him for adoption I asked them whether they could give me a photograph of him to keep. They just said that I'd given up all rights to him and so there was nothing they could do.

Ursula: I asked the people at the social services if, if anything ever happens to Andrew, like if he dies, could I be informed? They said 'No'. I asked the Roman Catholic adoption society that and they said 'Yes' and also they'd like me to give them my new address if I ever move.

Kara: You could be walking down the street, you know, you see [someone], and you think, this could be him, because you don't know what they look like ... You think that you could be walking past him in the street ... Though sometimes, when I think about my baby I miss him and I think 'I wonder what he's doing', 'I wonder how he is', I wonder all the things that you wonder. But then you think well maybe I'm wondering for some reason. Maybe something's happened to him. Maybe something like - how do you know that something's not happened to him and he has gone, maybe he has died through some - do you understand what I mean? It would be strange but you just don't know. It's the unknown. So your mind runs riot sometimes because you think maybe I'm sitting here wondering about this person who maybe doesn't exist any more. So it's all these strange thoughts and feelings you have and maybe that's - but that's how I feel sometimes. I think that's what its like when you've got no information - nothing whatsoever.

Fearing for the welfare of the child

Closely related to their general lack of information, many of the mothers described their anxiety in case the child should have come to any form of harm, developed an illness, or become miserable for any reason (Raphael-Leff, 1991). As Bouchier et al. (1991) also found, the need for factual information, to deal with unfounded anxieties, was paramount:

Quelia: I'll go through the rest of my life wondering 'Did I do the right thing giving her up?' 'Did she go to a happy enough home?' Other wee things like that.

Francesca: I cried a lot during the pregnancy. I was always crying. I wonder whether my bad moods affected his personality? Perhaps he gets depressed. What if the x-ray I had had done something? I would have ruined his life. I hope that he's not like me'. TEARS I'm sure he'll be alright. He's not unhappy - I hope'.

Iona: But I still think about Andrea and wonder how she is and where she is, wonder if she's happy ... I thought I was doing the right thing at the time by her, but now you hear so many horror stories. I have actually met people who have been adopted and they were not happy with their adoptive parents and I think 'Oh, my God, what if she has had an unhappy, miserable life?' - just all the questions we have gone over in this interview. What if she's not even alive any more, something has happened to her? I don't know any of these things, they'll always remain a mystery, unless she tries to get in touch with me. I would be quite happy to meet her.

The possibility of the child appearing unexpectedly and the effect on the present family was found by Bouchier to be a source of concern to the mothers. As noted by Fitsell (1989), the mother sought information which would help her to prepare herself and others in her family, such as her subsequent children, for the possibility of her child reappearing:

> Nadia: I do worry about the effect on the other children, especially my eldest son, if Andrew should happen to return. I am a bit anxious about his well being. But my sons know that this may happen and where my letter for Andrew is kept, in case I'm not there.

Fearing rejection

While hoping to obtain information to regain some form of contact with the child, each mother reported a nagging anxiety that the child might only make contact in order to exact some form of revenge.

> Kara: And I hope he's happy. I'd hate for him to find me because he was unhappy. It wouldn't bother me if he didn't find me. I think if he found me and told me that he had been unhappy that would be awful.

> Elena: If he did try to contact me, he might say 'Why did you do it, you're horrible?' You think to yourself that if you get in touch with each other everything will be rosy, but now I have started getting this fear that he might get in touch with me just to say 'I hate you' ... I'm worried that that might happen.

Conclusion

Although the searching described by each relinquishing mother may appear to have much in common with that part of the grieving process recognised in the literature, there are certain essential differences. The relinquishing mother's search is not only symbolic, although this long-term activity seems to be linked to incomplete grieving. Her search also has three practical functions of seeking information which may, first, allay her concerns about the welfare of her child. Second, the mother believes information is being denied her by adoption legislation. Third, she fears information is also being withheld from her child resulting in her ignorance of the real circumstances of her birth.

For the bereaved person searching contributes to a finite grieving process, of which the search is a similarly finite component. As Worden (1992) optimistically observes, yearning is a common experience of survivors which, when it diminishes, indicates that mourning is coming to an end. For the relinquishing mother, though, the search is extended by the legislative framework, perhaps indefinitely. It is necessary to consider whether her grieving process may be being similarly extended?

The fact that almost every mother I interviewed is still searching indicates that her grieving is not coming to an end:

Ursula: They always say that adoption is like a bereavement, but it's not it's worse than that. This is because when someone dies you know that that is it, but when you place a baby for adoption they are still around and so you keep on searching for them. I look for him all the time. When I see a tiny baby in a pram I think that it might be him being taken out by his foster mother. I'll always be searching for him up until the day I die. And I know that if he wants to he can come looking for me. I know that he may come knocking on my door when he is 18.

10 Being strong and feeling weak

In this chapter I examine the relinquishing mothers' accounts of their feelings of strength and weakness. These illustrate their perceptions of their ability to control the events surrounding their relinquishment; that is their feelings of being more helpless or more in control of their crisis situation. After scrutinising the mothers' reports and drawing conclusions, I compare the midwives perceptions of the strength of the relinquishing mother. In elucidating the mother's coping strategies, fundamentally important aspects of the mother's feelings about herself emerge, which are reflected in the midwives' comments. The concept of control is shown to be crucially significant.

Crisis and coping

In order to understand the relinquishing mother's perception of herself as feeling weak and needing to appear strong, it is helpful to consider the birth and relinquishment in terms of a crisis (Caplan, 1961). Among a range of characteristics which define a crisis, the person's inability to cope by using previously successful strategies, when under stress, is crucial.

Coping includes a wide range of behaviours which someone experiencing stress may employ in order to reduce the discomfort or pain of the stressor event (Littlewood, 1992). Individuals' use of coping styles has been shown to be extremely flexible, applying the strategy which seems most appropriate at a certain time in a given situation (Peterman & Bode, 1986). In spite of this, avoidance or denial is the strategy which is most widely used, being utilised so frequently in the grieving crisis that it is widely accepted as the first stage of grief (Kubler-Ross, 1970).

In the same way as Kubler-Ross described grieving in terms of being a dynamic process, the response to any stressful event is a process. This applies in that it involves a variable series of coping strategies being brought into operation as the situation develops. The initial cognitive response to crisis comprises a primary appraisal in order to categorise the degree of threat which it presents (Lazarus & Folkman, 1984). This is followed by a secondary appraisal during which the available options and coping resources are assessed and an action decision is taken. Thus, coping comprises a continuing series of such appraisals, resulting in changing interaction between the affected individual and the stressor (Rukholm & Viverais, 1993).

The response to a crisis varies according to a number of factors, and may include pathophysiological changes, such as increased tension, back pain or headache (Parry, 1990). Alternatively, the psychological component of the individual's coping style may be more pronounced; featuring anxiety, confused thinking, preoccupation, depression, together with denial, as mentioned already.

According to Littlewood (1992) a strategy which may constitute a coping style is 'learned helplessness'. This is a person's temporary perception of their inability to control their own circumstances, although whether it occurs depends on how the event is interpreted. Learned helplessness describes the debilitated behaviour of a person who is subject to some form of assault (such as electric shocks applied in a laboratory) over which they have no control. Learned helplessness comprises three main components, which are deficits in functioning. First, a deficit in motivation follows the person's inability to initiate any voluntary responses - on the assumption that to do so would be futile. Second, cognitive deficit causes the person difficulty in learning that in future responses may produce outcomes. There is difficulty in unlearning something that has been learned by possibly painful experience. The third feature of learned helplessness is the depressed affect, resulting from the conviction that changing anything is impossible. These features are based on the expectation that what has happened in the past will continue to apply in the future, that is, absence of control is unalterable (Garber & Seligman, 1980).

On the other hand 'locus of control', is the ability to take control of one's life as an enduring, personality characteristic (Wallston & Wallston, 1981). This phenomenon transcends the immediate situation and includes the expectancy that a person with certain personality characteristics will act in a certain way. Locus of control comprises a person's perception of what causes things to happen in their lives. Locus of control may be external, when the person tends to blame others or their environment for any negative events, or it may be internal, when the person blames herself or assumes responsibility. A person with an external locus of control really believes that the things that they do cannot influence outcomes. The converse is someone with an internal locus of control who believes that outcomes are contingent upon their actions. A tendency towards one extreme or the other results in that person being 'more internal' or 'more external'.

The need among bereaved mothers to be 'more internal' in their control over their situation was demonstrated by Gohlish (1985). She interviewed fifteen mothers of stillborn babies to identify the most helpful 'nursing' interventions. Twenty behavioural statements focussed on the mother's care; but the behaviours which the mothers considered 'most helpful' clearly related to taking control:

1. Recognise when I want to talk about my baby
2. Allow me to stay as long or as short a time in hospital as I wish
3. Let me decide if I want a single room or main ward
4. Ask me if I want a photograph of my baby
5. Explain to me that I may produce milk

6. Explain to me that I can see the baby after several days
7. Give me pain relief as often as I need.

Thus, it is apparent that a crisis, being a stressor, has the capacity to arouse feelings of either passivity or the need to assume control. To assess the extent to which this knowledge applies to a mother who loses her baby by relinquishment, I draw on the data in the recent study (Mander, 1992a).

The relinquishing mother's view

For each of the mothers, the decision to relinquish her baby for adoption resulted from her inability to care for her baby as she considered necessary:

> Nadia: Because Billy and I weren't well off we thought that we would not be able to give the baby a good home and the baby might suffer.

Being strong and feeling weak

Reporting the experience of relinquishing mothers in USA, Silverman (1980) shows the persistence of poor self-image, which I found in my recent study. Silverman's informants also recounted feelings of not being able to manage, which were exacerbated by the pressure applied by those who were older and, supposedly, wiser. Regret at not being able to stand up to such pressure emerged clearly. In both studies a poor self-image not infrequently included her own personal characteristics and abilities, which prevented the mother from keeping her child:

> Elena: I didn't seem able to bring him up. Maybe if they'd said something I would, but I did not feel strong enough, maybe I was immature, but I did not feel strong enough.

Particularly perceptively, Elena blamed her immaturity for her lack of strength, whereas Rosa differentiated her strength from the maturity she would have expected at her chronological age:

> Rosa: I was old enough really to have dug my heels in. I should have I suppose. But I wasn't really a very strong person. I could have been talked into things I think quite easily. I think the girls of today - they mature much younger [and] they grow up much quicker.

Francesca, like Elena a young teenager at relinquishment, linked her perceived lack of inner strength with its outward manifestation, bravery:

> Francesca: I wanted to appear strong, brave. I wanted to keep him, but could not say it as I had no-one behind me.

She went on to vividly describe the fluctuations in her feelings between what she felt was right and what was possible:

Francesca: I equivocated. One day I'd feel so strong and would decide to keep him and the next day I was weak and feeble and could not. Gillian was helpful as she promised to stay with me and look after me, but she refused to advise me about keeping the baby. I really wanted someone to tell me what to do.

She looked back on her decision with obvious regret, and with no conviction of its validity:

Francesca: I realised that I could not look after him because I was not strong enough, but I did not make the wrong decision. I don't know if it was the right decision, but I'd made a decision and I had to stick to it. It was because I was not strong enough on my own.

Because strength and bravery tend in western society to be viewed positively, comments reflecting midwives' views of the relinquishing mother suggest sympathetic admiration:

Molly: I think it is a brave thing for people to do nowadays when there are so many other options - like termination - to actually go through pregnancy, deliver the baby and give it up for adoption. I think that is very brave. It must be the hardest thing to do.

The role of others in providing strong support during the relinquishment appears frequently in the data. In the case of Francesca this support was found in a range of unlikely sources, including a new girl friend:

Francesca: Gillian was very supportive, but I still felt bad, I felt that I had given in and that I had not been a strong person. I was too weak and felt useless.

The absence of support was linked by the mother with her own limited abilities, as her reason for relinquishment:

Rosa: It was the fact that I couldn't see how to cope on my own.

In her account of the birthmother's grief, Silverman (1980) argues that resolution of her grief may follow acceptance of the necessity of the relinquishment. Silverman links this acceptance with the realisation of the mother's limited 'mastery' of her situation. It is clear from the mothers' comments that those in my recent study had not achieved this degree of 'mastery'.

Differentiating strength and weakness

The use of arguments emphasising the positive nature of adoption (See Chapter 11) may have given rise to some confusion in the mother's mind concerning the strength underpinning her relinquishment:

Iona: I thought was I in actual fact being very weak, not being strong, in handing the baby over. Was I being weak in that I could not take the responsibility of bringing up the child on my own under great difficulty? It would have meant enormous sacrifices in those days, and hardship. There was no creche. There weren't the same facilities for working mothers. I wouldn't have got things like supplementary benefit because you were a lone parent. I don't know how I'd've managed. I often wonder whether in actual fact what was looked on as a strength, giving your child up, wasn't in actual fact a weakness.

The strength underpinning the decision was further questioned by Rosa who considered the durability of the decision among others in her mother and baby home:

Rosa: There were one or two that changed their minds at the last minute. Most [of the babies] were adopted.

Feeling pressure to relinquish

Inevitably the strength/weakness of the relinquishing mother frequently became focussed on deciding or resisting pressure to relinquish. Pressure matters not only because of the threat to the mother's autonomy, but also because perceptions of pressure have been linked with continuing regret about the relinquishment (Cushman, et al., 1993). The mother encountered differing degrees of pressure to relinquish varying from none at all, through presenting no alternative, to that pressure which Lena described as 'blackmail':

Pamela: [The SW] was good, she always used to say 'You must do what you want to do'. I made the decision at seven months. Ben helped with my decision; he said I was to do what I wanted to.

Barbara: Mum also said that whatever I decided to do, they would support me. I never ever had pressure to give the baby up for adoption or to keep it. Whatever I wanted they would support me.

Lena: The woman in charge ... said 'You don't have to sign'. I just kept saying 'I do'. Because I thought I did. I didn't realise that I didn't really have to, even though she said it to me. Because at the same time I thought if I sign them [everything'll be OK].

Iona: I honestly don't know who made the decision ... at the interview we were told that the baby would be adopted at six weeks. It just seemed to go on from there ... But I don't know whether again [the SW] was prejudiced because she was running part of this adoption society, but she convinced me that all along this was the correct decision and I was definitely doing the right thing - having the baby adopted. It would go to a really good family ...

Francesca: When [my Father] found out I couldn't have an abortion, he said 'Adoption, adoption' and I said 'Yes, yes'. Then I went along with the plans, being so small and young, for my baby to be adopted to avoid further hassle, particularly with my Father.

Debra: It was not my decision - it was suggested, it was always suggested. ... I do really truly believe that they wanted the best for me and the baby and I have tended to agree with them. You don't like to admit that you didn't make the decision about adoption.

Marcia: I don't know [who decided]. I still don't know. Y'know I would have perhaps have liked to put her for fostering but I was told by the Children's Officer that it's not very good ... she said 'You could hurt your child like that' and I didn't want that.

Tanya: So it was decided that I would just have to carry on with the pregnancy and have the baby adopted. This was all decided for me by the way, nobody asked me. Even my Mum said 'If you love her you'll have her adopted'.

Lena: My Mom just kept saying if you sign the papers you can come home. So of course I signed them 'cos I thought I'll be able to go home. So she was doing quite a lot of blackmail really, but when you're a kid you don't see it that way 'cos I really thought my Mom was like god.

The observations made at the Post-Adoption Centre (PAC) (Howe et al., 1992) endorse the mother's perception of weakness, resulting in her inability to resist the pressure to relinquish and her enduring pain. By encouraging reflection, the PAC allows anger to emerge in the mother, which shows strength and the resolution of her grief.

The pressure which has been mentioned so far has been perceived by the mothers as being quite overt and either neutral or favouring adoption. Other mothers experienced what may be regarded as more subtle pressure, in the opposite direction and from a particularly disquieting source:

Quelia: One of [the staff] did say to me 'You're going to regret this for the rest of your life, if you give your baby up'.

Ursula: The staff wanted me to feed him. Whenever I came to see him he was beautifully dressed and everything to make him look more attractive to me. I felt there was some pressure there, but gently and nicely. Or was it just the way I was feeling? One time I was with him and a nurse came up to me and said 'Isn't he gorgeous?' I felt like hitting her, I had no choice but to agree. They asked me five times to feed the baby and I fed him twice. Each time I phoned up to ask about coming in they said and he's ready for you to feed him.

Aline: The sister on the ward said when I walked in 'Here's Mummy.' She said 'She's absolutely gorgeous, but she's a wee guts'. The sister saying that to me about being Mummy got to me a bit. I think that I wasn't really ready for it. It was like when I first went to see her in the ward. When we walked into the ward she said to me 'Are you Mummy?' That really got up my nose. I was quite cut up when she said that to me. On the whole [the staff] were really good to me ... I told the sister when she did my check yesterday that I was having second thoughts about giving her up for adoption. The sister said that she was glad that I was having second thoughts.

Feeling stigmatised

It is apparent that the mother contemplating relinquishment is in a particularly vulnerable position. She faces both overt and more subtle pressures in the form of advice, which is probably well-intentioned. Because of her feelings of low self-worth and lack of strength, her ability to withstand the intrusion into her decision-making about her baby's future, is reduced.

The negative feelings which I identified in the relinquishing mother may constitute a form of stigma. This is comparable with feelings encountered by people with HIV/AIDS, although there may be important differences (Silverman, 1994). For both groups, they are faced with some form of loss and hostile reactions by society. Similarly, for both the problem may be assumed to be associated with deviant sexual activity which, like loss, is taboo in western society. The definition of stigma (Goffman, 1963) features the violation of society's taboos, although Silverman suggests that these are not immutable, but vary with time, place, ethnicity, gender and social status.

The stigma of relinquishment differs from that of the person with HIV/AIDS. Because of the secrecy which envelopes relinquishment, it is never likely to become apparent; so any stigma is almost totally self-imposed. This self-perception features in Goffman's work. He identified the discrepancy between the societal view of who/what the person is and their own sense of identity. It is this discrepancy which constitutes the spoiled identity or stigma. Thus discredit may be imposed by society or by the individual; the latter applying in the case of the relinquishing mother. As mentioned above, acceptance of the circumstances of the relinquishment serves to end the stigma (Silverman, 1980 & 1994).

Midwives' views

The views expressed by the midwives relating to strength are largely congruent with those of the relinquishing mothers.

Being strong

In the same way as the relinquishing mothers reported feeling the need to appear strong or brave (see above), the midwives described the mothers in similar terms. Not uncommonly favourable comparisons were made with women who were thought to have taken an easier, less brave or strong, option:

Fanny: ... Y'know, I could never do it and I could never understand why she could. I thought that was more brave of her, than to have a termination or something. It can't be an easy thing to do.

Pressure to relinquish

Midwives are firmly convinced that pressure on the mother to relinquish her baby for adoption may be exerted in several different ways.

Situational pressures: Fanny recounted the pressures facing a young single parent living with her parents:

Fanny: I think her circumstances made her feel that [relinquishment] was the best answer in her situation although in the end she changed her mind. But her family situation, I think, must have put some pressure on her. Y'know she didn't want to bring another child into a household that wasn't hers. It was her parents', they'd already accepted one child into the house and she felt another one was too much to put on to them. 'Cos obviously she had to go back to work etc, which she had to do, to support herself. She was asking an awful lot of her parents. Both in terms of the care and accommodation.

As mentioned by Elena (above), some midwives consider that the difficulties of raising a child when unsupported may be just too much for a young woman:

Izzy: Sometimes it's a young sixteen year old girl because of either family pressures or she doesn't feel able to cope and is putting her baby up for adoption.

The age of the mother alone may be a factor affecting the effectiveness of any other pressure:

Lucy: I think probably on the whole it is their own decision. I would say that really would probably depend too on the age group of the person. Younger girls, I would say, probably they are more influenced by what their parents think than older women. Again, that is probably, even though they are young, they have probably made up their own mind too. It is difficult to be sure.

Queeny: It depends a lot on the family. If it is a young girl its likely to be the parents who take the decision. If it is an older girl then because there will be no partner around, it will be her own decision. It really depends on the situation.

Social class was introduced as an influencing factor:

Shirley: The kids from maybe a better social class are more or less pressured into it. They are young. They are afraid to leave home. Where will they go? What will they do?

Personal pressure: The family may be seen as applying pressure to the mother to relinquish:

> Emily: Quite often or usually there is some pressure on her from her family - often her mother - to give the baby for adoption.

> Kay: I would hope ultimately that [the decision] would be the mother's. But I don't think it is on many occasions. If it's a young girl and she's perhaps immature, I would imagine the parents probably influence her very strongly. Perhaps peer pressure, I don't know.

Health care providers and other professionals are seen by some midwives as applying pressure to the mother contemplating relinquishment:

> Betty: There may be pressure on a young girl by her family. Perhaps SWs and midwives may pressure her too.

Nancy clearly shows the difficulty of differentiating between giving (or not giving) information and applying pressure in a desired direction:

> Nancy: The [voluntary adoption society] is nearby so the mothers come here. And they tend to deal with it with their own hospital social workers. It is more the Society's social workers. We have difficulty in that they tend to seem to push the girl ... they don't tell her much about benefits etc if the baby was kept and I suppose that is where we come in and do our bit.

Changing social pressures: Some midwives identified social pressures as being associated with changes in the decision to relinquish:

> Joy: Previously there used to be a lot of family pressure [to relinquish]. Housing is more easily available now, so that these girls are better able to keep their babies, but it may not be in the right sort of area for a child to be brought up. More housing means that adoption has become less necessary. Although I think peer pressure on her to keep her baby must have some effect. The reason always used to be the stigma of having a baby when you're not married. That's all gone now.

> Dorothy: Some of them feel guilty because nowadays there is a lot of pressure on them to keep the baby, or they **feel** there is pressure put on them to keep the baby, that it is the right thing to do.

Avoiding applying pressure: Midwives' anxiety about any repercussions if they were seen to have influenced a mother's decision about relinquishment emerged clearly:

> Shirley: You need to spend time and talk to them, but you must never try to talk them into keeping the baby or putting their baby up for adoption. People must make up their own mind and they must be under no pressure from anybody. If you pressurise them to keep a baby and it didn't work out, then they are going to blame you.

> Dorothy: It is something she really has to decide herself. You wouldn't want to put pressure on her one way or the other because if you said 'I think you should have this baby adopted' and then she changes her mind, or if you said 'I think you should keep the baby' and she then she decides to keep the baby and something goes wrong, she could turn round and say 'It's all your fault'.

Mother's resistance to pressure: Shirley, a midwife with over thirty years experience, recounted her impressions of the way in which a mother being pressured to relinquish may resist and manipulate her situation:

> Shirley: Once the baby is born, close to the nursery, [the mother] wants to see the baby, she goes and sees it and then granny or grandpa [are persuaded] 'Come and see him', 'He's a lovely wee boy' and it is hard to resist a nice baby. They come round. I find this more and more often. But when the kid comes in, the baby is for adoption, because it is family pressure.

Despite overwhelming feelings of inability to cope, the relinquishing mother perceives the need to be strong and brave. This is actually how midwives tend to regard her relinquishment, in spite of perceptions from all the informants that the mother is under pressure from various directions to encourage her to relinquish. This section ends with the introduction of the possibility that the mother may exert some manipulative power.

Coping strategies

To help the relinquishing mother to cope with feelings of helplessness in the crisis situation in which she finds herself, she is likely to employ a range of coping strategies, some of which illustrate her particular needs.

Appearing strong

Probably because of her low self-esteem, there was an especially acute need for the mother to appear strong by behaving with dignity in the presence of carers. This need was clearly spelt out by Elena and commented on by some midwives:

> Elena: [In labour] I kept trying to be brave, put on a good front and behave myself properly. But I got so tired and I started to cry, and the nurse said 'You have been very brave up to now, so don't go and spoil it all'. So then I thought I'd better not cry. I was just trying to be brave all the time, so I didn't.

Active adopting

In the course of this research I became aware of terminology used by mothers and midwives which differs from the ordinary usage. Certain forms of words suggest that some mothers may regard themselves as being more in control of their crisis situation than the data mentioned above seem to indicate. According to Chambers' (1981) dictionary the verb 'to adopt' means 'to take voluntarily', requiring the verb to be used passively when referring to the child (who 'is adopted') or the relinquishing mother (who places her child to 'be adopted'). This conventional use of the terminology suggests a degree of passivity or weakness on the part of the relinquishing mother which is endorsed by the data given above. Some of the informants, however, used the verb 'to adopt' in the active form. For Francesca her activity reflected her involvement in the placement:

> Francesca: I chose the adoptive parents, because they sounded artistic ... when I decided that I was going to adopt.

> Kara: There were two other women adopting their babies in the ward at the time.

> Pamela: These break-ups in the family convince me that I did the right thing in adopting him. I don't have any doubts about placing him for adoption - it is the right thing for him.

> Vera: We all had the wish to keep our babies, some of the mothers said they didn't before the birth but after the baby was born they changed their minds. They all adopted them because they loved them.

> Leonie: The girl who is adopting her baby will want to have the whole thing kept quite secret and confidential.

Whether this terminology reflects a degree of control which is actually lacking, as implied by the data quoted already is difficult to assess. It may be being used as an ideal for which the mother and carers are striving. The mother may be demonstrating that the relinquishment was in fact a more active process than the data suggest, and that she was not the passive recipient of pressure as may appear. Similarly, the midwife may be attempting to more actively involve the mother in her relinquishment in order to facilitate her grieving.

This more active view of relinquishment may constitute a coping strategy for mothers and midwives to enable each of them to work through what would otherwise be a totally negative and near-intolerable event.

Ranking badness

Another coping strategy which was widely used by all of the informants, served to provide reassurance that the mother's behaviour was preferable to the way in which certain other women reacted to a similar situation. The strategy which emerged, which I refer to as the 'hierarchy of badness', allowed the mother to come to terms in gradual stages with the behaviour under scrutiny.

For the previous relinquishing mother her generally 'unacceptable' behaviour was initially seen as the most serious problem:

> Elena: I felt guilty because of my promiscuous behaviour, it was my religious upbringing making me feel like that.

Tanya: I think I was going through that probably rebellious time with my parents, when you think they're just trying to stop you from having a good time, when actually they're trying to protect you. I had been seeing this boy for quite a long time about a year or something and they did not like him. They did not approve of him. Which made it all the more attractive to go out with him. So I did!

As her perception of her situation developed, the really serious problem evolved to become the pregnancy or perhaps the forbidden sexual activity from which it resulted:

Vera: There are women where I work who are single parents and I am bitter about this because I was certainly not one to sleep around.

Tanya: But I think my Dad felt that it was dreadful that I got pregnant - that was terrible. But I think he would have felt that too if I'd married a catholic. It wasn't done in our family. I'm not sure whether it was the pregnancy or the sex that led up to it that caused my Dad to react badly. I think he would probably have gone just as berserk if he'd found out I was having sex with somebody, had I not been pregnant. I don't know. I don't think he thought about it at all, that was it that was just his immediate reaction. It was probably the fact that I was pregnant and then afterwards maybe when he thought about how I got that way it didn't help any.

At this level in the hierarchy of badness the mother compared her choice of relinquishment with a choice that she may have had to face, that of whether to seek termination of the pregnancy. Ursula contemplated how, although she considered termination of pregnancy to be far less acceptable than relinquishment, she would have found life easier in terms of being better supported had she chosen termination:

Ursula: Women who have abortions have support groups for them, but those of us who choose to have the baby adopted have nothing. Women should be able to choose whether to abort the pregnancy or continue with it, but those who continue should not be penalised.

Midwives similarly compared the relinquishing mother favourably with the mother having a termination:

Emily: If the midwife does not believe in abortion, it may be that she thinks that the mother has done the right thing in continuing in her pregnancy and be more sympathetic towards her.

With time, the previous relinquishing mother further adjusts her attitude to her experience and comes to regard her relinquishment as the most seriously adverse aspect. Thus, the relinquishment comes to constitute the peak of the hierarchy of badness:

> Rosa: It was all hushed up. They felt it was a disgrace for the family. It was awful the day when he was adopted, that was the most ghastly day of my whole life I think. I suppose I always felt guilty really, guilty having had him adopted. Not guilty of finding myself pregnant ... but I definitely have had guilt feelings all my life about giving him up for adoption. Having the baby adopted seems to have got worse as the time has gone on and the feelings about it ... [When I had my next child] I wasn't really ashamed of it as such, but I just didn't want anybody to know I suppose - not the fact that I had had a baby, but the fact that I had a baby adopted. Sometimes I think now, I wonder what they would say if I said .... Then I think I would never tell anybody, because I'm sure they would think I was awful having done what I did. I'm sure they would feel 'How could anybody do that'? Even after all this time, I would feel - I suppose this is why I never told my daughter really - the fact that I thought she would think I was terrible. What an awful thing to do.

The potential for a further level of the hierarchy is demonstrated by the subject of the case study. Aline, after opting to see her baby, found reassurance by comparing herself favourably with the mother who relinquishes her baby without having any contact with her:

> Aline: I was worried about how the staff would be though ... It wasn't as if I was not going to have anything to do with her. I couldn't've just had her wheeked away as soon as she was born. No, I couldn't've done that - I don't know how they can, when you have to give her a name.

Vera, who relinquished her child over thirty years previously, shows that this hierarchy would be alien to those with no experience of relinquishment. She reflected on society's attitude towards the relinquishing mother, although she neglects the possibility of societal attitudes having changed over time:

> Vera: People think that mothers should have their children with them and that it is wrong for a mother to part from her child. They are likely to assume that I gave my child up for my own sake, for selfish reasons and that I did not love him.

The painful need for a relinquishing mother to readjust her orientation to behaviour which she considers to be more bad or less bad is clearly spelt out in the experience of a relinquishing mother (Marsh, 1993). In a written confession to her anti-choice diocesan priest, this relinquishing mother condemns the lack of sympathetic support provided by the church following her relinquishment compared with that provided for women who have chosen termination of pregnancy.

It is apparent that the hierarchy of badness is not a static phenomenon. It is a dynamic process which, for the relinquishing mother, serves as a coping strategy to assist her through her pregnancy and which may eventually facilitate her grieving.

11 Doing the best

Terms such as 'doing the best' were used by a range of people involved in the process of relinquishment in my recent study (Mander, 1992a) and have also been observed by Farrar (1993). At first glance such terms appear to be intended to comfort the mother by providing reassurance of the appropriateness of her relinquishment. On closer examination, though, it becomes apparent that these comments, and the fact that they are reported, may be saying a lot more. They are comments which, when the mother reported them, suggested either some degree of coercion to relinquish or confirmation of the correctness of her relinquishment. It is only the timing of such comments in relation to actual relinquishment which differentiates whether they are intended as persuasion or as reassurance.

These comments invariably imply comparison between the relinquishing mother's lifestyle, particularly in terms of the material goods which she would be able to offer her child, and the lifestyle which she or others consider appropriate for her child. The latter usually correlates closely with the lifestyle which she imagines potential adoptive parents would be able to provide. This conflict is similar to that which is aroused in the mother between her surprisingly powerful inclination to keep her baby and her conviction that she is unable to (Howe et al., 1992).

In considering the use of 'doing the best' devices, I will consider first their obvious effects. I will then go on to consider other, potentially more insidious, effects of their use.

Obvious effects

These forms of words appear to have the obvious potential for directly affecting the relinquishment in one of two ways.

Encouraging contemplating relinquishment

When the mother was uncertain about her future and that of her child these comments were used to encourage her to consider relinquishment. Anthea described the overt pressure which was applied to her by social workers to begin thinking about relinquishing her children, when she had no intention of parting with them on a long-term basis. For her, an unstable marriage and housing problems convinced carers that the children would have a better future if they were adopted:

> Anthea: They said 'What can you give your kids? They can get a better life here, there's an [overseas] couple who want to adopt'.

The prominence of material considerations in making the adoption decision features in research by Macintyre (1977). She found that the invariable assumption that the mother keeps and cares for her own baby ceased to apply when a mother was found to be unmarried. In the same way, financial, employment and accommodation problems were explored minutely with an unmarried woman, whereas they would not have merited a second thought had she been married. It is necessary to question whether material things, being quantifiable, are used by carers as a proxy for other less tangible characteristics in the mother, which may make her less suitable to care for her child. This emphasis on material factors is articulated explicitly by Nadia, who was in a stable loving, but financially impoverished relationship with her baby's father:

> Nadia: Because we weren't well off we thought that we would not be able to give the baby a good home and the baby might suffer.

The benefits of the child being materially and financially secure were not always easily distinguishable from the benefits of the child having two parents:

> Rosa: I felt it would be better to give him up for adoption because then I thought he would get a better chance. They were a professional couple, I don't know which profession, but apparently he went to a professional couple who obviously probably had plenty of money.

> Barbara: She needed [two] parents and there were couples out there that couldn't have a baby, that could give all their love and give this child everything.

Exceptionally, Kara was able to recognise that there were non-material factors involved which made her decision to relinquish that much harder to take:

> Kara: I know I'd probably have done better for him in many ways.

For those mothers who were dependent on or in close contact with their parents their reassuring comments were accepted unquestioningly at the time:

> Debra: If my parents said 'That was the best thing', then that was best thing.

The united approach among all her advisers must have seemed overpowering, particularly to a young mother who had been ejected from her parental home:

> Elena: The mother and baby home was run by nuns, they all thought that adoption was the best thing. The social worker took the same line as the nuns, that adoption was the best thing all round.

'Doing the best' assumed a slightly different, possibly more sinister, meaning in an account given by Howe and colleagues (1992). A baby was being fostered and visited by his young mother, Christine, who was contemplating relinquishment. The highly expert foster mother forced her to provide baby care in which she had no experience, such as bottle-making and nappy-changing. When Christine showed her incompetence the foster mother retorted 'You've got to do what's best for the baby'. Thus, clearly indicating to Christine that her care was far from the best and that adoption was inevitable. In this way pressure to relinquish emerged more graphically and from a different source.

Confirming the decision and reducing dissonance

Later in the relinquishment process similar comments were offered as reassurance that the correct decision was being or had been made. For Jessica this 'reassurance' began before she left the maternity unit:

> Jessica: The doctors kept saying 'You're doing the right thing' when I had doubts, as I did all along.

In Hilda's experience this reassurance was linked with exhortations, to minimise the impact of her relinquishment and look to the future:

> Hilda: I signed the piece of paper. They all said it was for the best - 'Get on and pick up the threads of your life'.

As with other mothers who were given this form of reassurance by parents and other more formal carers, Iona questioned the motives involved:

> Iona: But I don't know whether, again, she was prejudiced because she was running part of this adoption society, but she convinced me that all along this was the correct decision and I was definitely doing the right thing - having the baby adopted. It would go to a really good family ...

The fervour with which this form of reassurance appears to have been proffered implies a lack of conviction in the mother that relinquishment was altogether the most acceptable or ideal solution to her situation.

Comments made by the midwives support the mothers' reports; in that adoption is perceived by carers to be definitely the preferable option in terms of both the care of and material provision for the baby:

> Amy: She was doing the best for the baby,

> Marie: I think certainly adopted parents would certainly care for these babies a lot better than the girls who are caring for them on social services [benefits].

> Florrie: Obviously, there are situations with very young girls who may be [in] poor family circumstances and a baby that was adopted would get a very good upbringing and be loved and all that.

> Irene: I think that she wanted her child to have the material things in life.

Some of the midwives perceived part of their role as being to reassure the mother that her relinquishment is not inappropriate. Zy's statement shows how providing comfort may incorporate 'doing the best':

> Zy: By talking to these mothers we are able to reassure them that they are not doing anything wrong by giving up their baby for adoption, but they are actually doing their best for the baby.

While using these terms to try to resolve the relinquishing mother's discomfort and dissonance, it may be that staff simultaneously attempt to deal with their own sorrow at this outcome to her pregnancy. Kay links her sorrow to obvious misgivings that adoption is not the ideal solution:

> Kay: I find it y'know 'lump in the throat' time. Y'know when an 18 year old girl comes in and says 'It's not right, just now. I've got to get my life together and I just can't care for a baby'. I know whenever I've seen babies given up [for adoption], it's always been a very difficult thing to do, but it's something they really believe is for the best ...

Reinterpreting with hindsight

For each relinquishing mother there was the recollection of how her perception of what was best for her child had changed as time has elapsed since her relinquishment. Iona hints at the uncertainty that has developed:

> Iona: I still feel that I probably did the right thing and she's had a better life than I could have given her.

For Elena, though, the result was feelings of guilt and concern that her child may not understand her reasons for arranging the adoption.

> Elena: But at the time, I still thought it was the best thing for the baby. But now, over the years, I am beginning to feel guilty and thinking 'Maybe it wasn't the best thing for the baby' - to be rejected by his natural mother. I'm haunted by that now ... But at the time I thought there'd be more money, a stable home, two parents - and in that way I thought it was for the best.

Vera took this concern a stage further, by contemplating the negative reactions of other people who might not realise that her relinquishment was intended to benefit her child:

> Vera: They are likely to assume that I gave my child up for my own sake, for selfish reasons and that I did not love him. I gave him up because I did love him. People might not realise that, so I don't tell anybody.

Media exposure of adoption and other child care arrangements which have gone badly wrong have served to aggravate the mother's anxiety:

> Iona: I thought I was doing the right thing at the time by her, but now you hear so many horror stories ...

Reinterpreting parental motives

The mothers who felt more responsible for their relinquishment blame themselves and personally experience serious misgivings. Similarly, those who consider their parents to have been more instrumental, reinterpreted their understanding of their parents' feelings. For Barbara this reinterpretation resulted in marginally more positive feelings towards her father:

> Barbara: But I suspect my Dad thought then, at the time, he was doing it for the best ... I think it was his way of protecting me ... as I say, although the relationship between [us] is so bad ...

Nadia has also developed a deeper understanding of her parents' motives with the passage of time:

> Nadia: I don't feel any bitterness [to my parents], I can't blame them, they did what they thought was right for me at the time. They must have felt terribly guilty about it.

For Elena there is greater difficulty in sympathising with the role that her mother and, probably even more, her father played in her relinquishment:

> Elena: She just kept saying 'It was for the best. Nobody needed to know'. Actually I think it was for my Dad ...

One relinquishing mother graphically described the remorse which her mother experienced after coercing her daughter to relinquish:

> Hilda: They know now that they done wrong. My Mother bursts into tears - 'We thought we were doing the best for you.'

Best for whom?

The question that implicitly emerges from the mothers' uncertain comments is more clearly apparent in the midwives' ideas. These raise the issue of the costs and benefits involved in adoption. The psychological costs may be seen as being paid by the mother, who may seek to reassure herself:

> Ginnie: The emotional trauma that these girls go through I think is overwhelming because they have to give the baby away and [one mother said] 'I have to give my baby away. But I know that my baby will be well cared for.'

The midwives perceived the benefits of adoption accruing not only in material terms to the adopted child, but also in a less tangible form to the adoptive parents. Thus, suggesting some indirect benefit to the relinquishing mother:

> Polly: I think the woman who is putting her baby up for adoption has a compensation in that she is making some other couple happy. It is not all loss as such because she is actually making life a bit more rewarding for someone else.

Thus it is apparent that, even when taken at face value as relating to the adoption decision, the reassurance which these phrases offer may raise more questions than it answers.

Impact of 'doing the best' on grief

It may be that the use of these terms has the desired effect of reassuring the relinquishing mother and the other people involved with her. It is necessary to consider, though, whether other, possibly inadvertent, effects resulted from this intended kindness. As already in this chapter, I consider the implications not only for the relinquishing mother but also for those near her.

While our knowledge of grief is largely derived from research with people grieving loss through death, I have shown in Chapter 6 that grief is a prominent feature of the reaction of the relinquishing mother to her loss. Thus, using grief as a theoretical framework facilitates our understanding of the implications of 'doing the best'.

A crucial aspect of grief work is the search for the meaning of the loss. This is achieved mainly by the retelling of the experience of loss and has been shown to facilitate resolution (Marris 1986; Stroebe & Stroebe, 1987). This is not always easy as health care providers 'freely offer' technical and other hard-edged information but there is difficulty in finding time to 'explore hopes and fears' (Marck et al., 1994). The mother needs to be able to talk about what it is that she feels she has lost without the listener, who may be experiencing personal discomfort, trying to change the subject or backing off (See Chapter 15). A 'conspiracy of silence' develops when carers inhibit the mother from talking through her feelings to find meaning (Howe, 1990).

Hermione Lovell et al. (1986) found that in her sample, previously-bereaved mothers were sufficiently assertive to be able to satisfy their need to talk through their loss. But Alice Lovell (1983) draws our attention to a discrepancy facing a grieving mother. She maintains that ordinarily each of us needs to communicate with our fellow beings, if only about the weather. In a crisis, however, our need to share our feelings is increased. The grieving mother, though, is faced with the prospect of not even being allowed to satisfy her usual need to talk, let alone her increased 'quota'. Lovell (1983) considers that this 'ironic discrepancy' aggravates her feelings of isolation and rejection.

The 'ironic discrepancy' may be due to the tendency of caregivers to try to rescue the mother from her grief by providing emotional comfort, which may have the unwanted side-effect of preventing her grief work from moving forward (Rando, 1986). The use of false reassurance in order to lighten the emotional load for the distressed client has been reported (Bradley & Edinberg, 1982; Roll et al., 1986), and attributed to social workers, family and friends. Philosophical and religious explanations, such as 'There must be a reason' and 'It's God's will' (Rando, 1986), serve the same purpose and have the same effects as 'doing the best'. The platitudes which the relinquishing mothers recounted are examples of 'saying something not known to be true', constituting examples of false reassurance. The result is an increase in the client's anxiety, and a rise in suspicions due to incongruity (Bradley & Edinberg, 1982). Rather than facilitating grieving, such reassurances impede its progress.

The need for the grieving mother to explore the meaning of her loss engenders two further requirements. These are, first, someone must be willing to listen (Rappoport, 1981) and, second, suitable opportunities to talk need to be created (Bond, 1986; Kellner & Lake, 1986). The difficulty in satisfying these requirements is shown by Worden (1992) who relates the unpreparedness of nearby family to listen. This may be due to family, like more formal carers, having their own grief to contend with as well as fears that 'dwelling on it' may be counterproductive.

Confronting their own feelings about such issues as unsupported pregnancy, is an essential precursor to staff providing appropriate care for this mother (Devaney & Lavery, 1980; Kellner & Lake, 1986). Without this the carer may rely on projecting herself into the mother's situation to decide care (Mander, 1992c) and have to resort to a range of coping strategies. According to Morse et al. (1992), the carer protects herself from the discomfort of becoming engaged in a patient's pain by blocking or ignoring her own feelings of empathy. She, thus, reduces her vulnerability and increases her ability to function at a suitably 'professional' level. Morse goes on to describe the crucial role of detachment in this scenario, which distances the nurse from the patient's suffering during certain situations.

One coping strategy is 'reflexive reassurance' (Morse et al., 1992), which is defined as 'a spontaneous reaction ... to counteract feelings of anxiety, uncertainty or worry about the circumstances in which patients find themselves'. This strategy has been labelled more descriptively 'optimistic assertion' (Teasdale, 1989). A 'parental' tone is employed, rather like 'nannying' to achieve comfort. Although 'reflexive reassurance' is ordinarily used by carers, it may also be utilised by patients to reassure those who are concerned about them. A loop of deceit develops, effectively silencing further interaction.

Another coping strategy used by carers is the inability to listen (Bond, 1986). It is likely to lead to emotional repression, carrying risks of unforeseen long-term emotional consequences. Research by Cullberg (1971) showed that the response of staff to situations of loss in childbearing included avoidance of the bereaved parents, projection of blame onto the parents and denial. Thus supporting the conspiracy of silence (Howe, 1990). To quieten the mother, cliches like 'doing the best' may be used to 'stem the tide' of emotion. In this way the grieving mother is robbed of her legitimate anguish. Simultaneously, her search for the meaning of her loss is impeded (Rando, 1986). Platitudes and reassurances have been shown to be examples of unhelpful behaviours encountered by others facing grief, such as widows (Stroebe & Stroebe, 1987; Osterweis et al., 1984).

Clearly, there are seriously harmful effects to the relinquishing mother, to the extent that the progress of her grief work is threatened. There may be other harms which derive from 'doing the best' type statements. The grief of the carer, parent, midwife or friend, while of a different degree, is similarly repressed.

The caring relationship may also be damaged. This is because the carer may, having effectively stemmed the emotional tide and restored superficial equilibrium, convince herself that she has benefitted the grieving woman. This may certainly appear to be the case because she has ceased to be distressed. Thus, the carer may mistakenly conclude that the relationship has been strengthened, whereas the reverse is more likely to be the case. This may be another example of a short-term benefit, which threatens the relinquishing mother's long-term well-being.

Conclusion

'Doing the best' comments appear to have been being used to resolve any persistent dissonance about a decision which is being advocated, considered or taken. The person making this comment appears to be seeking to resolve the doubts in the mind of the relinquishing mother concerning the appropriateness of parting from the baby. The effects of such comments on the relinquishing mother's grieving have been considered. It may be that, by curtailing or forbidding the mother's distress, they serve to foreshorten or artificially arrest her grief. This interpretation of the significance of these comments is endorsed by the statements made by relinquishing mothers which indicate that they are still, many years later, trying to convince or reassure themselves that what they did was right.

12 Being mother

The events around the time of the birth ordinarily mould the mother's relationship with her child. For this reason their significance cannot be overstated. These events, and the ensuing relationship, are fundamental to our understanding of mothering as well as other aspects of life and death (Bowlby, 1977). The extent to which the relinquishing mother experiences the psychological changes characteristic of childbearing may not be easily identifiable. The implications of these changes for both her care and her grieving deserve detailed attention. In this chapter I consider these perinatal events in terms of, first, the changes during pregnancy as described by the research literature and the relinquishing mothers. Second, I examine how the processes which begin during pregnancy are continued after the birth, how this knowledge informs our care of the relinquishing mother and the implications of this knowledge for her care. Third, I compare this material with the experience of the relinquishing mother who was the subject of the case study. I then go on to consider the impact of relinquishment for the mother's other children. This chapter concludes by focussing on the relinquishing mother's memories of her lost motherhood and how she and her family deal with these memories.

Changes during pregnancy and the relationship with the baby

Certain emotional events during pregnancy lay the foundation for the mother's reaction to her baby - which may comprise grief.

Attachment

Because, developmentally, the human baby is so immature at birth, she depends on care by others to survive. How her care and hence the survival of humanity is ensured has long been a topic for speculation. Our thinking has moved on since Freud's psychoanalytic ideas and his assumption that human babies have innate biological drives, such as hunger, which demand gratification. The behaviourists' ideas followed, focussing on attachment developing through reinforcement of learning. In the 1960s their biological explanations were modified when external factors, such as touch, were found to affect the mother-child relationship (Harlow & Harlow, 1966).

Simultaneously, ethology (studying animals in their natural habitat) added imprinting to our understanding of the mother-child relationship. This is the process by which, typically, a newly-hatched duck assumes the first moving object it sees to be its source of comfort and security; this object would ordinarily be its mother or 'primary caregiver'. The limited time-span for imprinting gives us the 'critical' or 'sensitive period' (Mussen et al., 1990).

Ethology was later integrated with psychoanalytic principles to support the thesis that attachment derives from neither drive-reduction nor prior learning (Bowlby, 1958). Thus, the human newborn emits signals or behaviours which keep caregivers near enough to meet her needs and ensure survival.

Attachment is 'A regulatory system hypothesised to exist within a person ... to regulate behaviours that maintain proximity to and contact with a discriminated protective person, referred to as the attachment figure. From the psychological vantage point of the attached person, however, the system's set goal is felt security' (Bretherton, 1987). Newborn behaviours initiate and maintain secure attachment to the caregiver (Brazelton, 1973).

Bowlby's thesis is that attachment derives from the need for security and safety and that babies form enduring attachments with only a limited number of individuals (1977). The role of attachment in healthy development is to provide a secure base from which a child may explore her physical and psychological surroundings, and to which she may retreat if threats become overwhelming (Bowlby, 1979:137).

Attachment and loss

Attachment is significant in relation to relinquishment because grieving is the inevitable eventual corollary of any warm loving relationship. These two contrasting aspects of attachment became apparent in Bowlby's research with toddlers separated from their mothers by the unusual situation of being admitted to residential care. His research identified a characteristic biphasic response involving protest, despair, unresponsiveness and tantrums. It became apparent that the absence of the attachment figure meant that the secure base no longer existed, engendering terror of the unknown. Bowlby (1979) equates adult grief, which may apply to relinquishment, with separation anxiety, when the security of a loving relationship is lost, leaving a frighteningly incomprehensible void.

Bonding

As a topic, bonding generates more heat than light. It is the first preliminary stage in the events which lead to attachment (Mussen et al., 1990). The plethora of research in this area has stimulated many changes in our care of the new mother and baby. Whether these changes are necessarily for the benefit of the mother-infant dyad is questionable (Herbert & Sluckin, 1985:123). Considerable attention has been given to early postnatal bonding, as it equates with 'love at first sight', formerly assumed to be fundamental to mother-love. However, in the context of relinquishment, events during pregnancy may be more significant.

Changes in pregnancy

Traditionally, we have assumed that the mother did not begin to love her baby until she laid eyes on her (Morrin, 1983). Hence, only recently has research focussed on the mother's prenatal relationship with her baby prenatally.

Following interviews with twenty mothers whose newborn babies had died, Kennell et al. (1970) were able to conclude that an affectionate mother-child relationship was present by the time the baby was due to be born. As many of the mothers had had no visual or tactile contact with their babies, postnatal stimuli to affection were excluded.

The mother's developing affection for her unborn child was measured, showing increasingly positive feelings as pregnancy progresses (Grace, 1989). Similar instruments were used to study the effects of maternal age, the experience of quickening and the physical symptoms of pregnancy on the developing relationship in eighty pregnant mothers (Lerum & Lobiondo-Wood, 1989). These researchers found that only quickening (first feeling fetal movements) has any effect on the relationship, and that is positive. The effects of ultrasound scans, which have been said to enhance the relationship, were unclear but mothers who were well-supported showed high levels of attachment. Unlike the two previous studies Zeanah et al. (1990) based their study of the prenatal mother-baby relationship on the mother's interpretation of fetal movements. The mother was shown to have sufficiently clear ideas about her baby's temperament during pregnancy to complete a questionnaire anticipating how the baby would react in given circumstances. It is impossible to judge whether the mother's interpretations of fetal behaviour derive from her own fantasies or from the actual movements, but the researchers correctly relate her interpretation to the developing relationship.

In her qualitative study, Stainton (1990) sought twenty-six couples' impressions of their unborn babies in the last trimester. She identified four different levels of awareness, coexisting simultaneously; in ascending order, they were the **idea** of the baby, awareness of her **presence**, awareness of her **specific behaviours** and awareness of her **interactive ability**. These interpretations of fetal behaviour suggest that knowledge of the psychosocial interaction with the unborn baby may have implications for our care of childbearing women in the same way as the more widely-used objective assessments because, as Stainton reminds us, a stronger mother-baby relationship during pregnancy facilitates mothering.

The limited benefits of ultrasound scans on the developing relationship in comparison with quickening are shown by Reading (1989). Lumley (1990) endorses these points and raises other disconcerting questions about routine investigations.

Our knowledge of the prenatal mother-baby relationship is still limited, hence attempts to influence its development are inappropriate. There is no doubt, though, that the strength of the mother's relationship with her unborn baby, results in grief if the baby is lost through death or relinquishment.

The experience of the relinquishing mother

The development of the relationship between the relinquishing mother and her unborn baby is inevitably affected by the prospect of their forthcoming parting. There remain, however, many features of their relationship prior to the birth which reflect the feelings of mothers in general.

Unequivocal loving: The feelings which are common to all mothers were expressed, with barely a hint of qualification, by the relinquishing mothers:

> Elena: I definitely did love the baby. I don't know how it happened so quickly, but I just did. It happened, I think, as I was getting bigger in the pregnancy. You feel close to the baby even before its born.

> Sandra: I could feel a sort of bond forming because she was kicking and that. I was sort of speaking to her when she was in my stomach, telling her things would be all right - things like that. I started to love my baby when she was in my stomach really, more or less right from the start, once I felt her moving about - from then onwards.

Us versus them: For the relinquishing mother who encountered a particularly traumatic pregnancy, her identification with and reliance on her baby as a confidante resulted in a shared feeling of strength. This is reminiscent of a physically tenuous pregnancy in which Douglas (1991) recollected 'A peculiar sense of forming a united front with the baby against the uneven odds':

> Francesca: At this time probably because I had no-one and nothing else to love. I started to feel something [for her] because no-one else loved me. I had no money and no support. I saw it as my baby and myself against the others.

> Jessica: During the pregnancy I used to talk to him, and to tell him about things, like how I was feeling at the time and how he'd get out. When I felt the movement inside, I felt very close to my baby. I had a strong feeling that it was him and me versus the rest.

Unwillingness to let go: Their 'united front' may have been one factor giving rise to the relinquishing mother's feelings of reluctance to part with her baby through birth. Jessica's and Francesca's accounts of near-dependence on their babies appeared in less well-defined forms in feelings of possessiveness recounted by other mothers:

> Quelia: Of course, as the pregnancy progressed, I liked being pregnant. Towards the end of the pregnancy I didn't want to have this baby. I wanted it to stay there all the time. I was quite happy with this bump. I wasn't very large. I really enjoyed being pregnant. The last three months when you could feel the baby moving about ... it's all yours then ...

Kara: I think I felt worse when I knew that it was coming to the end of the [pregnancy] and I knew that ... as long as I was carrying the baby he was mine.

It has not been possible to locate literature on whether mothers who are keeping their babies encounter similar unwillingness when faced with the prospect of sharing, rather than relinquishing, the baby with whom they have developed a unique relationship in pregnancy. The mother who has previously lost a baby through stillbirth does, however, experience a similar reluctance to give up her baby to birth. Lever Hense (1994) relates this reluctance more to concern about the baby's safety, than to parting or sharing.

Equivocating: Whereas many of the mothers were able to look back on feelings of unalloyed affection for the unborn baby, other mothers felt that their affection tended to vary.

Ursula: There were days when I felt so bad about this pregnancy. I just wanted them to take this lump off. It was awful and I hated it on those days. It was a bit like those women who've been raped say, they need to wash and wash and wash. That was how I felt - I hadn't been raped - but it was a similar dirty feeling. I felt really bad towards the baby. In spite of [all] this I eventually became attached to this baby. At the beginning of the pregnancy I had felt very protective towards him. My feelings swung between feeling very protective towards him to wanting a miscarriage.

Vera: I didn't feel any attachment to him during the pregnancy. I did feel movements during pregnancy, but not as many as you hear women talk about now. During the pregnancy I was not in any way resentful towards the baby even though he was going to cause changes in my life.

Such uncertain or ambivalent feelings are not uncommon among pregnant mothers (Oakley, 1979).

Feeling bad: A minority of the relinquishing mothers were unable to recount any positive feelings towards the unborn baby:

Tanya: As far as the pregnancy was concerned I felt that it was a most annoying lump in my stomach that I would be terribly glad when it was gone. I didn't feel anything at all for the baby. I just felt 'This damned thing, I'll be glad when its away'.

Lena: [On one occasion] my Mum started going on at me about - I can't remember what, but I went hysterical. I started punching myself and saying 'I hope it dies, I hope it dies'. I can always remember that. I just know I was very hurt, very lonely.

The midwife's perception of the relinquishing mother's feelings

The comments made by the midwives I interviewed show the difficulty that they may face in understanding the feelings of the relinquishing mother:

Bad feelings: The possibility of the mother convincing herself of unreal feelings towards her baby may account for some negative accounts, such as those by Tanya and Lena:

> Leonie: Maybe she might be blocking out [her] true feelings by pretending not to like the child, the child has been a big upset ... in her life, she may not want to admit that she could keep this baby and look after it.

Self deception/blocking: Blocking as a coping strategy was sometimes seen as helpful, but the duration of this deception must clearly be short:

> Gay: To conceal the pregnancy you don't think about it, you block it out of your mind.

> Ginnie: I wouldn't say [a relationship] doesn't exist. You can't be pregnant and not feel anything for the baby ... they are to be greatly admired that they can actually cut themselves off to a certain extent and say well I've had this baby but I can't keep it.

> Ruby: She may think there is less of a bond. In fact I think the bond is still there. Maybe they want to ignore it. They want to totally cut it out, but, the baby, it never existed for them, and it's been blocked out of their mind to a certain degree, I don't know, and the fact they never really acknowledged the existence of the pregnancy in the first place. ... the fact that you are carrying a baby you really mentally don't wish to acknowledge at all must be very difficult.

Denial: The use of denial to protect the mother from the unacceptable truth was seen by some midwives as an effective strategy:

> Irene: Normally during pregnancy the mother begins to form a bond with her baby. But the mother who is going to give her baby up [is] able to prevent this from happening so these women don't identify the baby with themselves. I think they must just cut off from the baby. They don't look at their tummies and think 'That is little Johnny kicking again'.

Loving: Most midwives admitted that the relinquishing mother tended to form a relationship with her unborn baby similar to any other mother:

> Florrie: I have always, always thought that it must be very very difficult to give up a baby for adoption. Because you know like ... its your baby and you love it and it is inside you.

> Marie: Obviously they make, form a relationship with their baby while the baby in still **in utero**. They feel it growing, they feel it moving and I'm sure they talk to it you know as a little person ... I think you must ...

Variable response: Despite recognising the affectionate feelings of the mother for her unborn baby, midwives perceived that the relationship was far from straightforward:

Josie: I think every mother does [love her baby] to a different degree even mum's who have babies up for adoption - they still love their children. I'm not quite sure of cases like rape and things like that, what they actually feel about it - that they're carrying it when they don't want it.

Deidre: I think it depends on the reasons why she is going to have the baby adopted. I think for some mums it has just been a disastrous mistake and it was possibly too late for a termination. I suppose in their case it is a relief. For other mothers, if circumstances have forced the adoption on them for whatever reason, I think they find it quite hard. They would have a strong attachment, a strong bond with the baby.

Difficulty understanding: The complexity of the relinquishing mother's feelings about her baby were recognised, together with our inevitably, and perhaps painfully, limited understanding of this relationship:

Valery: The mother who is giving her baby for adoption, maybe as early as three or four months decides she doesn't want this baby. I don't know how they feel when the baby kicks, whether it irritates them or not, but I imagine they wouldn't get so excited about it.

Bessie: There is an awful lot going on for [the relinquishing mother]. They are young girls, there is usually some trauma with their parents, they are forced to move away to have the baby and they have the baby with us and then go home again. It's really difficult to say how they feel about the baby.

Overload: The complexity of the feelings encountered by the relinquishing mother were regarded as being further aggravated by the other difficult psychological and emotional tasks which inevitably face her.

Kerrie: If the baby is for adoption, it's sometimes difficult [for her] to understand if it is a young girl. She may feel a lot of guilt or shame at having let her parents down. She gets a bit mixed up because she is worried about telling her parents and at the same time she has her feelings for the baby developing. Then there is all the pressure from her family to give the baby up for adoption. I think this girl will probably have all the same emotions, but she has a lot more on top which alters how she sees things.

Summary - feelings in pregnancy

The emotional changes which a relinquishing mother experiences as her relationship with her unborn baby develops are not dissimilar to other mothers' feelings. It is apparent that these changes may not be assisted by the complexity and extent of superimposed tasks which involve her family and her forthcoming separation from her baby.

Postnatal events and care

The well-known and influential research project on bonding (Klaus et al., 1974) was undertaken in the context of restricted mother-baby contact in USA maternity units. The control group of fourteen mothers was permitted the usual contact, that is, thirty minutes at feeding five times daily. The experiment or extended contact group of fourteen mothers cuddled their naked babies in bed with them for an extra five hours on each of their three days in the maternity unit. Observations and interviews were recorded at one and twelve months.

Despite many similarities, differences between the two groups were emphasised. During a paediatric examination, the experiment group showed greater reluctance to leave and they responded more to their babies' crying and maintained greater eye-to-eye contact during feeds. These researchers concluded that extended contact was essential for bonding; while others went as far as to suggest that without this contact adverse outcomes, such as child abuse, were more likely. Thus, bonding theory evolved into 'bonding doctrine' (Herbert & Sluckin, 1985; Sluckin et al., 1983).

Whether the changes in midwifery practice are justified by the results of the Klaus et al. study continues to be questioned on methodological grounds. Observer bias was a problem; but it is hard to envisage how a 'blind' study of attachment could be designed (Schaffer, 1977).

Advising about contact and care

The advice which the relinquishing mother is given about contact with her baby varies according to the currently fashionable psychological theory. Although her experience may sound unlikely, Gina gave birth to her son in another country at a time when the 'love at first sight' ethos prevailed (Tennyson, 1988). With hindsight, expecting a new mother to hold her baby without looking at him sounds preposterous:

> Gina: [The Nurse] said 'Don't look at him because it will be harder for you', but I did sneak a look ...
> RM: Why do you think she said that - about looking at him?
> Gina: She said it because presumably she thought it would be harder for me to give him away if I saw him. I can only presume that is what it would be - more difficult

The anxiety among a range of carers that the mother may change her mind about relinquishment, clear in Gina's words, is more explicit in Sandra's account:

> Sandra: Folk had been saying to me 'Don't see the baby' and all this sort of business.
> RM: Why do you think they told you ...
> Sandra: Maybe because they thought it would be better for me. Maybe they just thought it would be too upsetting for me to see the baby. To me, it would be upsetting not to see the baby. Once the baby was born I didn't actually see her at that stage, they whipped her away quickly so I didn't see her. They were very helpful in that respect.

RM: Why did you decide that?
Sandra: I thought if I was going to see my baby at all I wanted to have a pleasant memory of her. It was my decision. The SW had said 'Follow your own mind' ... A parting hug before parting. I would have liked to feed her. But I didn't want too much of a bond.

Sandra was given advice from a range of 'folk', some of whom may still have belonged to the 'love at first sight' school of thought. She also benefitted from the advice of a more forward-thinking social worker. Such differing approaches might have been confusing for a less practical person than Sandra. Unfortunately, Jessica also encountered differing ideas and continues to feel resentful, probably because inconsistencies in the advice and care she received resulted from poor communication which I have labelled a 'cockup':

Jessica: He was in my arms for about an hour. There was some kind of mix-up because when my parents came in at night he had been brought out to me again. By that time I was in a side room by myself I had him that night and I was quite happy with myself. The next day the nurses said 'That was it - I couldn't have any more contact'.

The changing pattern of advice to relinquishing mothers about contact and care proved to be a source of concern to more experienced midwives:

Dorothy: ... but I do know, it's years ago too, someone who had a baby and she had to look after it and care for it. She felt that it was awful [because] she had to put it up for adoption. She felt it was awful at the time, but it probably helped her in a way. The ideas have changed. What you were taught was wrong, but you begin to realise it wasn't wrong at all - like not letting her look at the baby, or even a stillbirth - not letting her look at a stillbirth.

Midwives' accounts suggested little variation in the advice they were prepared to offer. They tended to be unprepared to advise contact, with an overall conviction that the decision remains with the mother. This accords with the recommendations made for American nurses, where the emphasis appears to be on supporting the mother's decision about contact, regardless of what it is and how it changes (Ritchie, 1989) without mentioning that the carer may initiate discussion of this matter:

Cathy: I say 'You are the baby's mother. It is your baby, you must reach into your heart'. You can't advise or apply any pressure.

Gay: I would sort of give her points so that she could think on. And then if she didn't want to - Y'know ... Y'know so she'll probably see it at delivery and see the baby being put into a cot and then you would say 'Are you sure you don't want to see your little ... and have a hold ...?'

Nature of contact and care

The contact which the relinquishing mother may have with her baby is significant in this context because the grieving mother's confusion about who or what she has lost is likely to impede her grieving (Davidson, 1977). The lack of reality of a baby who is 'unknown' in the usual sense is best resolved by making contact with the baby (Kellner & Lake, 1986). Such contact has been found to cause no adverse reactions and Davidson (1977) found that there is less psychiatric pathology among mothers who did see their babies who had died. Similarly, Alice Lovell (1983), during a research project involving twenty-two mothers whose babies had died, found that of the twelve who saw their babies, none regretted having done so. These mothers were powerfully aware of the emotion-laden nature of their experience, but they thought that it was rewarding and appropriate. The ten mothers who chose not to see their babies recalled regret and described feelings of being 'in limbo'.

Contact with the baby may take a variety of forms. For the mother whose baby is stillborn there may be nothing beyond seeing, holding and, perhaps, bathing her baby. In comparison, the choices facing the relinquishing mother are probably infinite. At one extreme her contact may be merely visual, when further contact may be hindered by a lack of permission or by the mother's misgivings:

> Clara: The baby was put into a perspex cot as soon as she was born. I stared and stared at her but did not get to hold her at the time.

> Francesca: I had the baby in my room with me for some of the time, but I was scared to pick him up. When I was asked whether I wanted to feed him I said 'No' because I did not know what to do and in case I was expected to do it by myself. I was particularly anxious about the risk of harming him so I never picked him up.

Tactile contact was clearly important to many of the mothers. In the case of Nadia this arrangement seems satisfactory, but for Gina holding her baby resulted from unlikely organisation sufficient to warrant being a 'cockup':

> Nadia: It was a case of instant love but really I loved him already. I held him immediately he was born.

> Gina: At [the birth] I never saw my son. But under the regulations in [another country] I had to get taken out [of the maternity unit] in a wheelchair and I had to hold my baby in my arms and I had a sneaky look at him, of course.

Many of the mothers, such as Rosa, who stayed in Mother and Baby Homes were happy with the regime which these homes operated. The mothers particularly appreciated the opportunity the homes provided for unlimited contact, in the form of total care for the baby:

Rosa: We actually had the babies for the six weeks - we were in complete charge of them. It was actually very good because the staff were helpful at the Home from that point of view - you were able to really gen up on everything. Like feeding and looking after them and changing them.

The midwives were largely unenthusiastic for the relinquishing mother to care for her baby, tending to resort to allocating the decision to the mother. However, some midwives were able to contemplate certain benefits, as well as hazards, of such contact:

Queeny: ... [the baby] would be with her in the ward. It's always possible that if she decided not to see the baby she would spend the rest of her life wondering what it was like. I think that if she is at all unsure of whether she is going to give her baby up she should look after her baby for a wee while and that would help her to learn about the responsibility that a baby entails.

Devaney and Lavery (1980) describe a survey of fifty of the 113 unmarried adolescents who stayed at the 'Open House: Alternatives to Abortion' Scheme in USA. In a setting where it is usual for the relinquishing mother to at least see her baby, none of the respondents regretted the contact they had and most would have liked more. It may be that current recommendations for open adoption may be a logical progression in the direction of the greater contact sought by relinquishing mothers.

Deciding about contact and care

It is possible that the huge changes in maternity care since some of the informants gave birth may have reduced the value of their experiences of decision making, but certain themes remain relevant. The absence of a consistent approach was identified:

Clara: Contact with my baby was not encouraged or discouraged by the staff, they appeared to try to limit my contact to not more than twice daily after day three. This contact involved holding, looking and talking. The initiative to see my baby came from me. Staff usually let me, but were occasionally discouraging.

The mother being presented with a decision without having been involved in making it was not uncommon:

Gina: And when the baby was born he was taken away. I never saw him.
RM: Did anybody ask you if that was what you wanted.
Gina: Nobody asked me.

Hilda: ... the minute he was born they lifted him up to me, and I can mind I was absolutely shattered and I got a quick glimpse o' 'im. Then that was it - they said 'She's no tae get the bairn'. And that was it - he was ta'en away out of the room.

Nadia: What decision? It was never discussed.

The failure of the mother to be involved in the decision may have been due to no individual decision being necessary; in other words a policy operated:

Iona: The arrangement was ... she would be in the nursery - and I would never see her at all. They must obviously have been informed that the baby was to be adopted and I was not to see the baby at all, she was to be taken away as soon as she was born.
RM: Was that your decision?
Iona: I don't remember. I think it was the policy of the adoption society that I registered with - that this was what happened, or they thought this was best for the mother at that time. I just fell in with it I suppose.

Lena: I was just told that it was to be. I was told that when it was born they would take it away and that would be it. I wouldn't see it after it was born, that would be the best thing. ...

Tanya: I was in ... over two weeks all together with one thing and another. The baby stayed with me during that time. ... I fed her and did everything for her while I had her with me. It made me bond to her.
RM: How did you decide about the contact you would have with her?
Tanya: It was automatic.

Vera: I was concerned that I was going to have such a short time to care for my baby. To begin with it was only supposed to be six weeks. Although in the event it was three months because of his feeding problems. I felt at first that it was very hurtful to have him for such a short time. I enjoyed the time that I had him to look after.

Many of the relinquishing mothers reported how their attempts to make contact with the baby met with resistance in the staff:

Marcia: I went to see her once or twice, but the people were very sort of abrupt ... Y'know, as much as 'You have no right' - y'know, they let me see her, but, y'know, 'She's just put to sleep' and, y'know ...

Quelia: The decision was mine [to see Andrea in SCBU]. I decided I was going to go up to see her even if it was just the once ... When she was three days old I decided 'I've got to see her even if it is just the once'. I went up, and asked the nurse if I could hold her. She said 'She's in an incubator', and I said 'Please,I just want to hold her'. I actually managed to wangle round her.

Two of the relinquishing mothers who gave birth shortly before the interview were able to recount how they were able to take the decision about contact:

Olivia: I knew immediately that I would care for her while I was in hospital. When she was born Andrea was given to me immediately .

Ursula: I held him at birth and then he was whisked off to the SCBU. I made the decision about contact in pregnancy when I was asked if I would want to hold him. I agreed to and he was given to me at the birth, but it hurt too much and they had to take him from me to the SCBU. I went to see him a lot in SCBU.

While many ideas about maternity care may have changed and some practices too, there still exists among many mothers who have relinquished a feeling that she needs to protect herself from becoming too attached to her baby and that this may be achieved by limiting postnatal contact. That this feeling still pertains is evidenced by Sandra's comment (above) about avoiding 'too much of a bond', which was made when her daughter was under 12 months old:

Clara: My baby was cared for by the staff ... I wanted to avoid too much contact - to 'detach' myself from my baby. I did not do any care - no feeding or changing.

Kara: It's better having no contact. I think so.

Vera: [After being required to care for my baby] I don't know whether I'd encourage another birth mother to have contact with her baby, especially since nobody forces them to care for their babies now. I suppose it may be easier for some not seeing their babies at all.

The continuing existence of a certain wariness among mothers is clear. So, too, are the cockups relating to contact which cause confusion and pain for the mother and guilty embarrassment for the staff:

Elena: When the baby was born, I remember they wrapped him up and cleaned him the way they do. They handed him to me - which surprised me.

Hilda: My mother, when she got through to visit me, got to see the nurse ... she got in to see him and then they come back an' says she should not have got tae see him which made it sort of worse ['cos I hadn't].

In contrast to the general picture which has been presented of limiting contact, the midwives were able to report sensitive occasions when they had been able to encourage a relinquishing mother to make contact with her baby:

Izzy: I remember once helping a mum to change and feed her baby that was going for adoption. I know that it was not much, but it was very special for her because she felt that she was able to do something for her baby. Some of these mothers never get to do anything at all for their babies.

Nancy: [One] girl ... had cut off, she [said she] hadn't had a baby and 'What are you are talking about?', it was as if she had never had a baby. And eventually we decided to take her to visit her baby ... we took her downstairs because we just felt that she blanked out too much. It worked wonderful for her and she finally held her baby. It was actually very emotional, we brought the baby round and she held the baby and she spoke to the baby and told her baby how she was sorry about giving it up and just explained that she couldn't look after it. It was really very nice for someone who had denied for so long that they actually existed.

Nancy presents a clear, if rather extreme, example of how contact with her baby may facilitate the onset of grieving in a relinquishing mother.

Feeding

The importance of the relinquishing mother's decision about whether to have contact with her baby has been related to her necessity to grieve the loss around the time of parting for fostering or adoption. While her decision about whether to involve herself in feeding her baby is relevant to her grieving, it carries the additional significance that feeding is the time when any mother assesses her ability to function as a mother by satisfying her baby's needs. Thus, when feeding her baby, the relinquishing mother is able to recognise the fact of her motherhood. The reality of which must be accepted prior to grieving beginning.

The midwives were happy to facilitate contact between the mother and baby, and for some feeding seemed to constitute merely another aspect of that contact:

> Amy: I think if she wants to she could have a wee cuddle and maybe help feed the baby a few times, just so that she realises its a person.
>
> Carrie: I have seen women ... actually coming along and feeding the babies while they were in hospital, changing the nappies, seeing them and enjoying the contact with them, and sometimes being very emotional and upset ...

Carrie's comments suggest surprise at the relinquishing mother choosing to be so closely involved in the baby's care. Even greater surprise emerges from Nancy's account of a mother surreptitiously breastfeeding her baby:

> Nancy: There's no restriction on her at all to go down at any time and visit the baby. One girl we actually discovered was breastfeeding the baby downstairs each time she went in and the baby was going for adoption.

Other midwives' attitudes to the relinquishing mother breastfeeding ranged from incredulity to disapproving:

> Ottily: There was one mother I knew who was placing her baby for adoption and she breastfed it for a week before she gave it up. I think she must have been very strong to breast feed
>
> Queeny: I've never seen a mother like this breastfeed her baby. If she wished very strongly to breastfeed it would probably be all right. But I would explain to her about engorgement of her breasts happening when the baby came off. I wouldn't be trying to discourage her, but I think she ought to know. It would be nice for her at the time but there could be problems later.

The significance of breastfeeding in this context relates to the nature of the relationship between the breastfeeding mother and her baby, which is notoriously difficult to research (Lawrence, 1989). The early evidence on the mother-child relationship (see above) may lead to the conclusion that a secure relationship may be facilitated by breastfeeding (Brazelton, 1963). The Mother and Baby Homes to which some of the relinquishing mothers were despatched invariably required, as one of the conditions of being given a place, that the mother should breastfeed:

> Iona: I would work within the Home for a certain amount of time and do chores. I would have to look after the baby and breastfeed it for six weeks after it was born, before it was given for adoption ...

Following this information, Iona chose to stay with distant relatives, but the satisfying nature of the experience of breastfeeding a baby who is to be relinquished was confirmed by other mothers who took advantage of this system:

> Debra: If you could breast feed you were encouraged to do that. So I breast fed. I enjoyed that. It seemed natural to me. It seemed the right thing to do.

> Vera: I stayed there for three months after he was born. I was breastfeeding him to start with and he could not take the dried milk when the time came to take him off the breast and so I had to spend extra time breastfeeding him and bottle feeding him as well so that he would be able to go to the adoptive parents. I did enjoy caring for him and breastfeeding him. When ... I had to keep on breastfeeding him for much longer than usual I was pleased.

The tendency for midwives to discourage breastfeeding which has been noted already from midwives' comments, was also mentioned by relinquishing mothers whose babies were born long ago and recently, respectively:

> Marcia: ... actually I breast fed her for some time and then after they came and - because I didn't want to keep it - and then they said "It's going for adoption. You shouldn't breast feed it."

> Pamela: The only time he had a bottle when I was caring for him was one night when he was a bit upset. The sister said to me 'He's just sucking for comfort. You've got no milk in your breasts.' It was as if I was wasting everybody's time. I was very put out and very embarrassed, as if I should have known better. I felt that I might be harming him. Up until that time I had quite enjoyed feeding him. It felt right and complete.

In view of the significance and sorrow that the relinquishing mothers attributed to their inability to give anything to the child (Mander, 1992a), it is surprising that they did not realise the importance of the breast milk which they were able to provide.

Additionally, the midwives were able to explain clearly the part that memories contribute in facilitating grieving; this is because healthy grieving depends on having memories (Mallinson, 1989) on which to focus thoughts of the lost one.

Thus, in the absence of tangible memories, a focus for grief is lacking, which may inhibit its progress. The interventions which midwives utilise to help the mother create memories on which to focus her grief (Lewis, 1976), do not include breastfeeding.

Aline's experience

It is helpful to illustrate the continuing significance of the themes which I have identified relating to being a mother. Extracts from the case study show how Aline's feelings towards her baby changed from the realisation of the pregnancy in the third trimester through to three months after the birth:

> I've got no maternal feelings, in fact Fiona burst out laughing when I told her I was pregnant ...
>
> When the baby's born I would just like to see it very briefly to find out what sex it is and to make sure that it is all right. I would not want anything more to do with it. The little bugger is really giving me gip up here [under my ribs] kicking and pressing me.
>
> I've not had much in the way of feelings about it. There's not really been much time for any feelings to develop. I do think though that after the initial shock of discovering I was pregnant I have started to get more attached to it. I did find myself talking to it. This was particularly when it was not moving very much, I'd tell it to get on and start doing something. This was only when I was alone of course such as when I was lying in the bath I'd say 'Move you little bugger'. It was always an 'It' never he or she ... Yes I'd say I have become just a wee bit attached to it.
>
> [Privately after the birth the midwife told me that the medical notes said 'Mother does not want any contact with the baby'. Aline was asked during her admission whether this still applied and again during the birth.]
>
> I've been with Janice to see the baby. She's in an incubator, but she doesn't have a lot of tubes and things. ... They gave me a photo of her. D'you want to see it? They said they'd be taking some more photos and I could have some. I'll probably have some more to keep.
>
> I went to see her on Monday morning with Janice, I was a bit upset after that. It was just before you came to see me. On Monday afternoon I went to see her with my Mother. On Tuesday morning Kim came in to see me and we went along to see Andrea, she was about to be moved down to the ward ... I took my mother to see Andrea, she hadn't seen her except for a quick look at the birth.
>
> When I first went to see her in the ward, when we walked into the ward the sister said to me 'Are you Mummy?' That really got up my nose. I was quite cut up when she said that to me.

I'm going up to see Andrea this afternoon ... The SW thought it would be a good thing for me to see Andrea and the community Midwife asked me whether I'd seen her. I think that seeing her will help me to make up my mind about what I should do.

I haven't touched Andrea yet. But I decided last night that I will pick her up when I see her this afternoon. As long as its OK with the staff - if she hasn't just had a feed or something. She is my baby though, as the SW keeps on telling me.

I am going to pick her up because it would be unfair not to touch her or feel the size of her.

I have to name her and I could not have not seen her and give her a name. I did not plan to touch her. The SCU staff offered to let me touch her and to hold her. They said it would be OK if I change my mind. I felt a strong urge to pick her up, but I did not want to get attached to her. I feel now that I do want to hold her. Otherwise it would be unfair for her as well as to me.

[The staff] explained things. Like offering to let me feed her, they'd say you don't have to take over feeding her. It was entirely up to me what I did.

She's totally different now that I've seen her. [Blows nose] I have to keep thinking that she really is mine, part of me, a lovely wee thing. I have to think whether it is better for her to give her away. But I don't know if I want to give her away now. I'm worse when I'm on my own.

The SW says she'll be able to give me practical help if I do decide to keep her. She has reminded me more than once that I can still change my mind.

The uncertainty I'm feeling at the moment reminds me a bit of how I felt around the time my uncle died of cancer a couple of xmasses ago. I was the only person he told that he had cancer.

I've not done a lot of crying. I'm not really a cryy sort of person ... I do cry when I'm alone and doing some thinking.

Other children

Although the focus in this chapter has been on the relinquishing mother's relationship with the child she relinquished, it is necessary to remember that there are likely to be other children in her life. The implications of her relinquishment for her relationship with these other children deserves attention.

The relinquishment has the potential to affect other children in two ways: around the time of a subsequent birth and in long-term relationships:

Childbearing subsequently

In later pregnancies feelings of loss associated with relinquishment, which the mother thought were safely dealt with, are likely to be resurrected. This observation is similar to accounts of the feelings of bereaved mothers:

> Josie: In the case of the bereaved mother the baby is dead and it is all over; that is until she has a future pregnancy and all the memories will come flooding back.

That Josie's observation is relevant to relinquishing mothers is confirmed by Elena:

> Elena: I thought [the next birth] just brought it back in every way.

However the pain of the loss may not inevitably or invariably be resurrected:

> Nadia: The minutes after each birth have been the same for each of the children. The memories of Andrew's birth came back to me with subsequent births, but there was no pain or grief. It was OK.

The resurrection of latent memories results in comparisons between an idealised relinquished child and the actual new baby:

> Tanya: It comes back to me with the birth of each of my babies. Each one makes me remember the separation from Andrea. My elder son ... was so ugly. I compared him with Andrea when she was born and he really did not compare very well 'cos she was just perfection. After that I didn't compare them at all.

It is necessary to question whether such comparisons have any long-term implications for family relationships, as has been found in the 'replacement child syndrome' following losing a child through death (Cain & Cain, 1964: Oglethorpe, 1989).

It has been suggested that, in order to avoid resurrecting memories of sadness and loss, the mother's care should be provided 'well away from the hospital' (Kargar, 1990). Although this appears to be a kind suggestion, it may be construed as helping the mother to avoid the reality of her loss. The more supportive ambience which has been shown to achieve better pregnancy outcomes in bereaved mothers may have similarly beneficial effects in relinquishing mothers (Stray-Pedersen & Stray-Pedersen, 1984).

The possibility of the woman's avoidance of the reality of her loss having the potential to affect her care in a subsequent pregnancy arose, uniquely, in the account which Rosa gave of her second pregnancy:

> Rosa: I hadn't actually said - I never ever told anybody I had had a baby before. As far as I was concerned, when I had my [second child] she was my first baby. I can remember one nurse ... getting a bit narky when she suddenly discovered I had had a baby. She wasn't very pleased about it, y'know.
> RM: Would you say you were deliberately hiding this, or was it - ?
> Rosa: I don't think it was deliberately hiding it. I don't know what it was. I just know - maybe I was deliberately hiding it, its hard to say. I wasn't really ashamed of it as such, but I just didn't want anybody to know I suppose.

Having relinquished a baby previously is likely to affect the woman's subsequent childbearing experience. Although the effects are variable, the mother has been shown to utilise certain strategies to minimise them.

Relating to other children

The longer-term effects of relinquishment on the family are similarly variable. In relationships which openly share information about the relinquishment there may be no discernable effect:

> Gina: I have a son from my subsequent marriage and he has been absolutely wonderful. I told my son - he was 18 when I told him. He said 'Mum, you've got something to tell me haven't you?'

There may be undesirable effects on mother-child interaction, such as the protectiveness encountered by Hilda and the anxiety faced by Nadia:

> Hilda: I'm [confident] with them all but with Iain I'm very protective. I would not let anyone else have him; he did not get to go up to stay with my Mum until he was a year old. He was making up to me for everything else that I'd lost.

> Nadia: I do worry about the effect on the other children, especially my eldest son, if Andrew should happen to return.

In families in which the information is not shared, the mother may have to resort to deception to maintain the relationship, as shown by Ursula's experience of being pregnant with her second baby who was due to be relinquished:

> Ursula: I felt that I'd let my family down. I had to keep it a secret from my seven year old daughter. She lives with my mother and I saw her up until I was six months [pregnant], but then I told her that I was going to [another country] to work and continued to speak to her just on the phone.

Remembering the one who was relinquished

In view of the significance which is attached to memories facilitating grieving, the relinquishing mother's memories of her baby assume greater importance. These memories were almost invariably happy ones:

> Elena: I remember thinking he was lovely, he was perfect, and I got that sort of rush of love whatever you call it. It was great.

> Lena: She was nice - a pretty girl. She was like me when I was wee.

> Marcia: She was such a lovely - a lovely baby she was - a very gentle thing.

> Olivia: I always called her 'My Little Princess' and that is what I wanted her to be.

The mother's elation was usually modified by a variety of other feelings. Olivia's awareness of the temporary nature of her contact with her baby becomes apparent in her reference to her baby being 'mine', as some mothers mentioned (see above) of the relationship in pregnancy:

> Olivia: I was holding her, looking at her and talking to her. I was laughing and crying because I was so happy. She was so perfect and she was mine.

For some mothers the unpleasant memories related to physical aspects, exacerbating their significance:

> Pamela: I parted with Andrew in the hospital nursery. When I came home all I could hear was him crying.

> Gina: I do remember he was very dark with blue eyes. His one eye was sticky.

A few mothers were able to contrast their positive feelings after the birth with the negative feelings they had encountered earlier:

> Tanya: She was gorgeous. I didn't think that she had anything to do with the lump that I'd previously had in my stomach.

Although the mothers were concerned about their future contact with the one who was relinquished (See chapter 9), they had difficulty imagining this person as anything other than a newborn baby:

> Lena: [The midwife] gave me the bottle to give to her and they left me alone with her. I thought that was nice. 'Cos you didn't really go in the nursery to feed the children, they came to your bed. But they let me go in the nursery on my own. It was only the once. It was something I remember. It was the only time. I really got on my own with my baby. And really though it wasn't much I can remember holding her and I can remember feeding her. I always think about the baby. I don't think about when she's older now. But I only remember this baby, and what she was like.

The difficulty of envisaging an adult is aggravated by the lack of information provided for the relinquishing mother by adoption services. The result is that, while midwives are may help to create memories to facilitate grieving, the follow-up mechanisms are not in position to help the mother to prepare for any later contact, such as by providing updating information.

Conclusion

The mother who relinquishes her baby for adoption has been shown to experience the emotional changes around the time of birth which are common to all mothers. While midwives are accustomed to helping mothers who are keeping their babies to cope with these changes and, perhaps, to helping mothers who are bereaved to adjust to their loss and begin their grieving, some midwives appear to have difficulty relating their knowledge of these emotional changes to the relinquishing mother. It may be that, even if the midwife is able to facilitate the relinquishing mother's grieving, there is little likelihood of this being followed up by the other agencies involved.

13 Making decisions

It has been suggested that choice in childbirth has achieved the status of a shibboleth, in that it is the ultimate test of childbearing political correctness (Mander, 1993a). Thus, the lip-service which is openly paid to involving the healthy happy mother in decision-making about her care may be affecting practice. It is necessary to question the extent to which this autonomy is extended to the mother facing a less satisfactory outcome to her childbearing experience. In this chapter I focus on the decisions made by and for the relinquishing mother; included are her choices about her and her baby's future, as well as decisions about her care.

After a brief examination of decision theory, I look at the mother's decisions and the factors which influence them. Next, I consider an issue which was raised by each mother who had relinquished previously; this is how her relinquishment would have been unnecessary had her pregnancy happened later. On the basis of her developing interpretation of her relinquishment, I asked each mother the hypothetical question 'If you had your life over ... would you decide differently?' The mothers' answers demonstrate the stability of their decisions. Despite recommendations for 'patient autonomy', the data show that the provider and the recipient of care contribute variably to decisions about care, which is the last area to be considered.

Decision theory

Essentially based on mathematical principles, decision theory originated with the work of Pascal in the seventeenth century. Decision-making involves utilising available information to allow us to make the best of any given situation; this was defined by Pascal as the 'maximisation of expectation'.

Human beings have been shown to delay or avoid decision-making (Janis & Mann, 1977), probably due to fear of making the wrong decision and threatening their self-esteem. A further reason for delay is the preparatory processes preceding the decision, which are intended to reduce the likelihood of over-hasty and risky decisions (Thompson & Thompson, 1985). By way of preparation the individual must accept that all choices carry an element of risk, but then reduce this risk by gathering all the information possible on which to base the eventual decision (Jameton, 1984; Crisham, 1985). During information-gathering, contingency planning begins, using the 'What if ...?' device.

A crucial aspect of decision-making is the evaluation, which may precede implementing the decision. Known as anticipatory regret, it may modify the decision; a change of mind is likely if the decision has been the second best choice, if immediately unfavourable consequences threaten or if new information is acquired (Janis & Mann, 1977). The psychological consequences of the decision, in terms of commitment, correlate positively with the level of predecisional conflict. More adverse postdecisional consequences feature dissonance, which may require specific strategies to assist coping.

Many issues relating to decision making have been mentioned in other chapters, in discussing the experience of midwives and the relinquishing mother. It is now necessary to draw together these issues in order to demonstrate the part played by the mother and those near her. I hope to show the power which the mother exerts to control her decisions and, hence, her experience.

The mother's decisions

Some mothers were unaware of having **any** choices; the remainder felt severely limited in the options presented, from which to choose the future of herself and her baby.

Termination of pregnancy

Although it was rarely in the mother's mind, the possibility of termination of pregnancy tended to be presented to her as a relatively easy solution to her situation:

> Iona: I never even thought about abortion or anything like that. The question of an abortion was never raised and I think by the time everyone found out it was too late anyway.

> Quelia: I didn't fancy a termination. My Mum and Dad had actually talked about an abortion when I found out I was pregnant but I just couldn't go through with it.

> Lena: [My Mum] tried to arrange for an abortion, but by this time it was too late. ... so I just had to have it. Although I don't regret that, in that way. I'm glad I didn't have an abortion. I don't think I could've lived with it ... But probably at the time it would have seemed easier, but I'm glad I never.

> Sandra: The thing is, my parents, immediately they heard, they wanted me to have an abortion. They were thinking along those lines, that there was only one solution. But I said I couldn't go through with it. Besides the fact that I was too far on by that time.

Despite strong parental conviction that termination of pregnancy was the best solution, the mother often, like Sandra and Iona, found that her pregnancy was too far advanced for termination to be feasible. It is impossible to determine whether this was a deliberate, manipulative delaying tactic by the mother, or whether (as mentioned above) a decision was being avoided. Sandra may have been procrastinating but with a, to her, valid reason:

> Sandra: I just kept saying I wasn't sure because I thought he might be able to come back. I was keeping the decision right until I had to make a choice. I delayed the decision as long as I possibly could, yes, although I did fill in the forms in the early stages, just in case.

Kara, like some other young mothers, was persuaded to seek medical advice about termination of pregnancy. It took an unfortunate meeting with a gynaecologist to convince Kara that this was not the solution:

> Kara: I didn't know what I wanted to do really and I didn't want to have an abortion but I went through the process. I knew I didn't want - I don't know why I bothered - and [my GP] got me an appointment really quickly because I was quite far on.

Marriage

Another choice which was open to many of the mothers and which might have provided a solution was marriage to the baby's father:

> Quelia: [My parents'] first reaction was 'Are you getting married?' once things had calmed down. I had no intention of getting married ... I couldn't see why I should get married for the sake of a baby - not fair on the baby and not fair on us either.

Marriage proved unrealistic, because of opposition from the parents on the grounds of unsuitability or because of the carefully considered reluctance of the couple:

> Debra: We could have got married, but Father would not allow it.

> Rosa: I had said to [my Mother] that we weren't going to get married. I think probably she thought we would have got married and that would have been OK. Although Billy was kind of sympathetic and everything, he didn't want to get married at that particular time, unfortunately.

In spite of being forbidden, or unwilling, to marry him during the pregnancy, several mothers settled into a marital relationship with the baby's father after the relinquishment.

Termination and marriage were clearly not regarded as valid choices by the mothers I interviewed.

No alternative

As identified by Anderson and colleagues (1986) in a survey of twenty Australian relinquishing mothers, each mother in my recent study expressed her conviction that she was presented with no alternative to adoption:

> Marcia: [TEARS] I had no choice ... about placing Andrea for adoption ...
>
> Lena: Nobody told me about these [choices]. Nobody told me that I had any other options. 'Cos 'far as I was concerned I'd have to have this baby, have it adopted and that would be it. I wasn't told anything. I wasn't given any options. I really thought I had to do this, that I didn't have a choice - that I had to have it adopted. Nobody told me otherwise. That now really irks me I think I should have been told. 'Cos I wasn't given any other option.
>
> Gina: The baby was going to be adopted and there was no alternative. There was no chance whatsoever that I could suddenly have a baby and go back home with a baby.

Lacking resources

The mother's perception of a forced choice was reinforced by her awareness that her own, usually financial, resources were too limited to allow her to raise a child:

> Sandra: I would have had to get social security and single parent allowance. There wouldn't be enough to keep us ...
>
> Rosa: Unfortunately there wasn't a lot of money about. I couldn't see any way that I could bring up a child really. It came down to a lack of money. I never seemed to have any money. I seemed to be always wearing cast-offs ... I would have been really struggling. I wouldn't have been able to go out to work, because I wouldn't have had anywhere to leave him. I needed to go to work, I couldn't obviously rely on my mother and my aunt to keep me.

Lacking information

As mentioned by Lena (above), the limited information provided for the mother about adoption and the alternatives resulted in the impression that no choices existed. The need for accurate information to permit sound decision-making has been observed by other researchers (Farrer, 1993). Research by McHutchison (1986 cited in Farrer 1993) focussed on information-giving. She found that almost three-quarters of relinquishing mothers stated that information about adoption and the effects of relinquishment would have influenced and possibly reversed their decision. Farrer consequently questions whether withholding information is a deliberate strategy to ensure a continuing supply of suitable babies?

When I asked about how care might be improved, the need for information emerged powerfully:

Quelia: More information is needed about the details of the adoption process and papers to be signed, as I am now wary of signing anything.

Tanya: I wanted information from a birth mother who'd kept her baby, about the good things and the bad things about bringing up the baby by yourself. [Mothers] have to have the options presented to them. It's easier now for the birth mother to keep her baby and really the advantages and disadvantages need to be explained.

Contrary to Tanya's wishes, and according to Mech (1986), information from other relinquishing mothers tends to be discouraged by adoption agencies.

It is clear that, although the literature suggests that information-gathering is an essential precursor to decision-making, this is severely hampered for the relinquishing mother by her belief that there is no other solution. The absence of real alternatives in this context, as in other aspects of childbearing (Richards, 1982) cancels out any choice. Further, it may be that her inability to base her decision on sound information affects the stability of the mother's decision (see below).

Factors influencing the adoption decision

The possibility of the mother experiencing pressure to relinquish her baby for adoption has been mentioned elsewhere (See Chapter 10). Influential roles were played by the family, the adoption agency and finance. The mothers considered that these factors exerted pressure in favour of relinquishment:

Tanya: Even my Mum said 'If you love her you'll have her adopted'.

Francesca: I felt myself to have been pressured to choose adoption by the adoption agency, who had promised not to pressure me. Like when I was told about the unsatisfactory aspects of keeping a small baby in a foster home for a long time.

Hilda: I said to my Mum 'I have to go through wi' it'. They'd had to pay for my board in [Mother & Baby Home], and I thought 'They've paid out all that money so I have to ...'

The stability of the decision

The ambivalence of unmarried women in their decisions about keeping their babies was noted by Macintyre (1977) and was related to their care and 'exhortations'. Macintyre's sample, being more varied, was less concerned about the lack of information and its implications for decision-making. The effect on the durability of the decision emerged in two ways in my recent study.

Time over

The first way in which the stability of the decision emerged was when many of the mothers spontaneously volunteered that, in a hypothetical reliving of their experience, they would behave in a particular way which was either the same or different. In later interviews, because this issue was obviously important to the mothers, if she did not raise it I did.

For many mothers the answer was painfully clear and overwhelmingly negative:

> RM: If you had your time over ... would you do the same again?
> Debra: That's very easy. I would never ever do it again. Knowing what adoption is I couldn't recommend it to anyone.

> Clara: If I were to have another chance my decision would be to keep the baby.

> Elena: I wouldn't do it. I wouldn't get the baby adopted, no way. Even if I had to go on the streets until somebody helped me, I would just not do it.

> Hilda: [It was] all totally wrong - should never have happened. If I had my time again I would never do it. I wouldn't say I wouldn't get pregnant, but I would never gie it away.

While this powerfully negative reaction emerged from some mothers, others who had relinquished more recently seemed content with and prepared to - at least hypothetically - repeat their decision:

> Olivia: I am quite happy about having placed Andrea for adoption, I'm confident that it was the right thing to do in the circumstances. In the same circumstances I would probably do the same thing again.

> Pamela: If I had my time over again, if everything else was the same I would do the same again.

A mother whose relinquishment was incomplete when I met her expressed marked ambivalence about her feelings:

> Sandra: I know that I have made the right decision, but as I say there is still this guilt in my mind, because I know it is not what I really want to do.

A few mothers distinguished the repeatability of the experience for those involved. Quelia differentiated the implications for herself and her baby, while Ursula considered that, in view of her experience of maternity care, she would prefer termination of pregnancy:

> Quelia: No. Never. I loved my baby. [TEARS] I still regret it. I'll never say I'm glad, but I am glad I did it for her sake, but I regret it for my sake.

> Ursula: People had advised me that I should have an abortion because it was just a mass of cells, but I couldn't. If I had my time over again I would certainly have an abortion, after the way I've been looked after.

In an American study comparing relinquishing and parenting mothers (Remez, 1992; Kalmuss et al., 1992), both groups of mothers expressed satisfaction with their decision at six months. The significantly higher mean regret score in relinquishing mothers was associated with a large majority (78%) stating, like the more recent relinquishing mothers in my recent study, that they would make the same decision again.

Mothers today

The second way in which the stability of the decision emerged was through comparisons between her experience of pregnancy and the experience of current unsupported mothers. Perhaps not surprisingly, observations of the relatively 'easy' life of current single mothers were tinged with bitterness. Although some comments were surprisingly positive:

> Tanya: I really couldn't see that I had any option but to place the baby for adoption. There was no help with housing in those days and their was no benefit available for single parents.
>
> Rosa: You didn't get the help financially like you do now. I think it's good that people get more financial help and they also get more help from social workers - I should imagine they do.
>
> Gina: I really think today how wonderful it must be for women who are in the same circumstances - to have the opportunity to keep their child, to have the choice - I think that is wonderful. That is a tremendous step forward for women who are having children on their own - to have a choice, without being a pariah or something like that.

The statutory rights of single parents have certainly been extended since many of the mothers relinquished (Etchells, 1990). But it is necessary to question whether life has actually been made easier and whether Gina's optimistic interpretation is justified.

Dissonance

Despite the largely positive comments of a small number of recently relinquished mothers, these data have a general feeling of dissatisfaction with the adoption decision. It may be that this reflects some degree of post-decisional dissonance among the mothers. The inability of the relinquishing mother to locate suitably detailed information about the solutions available to her has been demonstrated, and it may be suggested that decision-making is impeded by this omission.

Additionally, many of the reasons given by the mothers for relinquishment relate to comparatively short-term phenomena, such as financial constraints and parental disapproval. On the basis of these phenomena, the mother takes a decision which, for her at least, has long-term and probably permanent implications. This 'short-termism' has long been recognised:

> It does not seem fair ... to surrender a child permanently in order to get whatever care he may need temporarily'.
>
> (Thurston, 1919, cited by Jackson, 1986).

The sorrow and foreboding is implicit in Rosa's comment:

> Rosa: I think if you could just say to somebody 'Look into the future. Think about it' then it would be easy for them to make the decision.

Decision-making in care

So far in this chapter I have focussed on the relinquishing mother and the factors which affect her decision-making. I now broaden my scope in order to contemplate the interaction between the mother and her carers, the midwives, in making decisions relating to her care near the birth.

Being constrained in decision-making

Throughout my recent study, the midwives were comfortable to discuss their care of the grieving mother, irrespective of whether her grief was associated with loss through death or through relinquishment. It soon emerged that midwives consider that their decisions about their care of this mother are constrained in many ways. The constraints include factors such as, first, the buildings in which care is being provided, that is the lack of suitably quiet single rooms in the postnatal area. Second, midwives perceive that 'unit policies' inhibit their autonomy in making decisions; an example would be whether the grieving mother would be cared for in the antenatal ward or in another setting:

> Amy: ... the decision is made by nursing staff and hospital policy. Here they always come to ante natal. 'Cos antenatal is the only place with single rooms. But when I worked up at [another unit] they went to postnatal because postnatal had single rooms there and they were a postnatal lady. It depends on the policy and the geography.

The third, almost inevitable, constraint on decision making comprises staffing difficulties and, the factor which is inextricably linked, the perception of pressure of work; these include not only staff shortages, which come easily to mind, but also the constant emotional readjustment for a midwife who is caring both for mothers with babies and for grieving mothers.

Deciding where to care

An important constraint which midwives profoundly feel adversely affects their ability to make decisions concerning their care of the grieving mother is the difficulty they experience in finding suitable accommodation for her while she is in hospital. The accommodation problem is partly due to midwives' anxiety that the grieving mother may have what are perceived as negative visual and verbal encounters with other mothers, including seeing happy mothers with their babies and being asked by them about the birth.

> Hilary: She has a single room so that she'll be protected from the other mothers who'd ask her 'What did you have?'. A single room acts as a warning to people who may be curious. Other mums always assume that all has gone well and don't think that things can go badly wrong. They certainly don't intend to be unkind in any way - in fact quite the opposite'.

Hughes (1986) indicates that other mothers were certainly not averse to having a bereaved mother alongside them while in the maternity unit, suggesting that midwives' anxiety about the unsupportive or actively harmful role of other mothers is unjustified. These findings are reinforced by the comments of the relinquishing mothers who found helpful support among other (keeping) mothers:

> RM: ... a 12 bedded room?
> Lena: Actually the women were OK. And they used to mother me. They realised I was just a kid. They were OK to me. ...
> RM: Would you have preferred a smaller room?
> Lena: No. I think before I had the baby I wanted to be in a room on my own. I didn't want anyone to see me. But I was glad really that I was 'cos even though it was [a big room] the women were all nice. We were all just girls together. They done their exercises and had a bit of a giggle and they all were nice to me.

Midwives also vividly recounted their anxiety that the grieving mother would be further disturbed by hearing babies crying. I was able to probe the reasons why the presence of other mothers and babies is viewed so negatively. The midwives were unable, however, to contemplate the possibility that this avoidance of other mothers and their babies might be associated in any way with a denial of the reality of the loss.

Midwives showed a reluctance to burden the mother with what they see as mundane decisions about her care. These decisions include such matters as the type of ward in which she is cared for, the size of room which she should occupy or, if larger, the mothers with whom she should share it (pregnant women, new mothers or mothers of babies in SCBU). Such decisions were attributed to unit policy. Sharing a room with another mother is considered to be unhelpful for the grieving mother, as the onset of her mourning is delayed and her support system may be impeded. That there may be problems, such as embarrassment or anxiety for those with whom she would be sharing a room, is of less concern, though Hughes (1986) states that mothers denied such negative feelings.

The reluctance of midwives to allow or encourage the grieving mother to make decisions about her care is unfortunate, as the choices open to this mother and her control over her situation are being limited. This suggests that midwives could make more use of research findings, such as Gohlish's (1985) study showing how highly control is valued by bereaved mothers.

Deciding how long to stay

Midwives are generally comfortable for the mother to decide how long she will stay in hospital. They tend to agree with the mother that it may be beneficial for her to return home early; the busyness, strangeness and noise of the maternity unit make it an inappropriate place for the mother to begin grieving and her own home environment and family surroundings are seen as being more conducive to a healthy resolution of her grief. This feeling is strengthened by the problems midwives perceive in relation to accommodation and to other mothers and babies. The general feeling is that the family provide more appropriate support, resulting in the mother being encouraged to return home quickly, possibly (for the bereaved mother) directly from the labour ward. The woman's physical condition, determined by a medical examination, is thought to be the ultimate deciding factor:

> Gay: They're usually home the next day. And I think maybe it should be really up to them whether they go or not, but then again it's not really the ideal situation, because they're still seeing pregnant ladies and they can still hear the babies crying and I suppose they think maybe that its better for themselves just to go on out home. Y'know and some people end up with an epis[iotomy] and things and it's quite painful and they're probably tired too. Make them aware of the options, that they can stay a bit longer.
> RM: What do you think is the best?
> Gay: Leave it up to the individual. Whatever they want to do.

As in Hughes' (1986) study some midwives find this desire for early discharge a constraint to providing appropriate and individualised care, and when it seems to be elevated to the status of unit policy they find it difficult to resist. A small minority of midwives suggested that the tendency to early discharge may not necessarily be for the benefit of the mother, while some regard it as a reflection of the limited accommodation and other facilities she can be offered in the unit. That early discharge may be associated with avoiding the reality of the loss, as found by Hughes (1986) was, again, not mentioned by my sample.

The widespread assumption of the mother deciding when to go home, contrasts with the observations by Alice Lovell (1984). She identified the mother's perception of being despatched home over-hastily and not for her benefit, but because the staff in the maternity unit had difficulty coping with her presence. The decision about the mother's transfer home, particularly who makes it, what influences it and how it relates to education about grieving, deserves closer attention.

For Lovell's sample the return home was not the panacea which some anticipate. The grieving mother found that friends and family had other preoccupations which limited the support available. Although convinced that the mother would find good support at home, the midwives were less certain of the role of these people in the maternity unit:

> Queeny: The patient is in control of who comes to see her ... If there is too much of a crowd (7 or 8) we may say something.

While this may reflect a common area of conflict, the implications for the grieving mother are particularly serious. We should give attention to the discrepancy between visiting in the maternity unit needing supervision and assuming that those at home are supportive. Although the midwives, like Queeny, were happy for the mother to decide who visited, I was unable to find out what help, if any, the mother was given in making and implementing this decision.

Who decides?

The data show that midwives have a clear perception of who should be making decisions regarding this mother's care. This is apparent in their conviction that decisions relating to her hospital accommodation should not be made by the mother.

Many decisions relating to the care of the grieving mother are effectively non-decisions; in that these matters are not decided by either the mother or by the midwife. Midwives considered that these 'decisions' were being imposed on them by a range of organisational and other factors. These aspects of care were those which have been given a degree of acceptance, resulting in them having been raised them to a level of 'custom and practice' which may impede their being questioned and which may be inconsistent with the professional status to which midwives aspire.

A third set of decisions, including when to go home and contact with the baby (See Chapter 12), have been shown to be avoided by midwives.

Conclusion

The need for mothers and for midwives to be autonomous in their decision-making, though potentially conflicting, is increasingly recognised (Mander, 1993b). The implications of this interaction emerged in an important study by Green et al. (1990). These researchers found that the provision of information enabling the mother to assume some degree of control over her experience of childbearing was fundamentally important to a healthy recovery from the experience:

> Women who did not feel in control, either of themselves or of their environment, were least satisfied and least likely to feel fulfilled, and had low postnatal emotional well-being.

The mothers in Green's study related their perception of being in control to the relationship with the carers, rather than the nature of the childbearing experience. Thus, information-giving and the negotiation of interventions between the mother and her carers permits decision-making to be individualised and control to be assumed by whoever is appropriate.

It has been suggested, however, that there may be an argument against involving a grieving mother in making decisions about care, because such responsibility superimposed on grief may become intolerable (Borg & Lasker, 1982). This argument is refuted by research undertaken in the context of babies dying neonatally (Benfield et al., 1978). These researchers compared the grieving of 19 parents who had shared the decision to limit care with the grieving of 21 parents whose babies had received total care. The mothers of the limited care babies demonstrated significantly less anger, irritability and 'wanting to be left alone'. The fathers in the limited care group encountered less sleeplessness, irritability, depression, crying and anorexia. Thus, Benfield and colleagues' finding that well-informed parents are able to contribute to taxing decisions about treatment and go on to adjust healthily to their loss, is highly relevant to the relinquishing mother.

It is clear that the need for the relinquishing mother to be the prime decision-maker is paramount. With appropriate information on which to base her decision the long-term implications of short-term decisions may be avoided.

14 Facing the future

The prospect of the future for the mother who relinquishes her baby comprises many aspects; one which comes less readily to her mind, but which emerged in my recent study (Mander 1992a), is the duration of her grief. Although the grief of relinquishment has unique features, it also shares much in common with grieving loss through death (See Chapter 6). Despite the widely succumbed-to temptation to set a time limit on grief, this is a pointless and potentially damaging exercise - a lesson learned painfully by a widow (Rose, 1990). Having been led to believe the 'one year myth', on the anniversary of her bereavement she was surprised to find herself feeling no better, and eventually feeling much worse.

When we contemplate how far into the future grief must be endured we have to rely on research such as that by Worden (1992) with widows. The completion of grieving, according to Worden, is characterised by the ability to think of the lost person without pain. Although, he does not suggest that the sadness will not continue for longer, perhaps indefinitely. As well as featuring resolution of the pain, the completion of grieving is marked by a more positive development; this is the ability of the bereaved person to, as Worden puts it, 're-invest his or her emotions back into life and living'. Re-investment starts with the realisation that it is possible to continue to exist, despite the loss of the loved one, and is followed by making plans for this continuing existence. The possibility of a future tends to be neglected by most authorities on grieving, whose concern with the future invariably ends with the assumption of the new bereaved identity (Parkes, 1976). Perhaps this neglect of the future is due to the usual focus of grief research - elderly people (Stroebe & Stroebe, 1987). In the case of relinquishing mothers the future life, being considerably longer, becomes more significant.

In this chapter I consider the implications for the mother's future life of her relinquishment and, particularly, her delayed grieving (See Chapter 6).

Lacking a future

Despite her grief, each of the mothers I interviewed was comfortable to contemplate her life following relinquishment. Others who were close to her, however, had experienced more difficulty:

> Lena: She [Mother] would hang it over my head - that there would be nothing for me anyway in the future.

> Tanya: I think my father had me so convinced that I had completely ruined my life, that that was it. My life was over, because I had done this. That was me, then I had no job, I had no money, no man was ever going to want to marry me - so I was never going to get married.

Perhaps the parents were trying to resolve their own grief at losing a grandchild, as well as less tangible ideals, by projecting their personal concerns on to their daughter's future. Alternatively, the parents may have needed to impress on a possibly impassive or resistant daughter the serious implications of her behaviour. These hypotheses imply long-term effects, which conflict with the relatively short-term view of the effects of relinquishment apparent in the next section.

Making a fresh start

The concept of beginning her life afresh reflected limited insight into the feelings of the relinquishing mother. Hence, it was almost invariably used to advise her. The form of this advice varied according to how it related chronologically to the relinquishment.

Advising retrospectively

In order to start her life anew some mothers found the advice being given retrospectively. She found herself being recommended to forget her child or, for Anthea, children:

> Anthea: 'You should forget about them, forget about them' - that was my mother. I said I would never forget them.

During her unassisted search, Marcia faced similar advice from the adoptive mother. Marcia tearfully showed me a particularly insensitive letter in which the adoptive mother urged 'You must forget about her'. Earlier in her search Marcia had encountered a Minister who was probably trying to help, but who succeeded only in raising false hopes:

> Marcia: Eventually [the Minister] told me 'Put it out of your mind and do not pray for her'.

In these examples, the advice may have incorporated personal feelings of loss, threat or failure respectively.

Advising prospectively

A marginally more constructive form of the advice to start afresh was faced by Debra. She was recommended, with a subtle implication that she should forget the past, to look forward:

> Debra: My mother said 'You must get on with your life'. I tried and tried to cope, it took a long time.

Advising maintaining continuity

In the same way as forgetting her loss and grief is quite unrealistic, so too is the recommendation to resume her former life. The desire for life to return to its previous stable and probably humdrum pattern reflects our human need for orderliness and security. Closed systems of adoption are most likely to achieve 'business as usual' (Marck, 1994). Jessica used this strategy when she initially sought to organise her life as it had been before her relinquishment. Her non-verbal communication indicated her rapid realisation that this was hopeless:

> Jessica: I really just wanted to get back to normal as quickly as possible. It did not happen like that (Laugh!).

In an attempt to achieve the 'normality' which Jessica mentions, a variety of strategies and subterfuges were employed by the relinquishing mother or, more likely, her parents (See Chapter 5.).

Transience of the experience

The relatively short-term nature of pregnancy is obvious. Such common knowledge appears to have been used to encourage the relinquishing mother to recover from her experience of childbearing. Unfortunately, the mother's advisers chose to ignore the long-term implications of pregnancy which are clearly apparent in successful childbearing, but less obvious with other outcomes. This form of encouragement was used prior to the birth to provide much-needed support for a mother with an unstable family background:

> Elena: I remember Mum used to write letters when [Dad made her] stop coming to see me [in the Mother & Baby home] saying 'It'll soon be over'.

In this way the experience of childbearing and relinquishment was anticipated as being only an acute experience. Again, there appears to be the expectation of a fresh start with a speedy return to normal.

The understanding provided by hindsight permitted some relinquishing mothers to see the falsity of such expectations. Unfortunately, though, those close to them did not have such clear insight:

> Lena: I done what I was told, 'cos she'd said ... it would all be all right. OK, when you're young you think that's fact, you never realise it's **not ever** going to be right again.

Ursula: Some people expect bloody miracles. They expect an immediate recovery from something like that.

Tanya: My Mum and Dad simply saw the pregnancy and the birth as a mistake. It was something that only lasted for a short time and when it was over that was it.

The way in which a mother was able to combine a number of strategies to attempt a new start emerges from Iona's words:

Iona: I wanted to put it all behind me. I wanted to make a fresh start. To all outward appearances, it was like that. Because no one mentioned it, because it was a closed book, because I was able to come back to [city] and sort of pick up the threads again after a while ... life went on. I think in a way I wanted it like that in order to make a fresh start, I wanted to forget what had happened.

Iona's contrast between the outward success of these strategies and their inner shortcomings indicate the conflict which she endured.

Another fresh start which mothers are encouraged to consider are new relationships. These may take the form of a new partner or of further childbearing:

Ursula: People try to reassure me. They say things like 'You'll get over it' or 'You can always have another'.

Subsequent relationships

My recent study provides data on the mothers' marital and similar relationships (See Chapter 3) and shows that a woman who has relinquished is likely to embark on a marital or similar relationship. The likelihood of her bearing further children is less clear, as I discuss below. Other researcher's data are considered here.

Marriage

The important study by Pannor and his colleagues (1978) involved thirty eight birth parents, of whom two were men. This study supports the findings of my recent study, in that following relinquishment three-quarters of their sample married at least once. The remainder never married. The tendency of most relinquishing mothers to marry is further supported by Australian data (Winkler & van Keppel, 1984). Of their sample of 213 relinquishing mothers, only 3.1 per cent never married

A larger study in Seattle examined the consequences of adolescent pregnancy McLaughlin et al., 1987). The lives and satisfactions of 123 young people who chose to 'parent' were compared with 146 who relinquished. The data show that the 'parenting' group were far more likely to marry quickly than the relinquishing group. The researchers suggest that this observation is due to the fact that parenters have assumed the role of mother, making them more likely to seek the role of spouse. They imply that the relinquishers' postponement of the role of mother and the role of spouse may be due to having no need of the latter due to not being the former. Whether this simple cause/effect mechanism is accurate is difficult to assess. The operation of some more complex effects is apparent in Tanya's account:

> Tanya: When we told Dad that we wanted to get married he said that he was surprised that anyone would want to marry me after they knew I had had a baby adopted. I can't help wondering if there was a feeling at the back of my mind that I'd better marry him in case it was my last chance. So I did marry him, but it didn't work out.

Childbearing

Like the sample recruited by Pannor and his colleagues (1978) of whom a majority (63%) bore subsequent children, most mothers in my recent study bore later children. Perhaps associated with their higher marriage rate, McLaughlin and colleagues (1987) observed that pregnancy rates as well as abortion rates were higher in those adolescents who 'parented', compared with those who relinquished. There are, however, important issues relating to childbearing which may be hidden by these simple statistics.

Replacement child: Without being prompted the mothers in my recent study indicated their fear of conceiving a replacement child:

> Kara: Sometimes you think if you had a baby you'd be saying you wanted it to be the same as the one that you gave away. And it won't be.

> Nadia: I was desperate **not** to conceive again. I really wanted to avoid having a baby who might be seen in any way as a replacement for Andrew.

Oglethorpe (1989) defines a replacement child as either one who is specifically conceived to replace one who has died or a child forced by its family into this position. The term, however, tends to be used rather loosely to describe any child who is born soon after a loss or disappointment (Floyd, 1981; Borg & Lasker, 1982; Bourne & Lewis, 1984; Lewis, 1979).

In their seminal paper on this topic, Cain and Cain (1964) report six families who had suddenly lost a child by through death following illness or accident. The psychiatric morbidity in, usually, the bereaved mother indicated unresolved grief, which resulted in the albeit hesitant decision to replace the lost child. Identification of the new child with its dead sibling was overpowering and frequent comparisons were made. Unfortunately for the replacement child unrealistic 'hyperidealisation' of the dead sibling often happened. In my recent study Ursula, contemplating a 'replacement child', recognised the risk of 'idealising' the one who was relinquished, with the potential for trauma:

> Ursula: Another problem is that Andrew is the perfect child. He has no bad points and will always be quite unique to me. Because when I first saw him he was perfect at his birth and every time I saw him after that he was being good.

Focussing on the prevalent psychiatric disturbances found among replacement children, Cain and Cain show the family pathology engendered by well-meaning but ill-informed people who had recommended 'having another':

> Ursula: Everybody round about keeps advising me to have another child to make me feel better. But no other child will ever be a substitute for Andrew and I'm not going to have a child as a form of therapy.

Infertility: As well as fears of another unplanned pregnancy limiting both social and sexual activity, the relinquishing mother expressed other fundamental anxieties:

> Jessica: I was scared to go out in case of meeting someone and the same thing happening again.

> Ursula: Now I find that I just can't make love. Its like all that bitterness and stress and then NO NO NO NO. I s'pose there is also the fear that I might become pregnant again.

> Jessica: I sometimes think well I'm thirty five now. I don't have that much time really to have a family ... I feel I've had my chance and gave it away. I might not get another one. I think about what happens if I can't for some reason have any more kids when my situation is different and I'm married. After I've given up my child.

Jessica's anxiety about future secondary infertility is shared with all the mothers in Rynearson's (1982) unusual sample of twenty previous relinquishing mothers undergoing psychotherapy (See Chapter 6.). He found that these anxieties inhibited social relationships with men and were associated with sexual dysfunction, as reported by Ursula (above).

Anxiety about secondary infertility featured prominently among the mothers I interviewed. Additionally, as described by Farrar (1993) as a 'cruel twist of fate', effects of the reality of infertility emerged strongly:

> Lena: And I always had a feeling that when my husband and me got married we could start a family soon. I used to wish I could get pregnant ... Then we found out we couldn't have any children and that was a big blow then. TEARS That was a real blow to me.

> Quelia: I know we're not going to have a family of our own now. I feel I've let Ben down an awful lot. We were only married two years when I had my hysterectomy done.

> Vera: We got married and didn't have any children but when I was thirty five Billy eventually persuaded me that we ought to try for a baby. But by then it was too late. I had my menopause early when I was thirty eight so we never did have another baby.

It is apparent that both the potential for as well as the reality of infertility engender pain in the relinquishing mother. It is necessary to consider whether anxieties such as these limit her ability to adjust to her loss.

Feelings and their duration

As I mentioned in the introduction to this chapter the duration of grief tends to be generally underestimated. This applies as much to the grief of relinquishment as to any other form of grief. It was Pannor (1978) and his colleagues in Los Angeles who, while researching open adoption, identified the enduring nature of the grief of relinquishment. These researchers recounted the parents' continuing feelings of loss, pain and mourning.

Continuing grief

In the same way as Connolly (1987) recounted how the relinquishing mother has to 'live with her absent child' so, in my recent study, each mother told me of the continuing nature of her sadness:

> Nadia: I find that the sorrow deepens, and that the guilt is always present.

> Debra: Its the hardest thing I've ever done, I'll never get over it. TEARS

Manifesting grief

For some mothers it was necessary for her to explain her grief in terms of the frequency with which it manifested itself:

> Elena: I think about him every day - it sounds stupid, but he's never away. He's always there in my thoughts, every day - not every minute of every day, but there is never a day that goes by that I haven't thought about him and wonder where he is and how he is.

> Gina: It is thirty years in [month] and I still can't talk about him without getting upset. TEARS It's an ache, it's something that never goes away, it's there all the time gnawing at you. It's not as if it's a yearly thing, the anniversary of his birth or Christmas, it can happen nearly every day.

Helping and not helping

There are certain ways in which the mother may expect or find help. Some told me how their grief was helped through contact with other relinquishing mothers:

> Clara: My feelings were bad for ten years. I thought about her almost every day and felt very guilty if I did not think about her. I still may cry when the kids aren't around. My feelings have eased through contact with the birth parents group and using the Birth Link register.

The effect of time in helping to resolve grief is more questionable. Writing from personal experience Quinton (1994) regards 'Time Heals' as a dangerous myth. Rynearson (1982) reports how the mothers in his sample experienced a diminution of their mourning responses with time, but he omits to specify the time span involved. Elena had been led to believe that time would help but, like Quinton, is not convinced:

> Elena: [The SW] did say the pain gets less. Maybe you just learn to hide it better, that's all. It's not as raw. I think you learn to bury it.

> Jessica: I can cope with [the pain] now, although I would never discuss it with anyone. The feelings have eased a bit but they are still there. I think of him only every second day.

> Kara: It never ever goes away. Everybody says it will just fade with time and it does to a certain extent but it's something that's always at the back of your mind.

Obviously, time is not the panacea which has been suggested. As I have established in Chapter 6, there is a crucial factor which may serve to prolong the mother's grief. This is her belief in the continuing existence of the one she relinquished and the possibility of being reunited with or, at least, making contact with that person. Although open adoption has been introduced in some countries to ease the mother's pain, there is evidence (Blanton & Deschner, 1990) that it may not have this effect.

Anticipating contact

Irrespective of whether it helps grieving or not and irrespective of whether a satisfactory relationship is established (Sachdev, 1992), the possibility of contact with the relinquished one features prominently in any future which the relinquishing mother foresees:

> Iona: I would be quite happy to meet her.

> Kara: Another six years and it could be all coming back into your life again - which doesn't bother me at all ... if I was planning on marrying or anything like that they would know that this person could appear on my doorstep which is my son. If he wants to find me then I won't hide from him at all.

> Tanya: I have arranged that when I die my sons will take care of it and give [a letter] to her if she should ever try to find me.

Perhaps because of the method of recruitment, the mothers in my recent study were largely positive about the possibility of future contact. In the study by Bouchier and colleagues (1991), however, the mothers expressed some wariness at the prospect.

Being concerned

Each mother told me of her concerns for the well-being of the one she relinquished. Her anxiety related to physical aspects, including being alive, dead, abused or neglected as well as psychological aspects (Marck, 1994). Debra's anxiety increased when she learned of a seriously ill child:

> Debra: I would like to know about Andrea's health. I hadn't ever thought about that before. I think we should be able to get that.

Some of the mothers, such as Francesca, were anxious that their behaviour during pregnancy, especially when related to denial or rejection, may have harmed the child:

> Francesca: I had been forcing myself into skin tight jeans which resulted in really terrible stomach cramps. Could they have damaged him? I feel responsible for his ill health and poor growth later on in the pregnancy. I feel really guilty. What if he is handicapped and it would be my fault. I would have ruined someone else's life.

Kara took her concerns a stage further, by wondering **why** she was wondering about her son's welfare:

> Kara: I wonder all the things that you wonder. But then you think 'Well maybe I'm wondering for some reason'. Maybe something's happened to him. Like - maybe he has died. D'you understand what I mean?

Clearly the mother who relinquished a baby continues to be concerned about the welfare of that person. These concerns constitute an argument in favour of the mother who so wishes being given non-identifying information on a regular basis (Triseliotis, 1991).

Conclusion

The future which the relinquishing mother faces has been shown to be likely to be affected by a number of factors. First, she must work through her grief sufficiently to accept that she has a future and then realise that her grief is not the short-term phenomenon which some may tell her. Second, her relinquishment carries clear implications for her future relationships. Third, her future is likely to be affected by certain preoccupations relating to her relinquishment, including her expectation of contact and concern for her child's welfare.

15 Being helpful

This chapter draws together issues relating to the care of the relinquishing mother. Other chapters, such as 5, 7, 10, 12, and 15, have focussed on specific aspects of her care which emerged significantly from my recent research (Mander, 1992a). This chapter presents a more general picture of her care and how it is perceived both by the mother and by those providing it. In considering the views of both, I hope to illuminate the beneficial aspects of care and recommend a strategy for further improvement.

Caring

A number of issues relating to the midwife's care of the relinquishing mother were raised by the mothers and the midwives (Mander, 1992). Many of these points are of concern to all mothers, but they assume a special significance for the mother relinquishing her baby.

Continuing caring

While midwives are becoming more aware of the need for continuity of care, continuity of carer (Flint, 1986) tends to be discounted as wishful thinking. The need for continuity arises from the burden of establishing relationships with a series of different carers, which is challenging even for a woman experiencing normal childbearing. The burden, however, becomes intolerable when superimposed on the psychological work of grieving. The midwives identified this problem:

> Trudy: I think it would be very nice if you could have a bit more continuity. I think if a woman is not intending to stay for very long [in the unit] ... the staff who looked after her could continue to look after her, without having to bring in a whole load of new people.

Some midwives suggested organisational approaches to improving continuity for the relinquishing mother, which would additionally prevent some of the errors in care or 'cockups' mentioned below:

> Wendy: With the constantly changing staff I think it's quite helpful if one person, identified as going to be the lead person in the care of this woman, has the responsibility for liaison. It's always more helpful. It gets very patchy otherwise. We try to identify one person who's going to be there for the next few days as a sort of lead person and to have the most to do with that mother.

This suggestion clearly has much in common with primary nursing (Wright, 1990), which is ignored in midwifery. Effie's alternative drew on her community background:

> Effie: These mothers usually go home quite early after the birth and they are seen by the community midwives from an early stage ... I suppose that a midwife from the labour ward or the postnatal ward could go out and see her at home. That way the relationship would be being maintained.

Debra, being a nurse, was in a good position to comment on her care. She was surprisingly positive. Her experience was of a Mother and Baby Home providing on-site midwifery care:

> Debra: The midwifery care was good. There was good continuity as I had met both of the midwives before at the AN checks and they delivered the baby. ... It was nice because we knew them. They did all the PN check-ups and everything. They were quite nice.

Being involved

The mothers were keenly aware of their rapport with the midwives caring for them. Most mothers, like Elena, were unprepared to attribute poor relationships to judgemental attitudes:

> Elena: There was the doctor and the midwife ... they said when the pain got too bad I was to press the button and they left. I don't think that was because I was getting the baby adopted, that was the policy of hospitals then with everybody.

> Marcia: I would say [the two midwives] were indifferent. I mean, they weren't unkind. They were just doing their job.

While Ursula was generally, and probably justifiably, mercilessly critical of her care, she was able to give credit for what support she did receive:

Ursula: Midwifery care. That needs a question mark in front of it! There was a student midwife who was lovely though. What did she do? She washed me!! But she sympathised and she chatted about everything and nothing which was just what I wanted. The sister midwife had talked over me to the other midwife about the other midwife's appearance.

The level of interest shown by the midwife appears to be significant to the mother, even though it may be manifested in touchingly simple ways:

Debra: The midwives which were involved were really nice ... They rubbed my back. They were concerned about me.

These comments endorse the observation by Brady-Fryer (1994) of the care of the mother of a preterm baby. She found that 'true concern and tactful presence' are able to make the experience endurable. Similarly, being company for the mother features prominently in the midwife's perception of her role in caring for the relinquishing mother. This function clearly relates to the traditional role of the midwife of being 'with woman' (Bennett & Brown, 1993):

Ottily: We are there to provide a safe environment for her to have her baby in, to provide her with company when she needs it and to be a counsellor available to her on a 24 hour basis.

The safety element emphasised by Ottily is, however, regarded by Zy as being not necessarily in the mother's best interests:

Zy: I see there is a danger of doing too much for these mothers - of protecting them too much from the reality of the situation.

Zy's comments may be interpreted as avoiding creating dependency in the mother, rather than recommending neglecting her when she is at her most vulnerable.

Teaching

A crucial part of the midwife's work comprises teaching. The material which is taught includes a wide range of topics, relating to childbearing and women's health. Inevitably, because of the trend towards smaller families in the UK, infant care requires considerable attention (Ball, 1993). Teaching the relinquishing mother about the care of her baby is closely linked with the degree of contact which the mother chooses or feels she is permitted to have with her baby (See Chapter 12.). Devaney and Lavery (1980) emphasise the significance of teaching for this mother, which was reflected by a mother in my recent study who was woefully undecided about relinquishment, and for whom being taught baby care was much appreciated:

Elena: The midwife gave us all demonstrations on how to look after a baby. She used Andrew, I remember, because he was so quiet, for bathing sessions. I didn't have a clue - it was a great help. I needed all the help I could get. But I was good at it once she showed me I could do it.

Francesca's contrasting experience also demonstrates the importance of the relinquishing mother learning about infant care:

Francesca: I was not taught how to care for the baby. Like when the other women were collected together to be shown a bath I was not asked to join in. I had the baby in the room with me for some of the time, but I was scared to pick him up. I felt different from the others. I wanted to learn, but was not taught. When they asked me whether I wanted to feed him I said 'No' because I did not know what to do. And in case I was expected to do it by myself.

For some midwives not teaching the mother about infant care is deliberate. I am uncertain whether this is a strategy to avoid promoting bonding or whether it is regarded as a waste of time in view of the likely relinquishment:

Polly: We just care for them as individuals. They are given the same post-natal care as any of the other ladies. Apart from not telling them how to deal with babies.

Among relinquishing mothers fear and ignorance of childbirth is likely to be superimposed on the usual anxiety of being admitted to hospital for the first time (Triseliotis, 1991). These anxieties may be compounded by a lack of child-birth education. Although 'the classes' are often criticised for being ineffective (Enkin, 1982), they are likely to at least prepare the mother for her admission (Kirkham, 1983). Persistant denial by the relinquishing mother often prevents early diagnosis of pregnancy and attendance at classes. Efforts are being made to make the prospect of childbirth education less intimidating to those often stereotyped as 'non-attenders' (Thomson, 1993). The teaching provided for Debra (see above) in a Mother and Baby Home is the only example in my recent research of a mother being given any of childbirth education.

Confidentiality

As I mentioned in Chapter 5., confidentiality was a source of concern to both the mothers and the midwives. Maintaining confidentiality not infrequently resulted in individualisaion of the mother's care:

Jessica: Fortunately, the midwife did not come to the house after the birth. If she had that would have made it very difficult.

Lucy: I have heard of some ladies who actually came up to the hospital for their post-natal examinations, as opposed to having a midwife go out to the home. I don't know whether that was for the benefit of their neighbours ...

Checklist

Although checklists are often recommended to ensure competent and comprehensive care (Brown, 1992), it is necessary to question whether these **aides memoires** may also depersonalise care (Mander, 1994)? Because the midwives were accustomed to using checklists with other grieving mothers, they wondered whether this would be helpful in the care of the relinquishing mother:

> Nellie: That [knowledge] comes with experience, there is nowhere else to get it from. But there's no actual checklist of any kind about the care of these girls. I don't know whether that would be helpful.

Summary

Although some of the mothers criticised their care, others were generally content:

> Nadia: On the whole I was very happy with the midwifery care.

Similarly, the views of the midwives varied. It was clear, though, that the consideration given to the mother grieving the loss of a baby through death was not necessarily accorded to her relinquishing sister:

> Hattie: I think they don't get nearly the care the woman gets who is having a stillborn baby.

The reason for this difference in care probably relates to a multiplicity of factors, but one factor may be the attitudes of those who provide care.

Attitudes of carers

Like Hattie (above), Bouchier and her colleagues (1991) found that a majority of relinquishing mothers were not at all satisfied with their maternity care. It may be that this unsatisfactory standard of care results from the situation in which the carers find themselves. As people who have been socialised into pronatalist attitudes (Fogel & Woods, 1981; Campbell, 1985) and who have chosen to work in an area which epitomises pronatalist ideals, midwives face a dilemma in caring for a mother contemplating relinquishment. The prevalent assumption in maternity, as generally, is that the mother both welcomes and cares for her child. When a mother appears to be doing neither of these, and may be perceived as rejecting her child, conflict emerges for the carers.

Devaney and Lavery (1980) suggest that this conflict may be resolved by regarding the mother in one of three ways: first, as sinful for her deviant sexual behaviour or, second, as heartless and unmotherly because of her planned relinquishment or, third, as stupid for failing to use contraceptives. Thus, carers feel uncomfortable with a woman who appears to have rejected a widely-held and, more importantly, personally-held, value system. This discomfort manifests itself in a number of ways:

Tanya: I was absolutely terrified. I think that they ... saw me as a nuisance. There was nothing said in words, but that's how it seemed to me.
Ursula: A hospital ... is not a courtroom where you are judged for what you have or have not done. This midwife did this, because when she read my notes her attitude to me changed. She had been kind and welcoming when I came into the labour ward, but after she read them she was chilly. I asked her 'Have you read my notes now?' She said 'Yes'. After I came home and the midwives came to see me they were so different ...

The midwives I interviewed were clearly aware of the risk of appearing judgemental and each sought to convince me that this did not reflect **her** behaviour:

Hilary: I personally try to avoid treating this woman any different from the other mums. I think that you should not let her think that you think she's heartless.

Kerrie: Some midwives may ask themselves 'How could you do that?' - such as ... give a baby up for adoption? Some midwives really cannot understand how women are able to do these things.

Kerrie's reference to the difficulty which carers face in understanding relinquishment may result in a poor standard of care (Lindsay & Monserrat, 1989) or in errors (see below). Some midwives attributed judgemental feelings to personal or occupational factors:

Betty: They may take on this manner because they have had a lot of contact with people with infertility. Staff dealing with infertile people and women having miscarriages tend to be hard and less understanding of these mothers.

Emily: Also a midwife's religion may play a part in it. If she does not believe in abortion it may be that she thinks that the mother has done the right thing in continuing in her pregnancy and be more sympathetic towards her. Midwives are not there to judge though.

Kay: Well some [staff] are quite dismissive of the baby being given for adoption. They don't agree with it. Because they don't like it they end up being slightly off-hand with the mother. Maybe they can't have children, y'know. Their attitude towards her is a bit negative.

Devaney and Lavery (1980) argue, in the context of the nursing care of unmarried adolescents, that carers should come to terms with their own personal feelings about relationships and marriage and motherhood, before being involved in the care of a mother contemplating relinquishment. These authors discuss, like the midwives (above), the possibly adverse effects of personal and occupational experience on care.

A common experience among the relinquishing mothers was the non-acceptance of factual information by staff, such as details of the lochia (Mander, 1992a). Each mother believed that this represented a judgement being made. Thus, the relinquishing mother felt she was being judged as being u 'unworthy', as proven by her pregnancy and relinquishment. This 'unworthiness' or inferiority operates like a stigma (Goffman, 1963) and becomes applied more generally to quite unrelated aspects of her behaviour, such as her ability to report factual information. The failure of certain clients or patients to be believed is widely recognised, being associated with their perceived deviance from societal norms and is associated with the more vulnerable client groups.

Being alone

The concept of isolation emerged in my recent study in two forms. The first form was the relatively short-term feelings which the mother encounters while in the maternity unit and the second was the more protracted feelings bound up with her grieving.

Isolation near the birth

The mother's need for company while in the maternity unit has been alluded to already (see above). Howe and colleagues (1992) refer to the 'harsh and lonely' experience of labour, which was experienced by many of the mothers I interviewed and which was anticipated by the midwives:

> Fanny: If she doesn't have anyone with her, obviously she'll need more psychological support from the midwifery staff that are with her.

> Gay: She'll probably need more assistance in labour because she might be doing it on her own, She might not have a mother or a partner or anything.

> Barbara: The birth itself wasn't a happy time because I was left on my own ... I remember screaming for my Mum and nobody being there holding my hand or just being there.

Although the isolation described by Barbara was the experience of many of the relinquishing mothers, those who gave birth more recently were more likely to have the support of a relative or partner. Devaney and Lavery (1980) describe the valuable role of this person, although it is necessary to question whether somebody as fundamentally involved as a close relative is able to offer effective support. For Aline, the subject of the case-study, her mother was present, but appeared to be too shocked by the speed of the labour and the prospect of relinquishment to be able to help Aline effectively. Perhaps the suggestion of a 'labor coach' (Devaney & Lavery, 1980) would be preferable in those cultures where known midwifery support is not available.

Following the birth, the postnatal stay presents a slightly different experience of isolation. Some mothers were accommodated in a special part of the unit:

> Hilda: I was just shut away on my own down the stairs. If I'd been upstairs I'd've seen mums and babies and that would have been me - I'd've had to have my bairn wi' me ... Perhaps that's why they put me there.

My personal recollection of care in the 1960s is that part of the rationale for segregating relinquishing mothers was not to protect her, as Hilda suggests, but to protect other mothers. The prevalent fear was that the relinquishing mother, due to her unconventional lifestyle, may harbour infection, now known as sexually transmitted, to which other mothers and babies were vulnerable. The fallacies inherent in this argument are transparent.

The isolation of the accommodation was perceived differently:

> Iona: I think [a single room] was the one kind act. I don't know whether it was because I was an embarrassment that I was stuck in there, or whether it was for my sake. I felt terribly lonely and I didn't have many visitors - obviously the nursing staff weren't wanting to stay and chat. I was protected from mothers and babies.

> Pamela: I wanted to be alone and to think things through. But, if I had been in a single room I would have developed a stronger attachment. I would not have liked to be in a single room as I would have been more isolated, the others provided some distraction for me.

The physical isolation faced by many mothers postnatally was compounded by feelings of being different which resulted from the anticipation of relinquishment. In other situations these feelings have been compared with being 'the ghost at the banquet':

> Pamela: I felt isolated in that I was going to give my baby up.

Enduring loneliness

Feelings of isolation and the uniqueness of the experience typically feature in grief (Penson, 1990). According to Stroebe and Stroebe (1987) such feelings may be moderated if family and friends are able to stand by the bereaved person. The isolation experienced by the relinquishing mother is partly due to her grief, but is compounded by other factors. As mentioned in Chapter 14., fear of social contacts may result from anxiety about another unplanned pregnancy. Other feelings aggravate the mother's isolation, such as low self-worth and deserving punishment:

> Iona: I felt the lowest of the low, just so degraded.

> Pamela: I tell myself 'You must stop punishing yourself'. I feel I am punishing myself for giving a life away.

Closely linked are guilty feelings:

> Clara: There was a lot of guilt. I thought giving up my baby might be my punishment [for becoming pregnant].

> Gina: I was very ashamed. I think guilt, guilt-ridden, ashamed, defiled ...

Iona: All I could think of was what would my life be like? I would have to wear sackcloth and ashes for the rest of my life.

Lena: Och aye. I used to feel ashamed like dirt for years ...

Howe and colleagues (1992) contemplate the possibility that the secrecy (see Chapter 5) which invariably surrounds relinquishment may be responsible for the mother's feelings of isolation. Part of these workers' strategy to help the mother to deal with her feelings of isolation is to encourage contacts, through group meetings, such as those held at the Post-Adoption Centre (Raphael-Leff, 1991).

Making errors in care

It may be argued that all mothers should receive the highest quality care; whether this is a realistic recommendation is debatable. It is unquestionable, though, that certain groups of mothers are more vulnerable to harm or pain due to errors and omissions in their care. I would include grieving mothers among these vulnerable groups. In my recent study, however, many of the mothers recounted incidents which constitute substandard or faulty care. I have termed these experiences 'cockups', whereas other researchers more circumspectly use terms such as 'painful situations' (Forrest, 1989) and 'awkward moments' (Benfield et al., 1976).

Some of these experiences relate to people being in the wrong place at the wrong time:

Clara: I cried at parting from Andrew, particularly when I accidentally bumped into the social worker with him all dressed and ready to go out.

Jessica: Just after I'd had him my Mum was sitting outside, and a nurse was in the next room looking after him and talking to him. The nurse said to him 'What a shame nobody loves you'. It broke her up to hear her saying that.

Sandra: In fact [although arranged otherwise], my parents actually saw the baby. My mother didn't have any choice. She went in to have a word with the staff nurse ... and she was feeding the baby. So my mother didn't have any choice but to see her.

That such errors of care are not merely historical artifacts is evidenced by the experiences of Aline, the subject of the case study. An example is her experience within minutes of learning the awful news of her pregnancy:

Aline: There was a student midwife in the AN Ward. She read my notes which (I think) said that I was devastated. The student asked how I was feeling and held my hand. She was unable find the baby's heart and so she got the sister. Sister bounced in saying 'What a lovely surprise' and wasn't I pleased? The student pointed to some comment in the notes, Sister looked aghast, found the baby's heart and left quickly.

Some may find reassurance in the fact that such potentially damaging cockups are not unique to the UK health care system. The 'awkward moments' encountered by grieving mothers in USA include ordinarily innocuous questions such as 'What did you have?' from casual acquaintances or mothers in the maternity unit (Benfield et al., 1976). More serious incidents are attributable to failures in health care, such as an obstetrician enquiring after a stillborn baby. Like Benfield's latter example, many cockups are due to a failure of communication about the mother's special circumstances, individual needs and plans:

> Jessica: [Andrew] was in my arms for about an hour. There was some kind of mix up, because when my parents came in at night he had been brought out to me again. By that time I had been put in a side room by myself. I had him that night and I was quite happy with myself. The next day the nurses said that was it! I couldn't have any more contact! Then one of the midwives said to me 'That bond hasn't got to be there. You can't bond. You can't see him any more'.

> Anthea: They wouldn't tell me where Andrea and Andrew were going [to be adopted], of course. I didn't even know they were going to [another continent]. One of the wee nurses who was in the Home let it slip that it was an [overseas] couple who were wanting them.

> Elena: [At the birth] they wrapped him up and cleaned him the way they do. They handed him to me - which surprised me because I thought if they know I'm on the adoption file ... but maybe they didn't. I thought 'Surely they wouldn't do that so that you couldn't form a bond'. I was very surprised.

These data show that communication may be faulty, with the potential for harm to the mother. In the next section I consider the benefits as well as the problems associated with communication.

Talking and listening

The term 'communication' refers to a wide range of activities which have been explained in the form of a continuum (Macleod Clark & Bridge, 1981). Purely factual information lies at one end of the continuum which extends, through support and reassurance, to the sharing of emotions and feelings at the opposite extreme. Although the significance of factual information should not be underestimated, as the examples of cockups given above indicate, the more human aspects of communication feature crucially in the care of the grieving mother. These aspects complicate communication to an extent which may not be apparent in the continuum analogy.

Communication is fundamental to an effective healing and/or caring relationship (Hockey, 1984). It is by listening, talking and using body language that we share the anxieties of those for whom we care (McCorkle, 1974). Although some may assume that communication is little more than speaking, its intricate nature means that carers are not automatically competent in this task. This is associated with the complexity of aspects of the carer's personality being reflected in a similar complexity in the client/patient (Candlin, 1992). Thus, when communicating we need to take account of the mother's wider concerns, such as her cultural environment which, when she is in hospital, is alien. In order to communicate effectively we must 'enter the world of the client' if she is to 'enter the consciousness of the carer' (Candlin, 1992); this is a basic requirement if the relationship is to be genuinely therapeutic.

Although 'talking to patients' has in the past been viewed by our nursing colleagues as a 'pleasant optional extra which does not contribute directly to the patient's well-being or rate of recovery' (Macleod Clark & Bridge, 1981), even for some midwives it is still accorded little importance:

> Amy: Anything I'd do for this woman? Just talking to her ...

Many of the midwives, though, viewed seriously the need for the mother to have space to articulate her feelings, particularly about her relinquishment decision:

> Hilary: She'll wonder whether she is doing the right thing to give her baby up for adoption. We would give her the opportunity to talk about her decision. We would help her to talk it through.

> Ottily: I felt that I was able to help [that mother] with her decision about giving her baby for adoption. Mainly by listening to her talking about it. These women do need opportunities to talk about the adoption.

A mother who gave birth recently reported her satisfaction with her opportunities for communication:

> Aline: The nurses there were good. They gave me lots of time. Two of them stayed with me and we talked for at least ten minutes each. They were staff nurses - Lee and Shona. Awful nice.

The comments by the midwives and mother suggest that the pattern of communication is balanced, rather than dominated by the carer.

Pitfalls

Certain problems with communication for both mother and midwife, were identified during my recent study.

Watching what you say: The first problem related to two points mentioned already in this chapter. The usual assumption is that maternity is an invariably happy area. Thus, difficulty may arise for staff when faced with grief. Additionally, anxiety about a verbal cockup may inhibit the midwife from saying anything meaningful to the mother:

> Josie: If they've already decided that the baby is going for adoption it is sometimes very difficult. You've got to keep remembering not to keep saying 'Your going to have a happy little bundle at the end of it and you'll look forward to looking after it'. Things like that, you've got to watch ...

> Valery: Right away, when you walk into the room, your approach is different. Normally it's 'Good morning' and you're cheerful and everything like that. So even your approach is different - you can't be like that. I just chat about anything normally, whereas I have to watch that I don't say anything silly ... you have to watch what you say. Because I have to watch what I say, I'm a bit more nervous.

The strategies which midwives ordinarily use to encourage a mother in labour or to establish a rapport postnatally are thought inappropriate for a relinquishing mother. The anxiety thus engendered is unlikely to facilitate the relationship with the mother.

Finding the opportunity: Because of the demands of their work, the midwives told me, finding time and opportunities to be with a grieving mother could be problematical:

> Carrie: At times you physically just don't have the amount of time you would like to spend with the woman. There are some times in the ward when it is just so busy you don't - you can't, no matter how much you want to, you can't give this woman the sort of time that you would like to give her. So I suppose you are not grieving as you would like to with her, or show that you going through the emotions with her.

Further, although the midwife might be able to identify a suitable time in her work schedule to spend with a grieving mother, this allocated time might not coincide with when the mother felt ready to 'open up'. For Elena an opportunity was ruined by the intrusion of her Mother:

> Elena: The midwife visited me at home. I wanted to open up to her to tell her how I really felt, but my Mother walked in at just the wrong moment.

Clearly, the carer takes the opportunities which present themselves to encourage the mother to articulate her feelings. It may be possible for the carer to make opportunities by bringing the topic into the open by using phrases such as 'I am sorry about ...'. In this way 'open awareness' (Glaser & Strauss, 1965) may be deliberately employed.

Defence mechanisms: The stress engendered in the carer by the involvement necessary for genuinely effective communication (see above) should not be underestimated (Candlin, 1992). The carer's fear of such emotional involvement with those for whom she cares has been identified as resulting in a number of defensive strategies (Menzies, 1969). These strategies, intended to protect the carer from anxiety, serve largely to dehumanise and devalue the care provided:

Francesca: I tried to talk to the midwife with me in the labour room, but I only got 'Yes, yes, yes' before she zoomed out.

Lena: The staff told you about your stitches being sore and things like that, but they didn't tell you a lot.

Marcia: (The midwives) never said anything, just push or whatever.

Nadia: The staff in the hospital were all kind, but they did not talk to me. I would have liked someone unconnected with the adoption to listen to me.

Stress engendered in staff by perinatal loss, was formerly 'dealt with' using defence mechanisms, such as those identified by Cooper (1980) in her research on the care of parents of a stillborn baby. The mothers felt they had been 'falsely reassured and not listened to seriously'. Attempts are now made to resolve the stress more healthily by talking about it openly (Mander, 1994).

Distancing herself

Some of the mothers recounted their reluctance to confide in members of staff. This tended to be more due to the conviction that nothing would be gained from sharing her sorrow, rather than the existence of a wide and supportive circle of alternative confidantes.

Pamela: I did not really want to talk to the nurses.

Quelia: I didn't really talk to the staff. [Relinquishment] was a decision that I'd made myself. I'd decided that I was going to give her up and I just felt 'No-one else knows me as well as I know myself'. I couldn't really relate to any of the staff.

Vera: The staff never discussed anything about the adoption with me. I think I may not have encouraged people to talk. I was very shy and withdrawn. I think it was because I had such a strict upbringing. I think that I probably would have opened up to the staff with a little encouragement.

Perhaps carers should take note of the need for 'a little encouragement' to which Vera refers. Although being encouraging without being intrusive begs the question of how to encourage this mother to open up?

Conclusion

In this chapter I have shown that the effectiveness of the care of the relinquishing mother hinges on her relationship with her carers. Fundamental to this relationship is the ability of both to communicate. The midwife should be able to communicate her continuing availability to and support for the mother. The mother needs opportunities to voice her need for help, support and the chance to share her feelings. Alternatively, the mother's wish for independence may predominate, albeit with the midwife being present in the background to act as a safety net in the event of sorrow becoming overwhelming. Swanson's theory (1991) of caring perinatally includes these aspects of care. She summarises care in terms of '(i) Knowing, (ii) being with, (iii) doing for, (iv) enabling and (v) maintaining belief'; the first, fourth and fifth concepts equate with the care needs identified in my recent study.

An intervention which has been introduced to assist mothers to articulate their hopes and expectations of their birth experience (Crooke & Smith, 1988) and which may be relevant for relinquishing mothers are 'birth plans'. The pioneering work by Simkin and Reinke (1980) in Seattle focussed largely on communication with carers in drawing up the birth plan; flexibility also featured prominently, as in subsequent work. There is also a tendency for those writing about birth plans to dismiss, at length, traditionally negative views of mothers utilising birth plans (Crooke & Smith, 1988; Swinnerton, 1990), including reference to over-demanding natural birthers with middle class values.

A report of a survey of birth plans in Huddersfield (Jackson, 1986) suggests that women may actually seek interventions such as pubic/perineal shaving. Kitzinger (1992) perceives such requests (episiotomy in her example) as opportunities for carers to probe the reason behind the request and to educate the mother about the value of such interventions.

According to Kitzinger (1992) birth plans improve continuity of care, particularly when continuity of carer is uncertain. She also links their use with increasing the mother's control over her birth experience through increasing her input into decision-making. The relinquishing mother's contribution to decision-making is limited (See Chapter 13), but it is necessary to consider whether a birth plan would, through her increased involvement, facilitate her empowerment.

It may be that like 'choice' in the early 1990s (Mander 1993c), 'empowerment' is in danger of becoming a shibboleth of political correctness. Skelton (1994) reminds us of the need, in view of empowerment's political connotations, to handle this word with care. It is particularly necessary to take account of the wide-ranging implications of empowerment, and for carers to remember that this concept does not merely apply to the service which they provide.

Despite Skelton's timely warning, empowerment is a valuable concept in the care of the mothers I have been describing as 'vulnerable' and who might equally be said to be 'disempowered'. By using a birth plan, the relinquishing mother is more likely to be assisted in communicating her perception of the situation in which she finds herself and become able to resolve, with carers' help, the dilemmas which face her. That making someone 'able' is the original meaning of 'empowerment (Gibson, 1991), reflects its relevance in this context. In her analysis of this concept Gibson (1991), like Skelton (1994), reminds us of the serious implications of changing the traditional balance of power in health care which empowerment involves. She contemplates the likely consequences for carers as well as for clients. Particularly significant are the implications of empowerment for the interaction between the carer and the client; this will certainly be changed and, hopefully, improved.

It may, however, be that some clients are unable or unwilling to assume the responsibilities which empowerment carries with it; the option to reject it is a basic characteristic of empowerment.

A birth plan used by relinquishing mothers in USA is discussed and illustrated by Lindsay and Monserrat (1989). While some of the issues raised are clearly inappropriate to the UK health care system, such as medical involvement in deciding the mother's accommodation, the general principle is shown to be applicable. These authors emphasise the importance of the birth plan being drawn up well in advance of the due date. They also remind us of the need for interdisciplinary cooperation in the preparation of this document, a point brought out in my recent research (See Chapter 5.). Their account endorses the flexibility which is crucial to drawing up a birth plan (Simkin & Reinke, 1980), and becomes even more significant in the context of the relinquishment decision. Of fundamental importance is the mother's understanding of her role in decisions about her baby and, primarily, her realisation that her baby is hers until the legal process is complete (Lindsay & Monserrat, 1989). It may be through this realisation that a birth plan serves to empower the relinquishing mother.

16 Conclusion

Looking back on my own, what appears now, risky teenage behaviour I recognise that the behaviour of others must have been even riskier. Did luck play a part in their misfortune or my good fortune? Ignorance may be blamed, as it is by some of the mothers I recently interviewed. My staunch Church of England background may be given the credit, but this has much in common with those whose story I tell and whose experience is very different. Repeatedly while listening to each of the relinquishing mothers, I experienced a feeling of **deja vu** due, I believe, to a common experience of adolescence, common family values and common family orientation and inhibitions. I am left with the question of what it is that results in me researching this subject while she is still trying to recover from it?

This research project is significant for a number of reasons. It shows us that the care of one vulnerable mother has many aspects in common with the care of other vulnerable mothers, even though her vulnerability may originate quite differently. The care of the vulnerable mother is the benchmark which we should use inform our thinking about mothers who appear more fortunate; it should set a standard to ensure that their care is of an equivalent quality.

That I was able to largely complete this study shows that highly sensitive topics are researchable. Thus, I have shown that what may be thought to be a 'no go' area for researchers is no such thing. It may be that those who thought so need to revise their ideas.

My recent study has demonstrated the irrelevance of stereotypes in the context of relinquishment. Although I am very conscious of the volunteer nature of my sample, the mothers particularly, and the midwives to a lesser extent, comprise quite heterogeneous groups. Although I make no claims to generaliseability, the sample of relinquishing mothers is different from the narrow range which might ordinarily be expected to join self-help groups. Equally, this research has shown that these mothers' relinquishment did not result from 'chip shop wall' conceptions (Cameron, 1989).

I have shown the double standards and paternalism operated in applying secrecy by those intended to provide care. The danger exists that such attitudes may be counterproductive to resolution of the mother's grief. The relevance of the imbalance of power in this mother's care begins to emerge, as do her attempts to assume control.

The equivalence of grieving loss through death and loss through relinquishment is clearly established. The possibility of the reappearance of the relinquished one serves to impede, by delaying or prolonging, the mother's grief.

I have illustrated the huge contribution of the family to the relinquishment process. The mother's parents' marked input contrasts with the less significant, though often ongoing, role of the baby's father. The comparative powerlessness of the mother reappears, set against the often compulsorily united front of her family.

The complexity of recognising or self-diagnosing pregnancy emerged. I have suggested that the mother's diagnosis is not assisted by health care providers. Carers' diagnostic skills are shown not to be infallible.

I have demonstrated the significance of the relinquishing mother's search in practical as well as psychological terms. The mother's relative powerlessness is manifested in relation to the unhelpfulness of the legislative framework governing contact. The impact of a thwarted search on the mother's grieving has been considered.

The mother's feelings of weakness and vulnerability when wanting to be strong have been shown to reduce her perception of control. I have identified strategies used by the mother and others to imply her control. The ability to cope with negative value judgements, through the hierarchy of badness, has emerged.

Certain communicative strategies by carers and others have been shown to be unhelpful to the mother's grieving. These strategies operate by limiting her scope for her expression of her grief and may be used to protect the carer from potentially painful involvement.

I have traced the development of the relinquishing mother's affectionate feelings for her baby through her words and those of her carers. The pressure on the mother not to see her baby and then to relinquish has been shown to have changed. Midwives report a marked reluctance to advise the mother about contact, but the case study suggests that the direction of pressure relating to contact has been reversed. This reversal may be associated with the changing views and increasing stigma relating to adoption (Howe et al., 1992). The implications for grief and relinquishment are not yet clear.

My recent study has shown that the mother's decision-making both in terms of the outcome of her pregnancy and her care is strongly influenced by those around her, if and when she is offered any opportunity to be involved in decision-making.

I have contrasted the long-term implications of relinquishment for the mother's relationships and childbearing with the expectation of the transitory nature of relinquishment. Also, the long-term effects of relinquishment have been contrasted with the pressure on her to regard it as a short-term event. These contrasts lead to the question of whether adoption is a solution with unknown long-term implications to a relatively short-term problem?

The ability of carers to help the relinquishing mother is a function of their ability to communicate with her. Effective communication, in this context, demands a degree of involvement beyond everyday talking and listening, requiring the carer to 'enter the world of the client' (Candlin, 1992). Communication with the relinquishing mother is likely to be facilitated by the use of a birth plan. In this way her care is more likely to meet her needs and she is able to assume control over her situation and become empowered.

This study has demonstrated the disempowerment of the relinquishing mother and her vulnerability to a variety of influences. These influences are variable in nature and inconsistent in direction, and may not benefit the mother on a long-term basis. Strategies for changing her disempowered status have been suggested.

The assumption of power by those caring for the relinquishing mother has been described as 'seductive' (Triseliotis, 1989). This study has demonstrated the existence of an imbalance in the power relationship between this mother and her carers. The implications of this imbalance on her grief and recovery from her loss are immense (Cushman, 1993). It may be that the relinquishment of power by her professional and other carers is overdue.

References

Aamodt, AM (1982), 'Examining Ethnography for Nurse Researchers' *Western Journal of Nursing Research*, vol. 4, No. 2, pp. 209-21.

Abdella, FG & Levine, E, (1986), *Better Patient Care through Nursing Research* 3rd Edn , Macmillan, New York.

Altschul, A & Sinclair, HC, (1981), *Psychology for Nurses*, 5th Edn, Bailliere Tindall, London.

Anderson, H., Sharley, A & Condon, J, (1986), 'A Total Eclipse of the Heart' *Women's Health in a Changing Society*, Australian National Conference.

Antle May, K, (1989), 'Interview Techniques in Qualitative Research: Concerns and Challenges' in Morse, JN, *Qualitative Nursing Research: A Contemporary Dialogue*, Aspen, Rockville Maryland.

Baggaley, S, (1993), *Personal Communication.*

Bailey, FG, (1991), *The Prevalence of Deceit* Cornell UP London.

Ball, JA, (1993), 'Physiology, Psychology and Management of the Puerperium' in Bennett, VR & Brown, LK *Myles Textbook for Midwives* Churchill Livingstone, Edinburgh.

Barth, RP, (1987), 'Adolescent Mothers' Beliefs about Open Adoption', *Social Casework*, June pp. 323-31.

Beauchamp, TL, & Childress, JF, (1989), *Principles of Biomedical Ethics*, 3rd Edn Oxford UP.

Becker, H, (1970), *Sociological Work: Method and Substance*, Aldine, Chicago.

Benet, MK, (1976), *The Politics of Adoption*, Free Press, New York.

Benfield, DG, Leib, SA & Reuter, J, (1976), 'Grief Responses of parents after referral of the critically ill newborn to a regional center', *New England Journal of Medicine*, 294, pp. 975-78.

Benfield, DG, Leib, SA & Vollman, JH, (1978), 'Grief Response of parents to Neonatal Death and Parent Participation in Deciding Care', *Pediatrics*, Vol. 62, No. 2, Aug, pp. 171-6.

Bennett, VR & Brown, LK, (1993), *Myles Textbook for Midwives*, Churchill Livingstone, Edinburgh.

Bernstein, R, (1966), 'Are We Still Stereotyping the Unmarried Mother?' in Roberts, RW, *The Unwed Mother*, Harper & Row, New York.

Blanton, TL & Deschner, J, (1990), 'Biological Mothers' Grief: The Postadoptive Experience in Open Versus Confidential Adoption', *Child Welfare* Vol. LXIX, No. 6, Nov-Dec, pp. 525-35.

Bluford, R Jr & Peters, RE, (1973), *Unwanted Pregnancy*, Harper & Row New York.

Bogdan, RC & Biklen, SK, (1982), *Qualitative Research for Education: An introduction to theory and methods*, Allyn & Bacon, Boston.

Bok, S, (1984), *Secrets: On the Ethics of Concealment* Oxford UP.

Bond, M, (1986), *Stress and Self-Awareness: A guide for nurses*, Heinemann, London.

Borg, S & Lasker, J, (1982), *When Pregnancy Fails*, Routledge Kegan Paul, London.

Bouchier, P., Lambert, L & Triseliotis, J, (1991), *Parting with a child for Adoption: the mother's perspective*, British Agencies for Adoption and Fostering Discussion Series No. 14, London.

Bourne, S & Lewis, E, (1984), 'Pregnancy after Stillbirth or Neonatal Death' *Lancet*, July 7:2 pp. 31-33.

Bowlby, J, (1958), 'The Nature of the Child's Tie to his Mother' *International Journal of Psychoanalysis*, Vol. 30, p. 350.

Bowlby, J, (1961), 'Processes of Mourning', *International Journal of Psycho Analysis*, Vol. 44, p317.

Bowlby, J, (1969), *Attachment and Loss Volume 1: Attachment*, Hogarth, London.

Bowlby, J, (1977), 'The Making and Breaking of Affectional Bonds I & II', *British Journal of Psychiatry*, Vol. 130, pp. 201-10 & 421-31.

Bowlby, J, (1979), *The Making and Breaking of Affectional Bonds*, Tavistock, London.

Bowlby, J, (1980), *Attachment and loss Vol. 3 Loss, Sadness and Despair*, Basic Books, New York.

Bradley, JC & Edinberg, MA, (1982), *Communication in the Nursing Context*, Appleton Century Crofts, New York.

Brady-Fryer, B, (1994), 'Becoming the Mother of a Preterm Baby Chapter 6 in Field, PA & Marck, PB *Uncertain Motherhood: Negotiating the Risks of the Childbearing Years*, Sage, London.

Brazell, K, (1960), *The Confessions of Lady Nijo*, Doubleday, New York.

Brazelton, TB, (1963), 'The Early Mother-Infant Adjustment', *Pediatrics*, Vol. 32, p. 931.

Brazelton, TB, (1973), *Neonatal Behavioral Assessment Scale*, SIMP, London.

Breakwell, GM, (1993), 'Psychological and Social Characteristics of Teenagers who have Children', Chapter 8 in Lawson, AL & Rhode, DL, *The Politics of Pregnancy: Adolescent Sexuality and Public Policy*, Yale UP.

Bretherton, I, (1987), 'New Perspectives on Attachment Relations', in Osophsky, JD, (Ed), *Handbook of Infant Development*, Wiley, New York.

Bromley, DB, (1986), *The Case-Study Method in Psychology and Related Discplines*, Wiley, Chichester.

Bronfenbrenner, U, (1961), 'Some Familial Antecedents of Responsibility and Leadership in Adolescents', in Petrullo, L & Boss, BM, *Leadership and Interpersonal Behavior*, Rinehart & Winston, New York.

Brown, Y, (1992), 'The Crisis of Pregnancy Loss: A team approach to Support', *Birth*, 19:2 June, pp. 82-9.

Buckland, A, (1989), *Personal Communication.*

Burgess, RG, (1982), 'Elements of Sampling in Field Research', in Burgess, RG, *Field Research: A Source book and field manual*, Allen & Unwin, London.

Burnell, GM & Norfleet, MA, (1979), 'Women Who Place Their Infant Up for Adoption: A Pilot Study', *Patient Counselling and Health Education*, Summer/Fall, pp. 169-72.

Cain, AC & Cain, BS, (1964), 'On Replacing a Child', *Journal of the American Academy of Child Psychiatry*, 3, pp. 433-56.

Cameron, JU, (1989), *Personal Communication.*

Campbell, DT & Stanley, JC, (1963), *Experimental and Quasi Experimental Designs for Research*, Rand McNally, Chicago.

Campbell, E, (1985), *The Childless Marriage*, Tavistock, London.

Candlin, S, (1992), 'Communication for Nurses: Implications for Nurse Education', *Nurse Education Today*, Vol. 12, No. 6, December, pp. 445-51.

Caplan, G, (1961), *An approach to Community Mental Health*, Tavistock, London.

Chambers, (1981), *Chambers Twentieth Century Dictionary*, Ed MacDonald, AM, W & R Chambers, Edinburgh.

Chaney, PS, (1981), *Dealing with Death and Dying: Nursing Skillbook*, Intermed Communications Ltd, Horsham pennsylvania.

Clark, GT, (1991), 'To the Edge of Existence: Living through grief', *Phenomenology and Pedagogy*, Fall Issue.

Clulow, C & Vincent, C (1987), *In the Child's best Interests*, Tavistock, London.

Cole, ES, (1984), 'Societal Influences in Adoption Practice', in Sachdev, P, *Adoption: Current Issues and Trends*, Butterworths, Toronto.

Connolly, M, (1987), 'The Experience of Living with an Absent Child', *Phenomenology and Pedagogy*, Vol. 5, No. 2, pp. 157-72.

Connor, S (1994), Denial, Acceptance and Other Myths in Corless, IB, Germinobb & Pittman, M, *Dying Death and Bereavement: Theoretical Perspectives and Other Ways of Knowing*, Jones & Bartlett, London.

Cook, AS & Oltjenbruns, KA, (1989), *Dying and Grieving: Lifespan and Family Perspectives*, Holt Rhinehart & Winston, New York.

Cooper, JD, (1980), 'Parental Reactions to Stillbirth', *British Journal of Social Work*, 10, pp. 55-69.

Corbett, M-A & Meyer, JH, (1987), *The Adolescent and Pregnancy*, Blackwell Scientific, Boston.

Costigan, BH, (1964), 'The Unmarried Mother: Her Decision Regarding Adoption', University of Southern California DSW Au Doctoral Dissertation in *Social Services Review*, Vol. 39, p. 346.

Craig, Y, (1977), 'The Bereavement of Parents and their Search for Meaning', *British Journal of Social Work*, Vol. 7, No. 1, pp. 41-54.

Crisham (1985), cited in Scott, RS, (1985), 'When it isn't Life or Death', *American Journal of Nursing*, Vol. 85, No. 1, pp. 19-20.

Crooke, IL & Smith, VA, (1988), 'Birth Plans', *Maternal and Child Health*, May, pp. 116-21.

Cullberg, J, (1971), 'Mental Reactions of Women to Perinatal Death', in *Proceedings of the Third Congress of Psychosomatic Medicine in Obstetrics and Gynaecology, Basel*, Karger, London.

Cunningham, DJ, (1977), 'Stigma and Social Isolation', HSRU Report no. 27 University of Kent.

Cushman, LF, Kalmuss, D & Namerow, PB, (1993), 'Placing an Infant for Adoption: The Experiences of Young Birthmothers', *Social Work*, Vol. 38, No. 3 May pp. 264-72.

David, HP & Baldwin, WH (1979), 'Childbearing and Child Development: Demographic and Psychosocial Trends', *American Psychologist*, Vol. 34, pp. 866-71.

David, HP., Dytrich, Z., Matejcek, Z & Schuller, V, (1988), *Born Unwanted: Developmental Effects of Denied Abortion*, Springer, New York.

Davidson, G, (1977), 'Death of the Wished-For Child: A case study', *Death Education*, Vol 1, p. 265.

Davis, DL, Stewart, M & Harmon, RJ, (1988), 'Perinatal loss: Providing Emotional Support for Bereaved Parents', *Birth*, 15:4 Dec, pp. 742-6.

Denzin, N, (1970), *The Research Act in Sociology: A Theoretical introduction to Sociological Methods*, Butterworths, London.

Deutsch, H, (1945), *The Psychology of Women Vol. 2 Motherhood*, Grune & Stratton, New York.

Devaney, SW & Lavery, SF, (1980), 'Nursing Care for the Relinquishing Mother', *Journal of Obstetrical, Gynecological and Neonatal Nursing* Nov/Dec, pp. 275-8.

Dickinson, J, (1988a), 'Hitting on a Successful Remix for a Family', *The Guardian* July 20.

Dickinson, J, (1988b), 'Performing Miracles for a Silent Child', *The Guardian* July 22.

Diesing, P, (1972), *Patterns of Discovery in the Social Sciences* London, Routledge Kegan Paul.

Dingwall, R, (1977), *Aspects of Illness*, Martin Robertson, London.

Dixon, M, (1988), 'Multiple Births (Letter)', *Midwives Chronicle*, Vol. 101, No. 1206, July, p. 210.

Dohrenwend, BP & Dohrenwend, BS, (1974), *Stressful Life Events their Nature and Effects*, Wiley, New York.

Douglas, J, (1991), 'Fight for life', *Nursing Times*, Jan 23, Vol. 87, No. 4, pp. 36-8.

Dukette, R, (1979), 'Adoption: Sleeping Beauty Awakes', *Social Thought*, Vol. 5 Fall.

Dukette, R, (1984), 'Value Issues in Present Day Adoption' *Child Welfare*, Vol. 63, No. 3, May/Jun, pp. 233-43.

Elbourne, D, (1987), 'Subjects' views about participation in a randomised controlled trial', *Journal of Reproductive & Infant Psychology*, Vol. 5, No. 1, Jan-Mar, pp. 3-8.

Engel, GL, (1961), 'Is Grief a Disease?', *Psychosomatic Medicine*, Vol. 23, No. 1, pp. 18-22.

Enkin, M, (1982), 'Antenatal Classes', IN Enkin, M & Chalmers, I (Eds), *Effectiveness and Satisfaction in Antenatal Care*, SIMP, London.

Etchells, A, (1990), 'Money Matters', *Nursing Times*, Jan 31, Vol. 86, No. 5 Cover.

Farrar, P, (1993), *The Crisis of Surrender: The Role of Professionals*, Paper presented at The Royal Women's Hospital Brisbane, Seminar on 'Women in Crisis: The Role of Professional Carers'.

Faulkner, A, (1984), *Recent Advances in nursing: Communication*, Churchill Livingstone, Edinburgh.

Field, PA & Morse, JM, (1987), *Nursing Research: The application of Qualitative Approaches*, Croom Helm, London.

Fielding, NG & Lee, RM, (1991), *Using Computers in Qualitative Research*, Sage Publications, London.

Fitsell, A, (1988), *Birth Mothers' Groups at the Post-Adoption Centre*, Post Adoption Centre, London.

Fitsell, A, (1989), 'Relinquishing Mothers Share Experiences', *Adoption and Fostering*, Vol. 13, No. 4, pp. 39-41.

Flint, C, (1986), 'The 'Know Your Midwife' Scheme', *Midwife, Health Visitor & Community Nurse*, Vol. 22, No. 5, pp. 168-9.

Floyd, CC, (1981), 'Pregnancy after Reproductive Failure', *American Journal of Nursing* Vol. 81, pp. 2050-2053.

Fogel, CI, (1981), 'High Risk Pregnancy', in Fogel, CI & Woods, NF, *Health Care of Women: a Nursing Perspective*,Mosby, St Louis.

Forrest, GC, (1983), 'Mourning Perinatal Death', in Davis, JA, Richards, MPM & Robertson, NRC, *Attachment in Premature Infants*, Croom Helm, London.

Forrest, GC, (1989), 'Care of the Bereaved after Perinatal Death', in Chalmers, I., Enkin, M & Keirse, MJNC, *Effective Care in Pregnancy and Childbirth*, Vol. 2, Oxford University Press.

Fox, RC, (1968), 'Illness in SILLS, D, (Ed), *International Encyclopaedia of the Social Sciences*, Free Press/Macmillan, New York.

Franklin, AW, (1954), 'Discussion on Adoption', *Proceedings of Royal Society of Medicine*, Vol. 47, pp. 1044.

Freidson, E, (1971), *Profession of Medicine*, Dodd Mead, New York.

Freilich, M, (1970), *Marginal Natives: Anthropologists at Work*, Harper & Row, New York.

Freud, S, (1917/59), 'Mourning and Melancholia', *Collected Papers*, Basic Books, New York (Originally published in 1917).

Gans, HJ, (1982), 'The Participant Observer as a Human Being: Observations on the Personal Aspects of Fieldwork', in Burgess, RG, *Field Research: A Sourcebook and Field Manual*, George Allen & Unwin, London.

Garber, J & Seligman, MEP, (1980), *Human Helplessness: Theory and Applications*, Academic Press, New York.

Gibson, CH, (1991), 'A Concept Analysis of Empowerment', *Journal of Advanced Nursing*, Vol. 16, pp. 354-36.

Gillon, R, (1986), *Philosophical Medical Ethics*, John Wiley, Chichester.

Glaser, BG & Strauss, AL, (1965), *Awareness of Dying*, Aldine Publishing, Chicago.

Goffman, E, (1963), *Stigma: Notes on the Management of a Spoiled Identity*, Englewood Cliffs, Prentice Hall.

Gohlish, MC, (1985), 'Stillbirth', *Midwife Health Visitor & Community Nurse*, Vol. 21, No. 1, pp. 16.

Golberg, DP, (1972), *The Detection of Psychiatric Illness by Questionnaire*, Maudsley Monograph No. 21, Oxford University Press.

Grace, JT, (1989), 'Development of Maternal-Fetal Attachment During Pregnancy', *Nursing Research*, July/August Vol. 38, No. 4, pp. 228-32.

Green, JM., Coupland, VA & Kitzinger, JV, (1990), 'Expectations, Experiences and Psychological Outcomes of Childbirth: A prospective Study of 825 Women', *Birth*, No. 17, Vol. 1, March, pp. 15-24.

Gross, HE, (1993), 'Open Adoption: A Research-Based Literature Review and New Data', *Child Welfare*, Vol. LXXII, No. 3, May/June, pp. 269-84.

Harlow. HF & Harlow, MK, (1966), 'Learning to Love', *American Scientist*, Vol. 54, No. 3, pp. 244-72.

Harris, J, (1985), *The Value of Life*, Routledge Kegan & Paul, London.

Harris, M, (1968), *The Rise of Anthropological Theory*, Thomas Y Crowell, New York.

Helman, C, (1985), *Culture, Health and Illness: An Introduction for Health Professionals*, Wright, Bristol.

Herbert, M & Sluckin, A, (1985), 'A Realistic Look at Mother-Infant Bonding', in Chiswick, ML (Ed), *Recent Advances in Perinatal Medicine: 2* Churchill Livingstone, Edinburgh.

Herz, F, (1980), 'The Impact of death and Serious Illness on the Family Life Cycle', in Carter, E & McGoldrick, M, (Eds), *The Family Life Cycle* Gardner, New York.

HMSO (1967), *The Abortion Act*, London.

HMSO (1975), *The Children Act*, London.

Hockey, L, (1984), 'Conclusions Chapter 9', in Faulkner, A *Recent Advances in Nursing: No. 7 Communication*, Churchill Livingstone, Edinburgh.

Hoggett, B, (1984), 'Adoption Law: An Overview', in Bean, P, *Adoption Essays in Social Policy Law and Sociology*, Tavistock, London.

Holm, K, (1983), 'Single Subject Research', *Nursing Research*, July/August, Vol. 32, No. 4, pp. 253-5.

Holmes, RH & Rahe, RH, (1967), 'The Social Readjustment Rating Scale', *Journal of Psychosomatic Research*, Vol. 11, pp. 213-8.

Howe, D, (1990), 'The Loss of a Baby', *Midwife, Health Visitor & Community Nurse*, Jan/Feb, Vol. 26, Nos 1 & 2, pp. 25-6.

Howe, D, Sawbridge, P & Hinings, D, (1992), *Half a Million Women: Mothers who lose their Children by Adoption*, Penguin, London.

Hubbard, GL, (1947), 'Who am I?' *The Child*, Vol. 11, No. 8, February, pp. 130-33.

Hughes, P, (1986), *Solitary or Solitude: Views on the Management of Bereaved Mothers*, Unpublished Diploma of Nursing Dissertation University of Wales.

Hughes, P, (1987), The Management of Bereaved Mothers: What is Best? *Midwives Chronicle*, August, Vol. 100, No. 1195, pp. 226-9.

Hurme, (1991), 'Dimensions of the Grandparent Role in Finland', in Smith, PK, (Ed), *The Psychology of Grandparenthood: An International Perspective*, Routledge, London.

Illich, I., Zola, IK., McKnight, J., Caplan, J & Shaiken, H, (1977), *Disabling Professions*, Marion Boyars, London.

Inglis, K, (1984), *Living Mistakes*, Allen & Unwin, Sydney.

Jackson, DD, (1986), 'It took Trains ... *Smithsonian*, Vol. 17, pp. 94-103.

Jackson, P, (1986), 'The Huddersfield Birth Plan', *Maternal & Child Health*, January, pp. 16-17.

Jaffe, ED, (1982), *Child Welfare in Israel*, Praeger, New York.

Jameton, A, (1984), *Nursing Practice: The Ethical Issues*, Prentice Hall. Englewood Cliffs NJ.

Janis, IL & Mann, L, (1977), *Decision-Making: A Psychological Analysis of conflict Choice and Commitment*, The Free Press, New York.

Jick, TD, (1983), 'Mixing Qualitative and Quantitative Methods: Triangulation in Action', in Van Maanen , J, (Ed), *Qualitative Methodology*, Sage, Beverley Hills.

Jolly, J, (1987), *Missed Beginnings*, Lisa Sainsbury Foundation Series, Austen Cornish, Reading.

Jolly, J, (1989), *Personal Communication.*

Jones, A & Jones, K, (1991), 'Accepting Motherhood', *Nursing Times*, May 15, Vol. 87, no. 20, pp. 56-8.

Jones, A, (1989), 'Managing the Invisible Grief', *Senior Nurse*, May, Vol. 9, No. 5, pp. 26-7.

Jones, WHS, (1926), *The Doctor's Oath: An essay in the History of Medicine*, Cambridge UP, Cambridge Mass.

Kallmuss, D, Namerow, PB & Bauer, U, (1992), 'Short Term Consequences of Parenting Versus Adoption among Unmarried Mothers', *Journal of Marriage and the Family*, Vol. 54, p. 80.

Kargar, I, (1990), 'Special Pregnancies', *Community Outlook*, June, pp. 12-18.

Keen, E, (1975), *A Primer in Phenomenonological Psychology*, University Press of America, Lanham.

Kellner, KR & Lake, M, (1986), 'Grief Counselling', in Knuppel, RA & Drukker, JE, *High Risk Pregnancy*, WB Saunders, Philadelphia.

Kennell, JH, Slyter, H & Klaus, MH, (1970), 'The Mourning Response of Parents to the Death of a Newborn Infant', *New England Jnl Of Medicine*, Vol. 283, No. 7, Aug 13, pp. 344-9.

Kenyon, S, (1985), 'No Grave, No Photograph, No Baby', *Nursing Mirror*, July 17, Vol. 161, No. 3, pp. 521-3.

Kirkham, MJ, (1983), 'Admission in Labour: Teaching the Patient to be Patient?', *Midwives Chronicle*, February, Vol. 96, No. 1141, pp. 44-5.

Kitzinger, S, (1992), 'Birth Plans', *Birth*, Vol. 19, no. 1, March, pp. 36-7.

Kottow, MH, (1986), 'Medical confidentiality: An intransigent and absolute obligation', *Journal of Medical Ethics*, Vol. 12, pp. 117-22.

Kubler-Ross, E, (1970), *On Death and Dying*, Tavistock Publications, London.

Laurence, KM, (1989), 'Sequelae and Support for Termination carried out for Fetal Malformation', IN van Hall, EV & Everaerd, W *The Free Woman: Women's Health in the 1990s*, Parthenon, Carnforth.

Laws, S (1992), 'Its just the Monthlies ...', *Journal of Reproductive and Infant Psychology, Vol. 10, No. 2, pp. 117-128.*

Lazarus, RS & Folkman, S, (1984), Stress, Appraisal and Coping, Springer, New York.

Lee, R, (1993), *Doing Research on Sensitive Topics*, Sage, London.

Leigh, D, Pare, CMB & Marks, J, (1977), *A Concise Encyclopaedia of Psychiatry*, MTP Press, Lancaster.

Leininger, MM, (1985), *Qualitative Research Methods in Nursing*, Grune & Stratton, Orlando.

Lerum, CW & Lobiondo-Wood, G (1989), 'The Relationship of Maternal Age, Quickening and Physical Symptoms of Pregnancy to the Development of Maternal-Fetal Attachment', *Birth*, Vol. 16, No. 1, pp. 13-17.

Lever, Hense, A, (1994), 'Livebirth following Stillbirth Chapter 5', in Field, PA & Marck, PB *Uncertain Motherhood: Negotiating the Risks of the Childbearing Years*, Sage, London.

Levine, RJ, (1986), *Ethics and Regulation of Clincal Research 2nd Edition*, Urban & Schwarzenberg, Baltimore.

Lewis, E, (1976), 'The Management of Stillbirth: Coping with an Unreality', *Lancet*, Sept 18 pp. 619-20.

Lewis, E, (1979), 'Inhibition of Mourning by Pregnancy: Psychopathology and Management', *British Medical Journal*, July 7, pp. 27-28.

Lindemann, E, (1944), 'Symptomatology and Management of Acute Grief', *American Journal of Psychiatry*, 101, pp. 141-9.

Lindsay, J & Monserrat, C, (1989), *Adoption Awareness: A Guide for Teachers Counselors Nurses and Caring Others*, Morning Glory Press, California.

Lipson, JG, (1989), 'The Use of Self in Ethnographic Research Chapter 5', in Morse, JM, *Qualitative Nursing Research: A Contemporary Dialogue*, Aspen, Rockville.

Littlewood, J, (1992), *Aspects of Grief: Bereavement in Adult Life*, Tavistock/Routledge, London.

Lobiondo-Wood, G & Haber, J, (1986), *Nursing research: Critical appraisal and utilisation*, Mosby, St Louis.

Lovell, A, (1983), 'Women's Reactions to Late Miscarriage, Stillbirth and Perinatal Death', *Health Visitor*, Sept, Vol. 56, pp. 325-7.

Lovell, A, (1984), *A Bereavement with a Difference: A study of late miscarriage, stillbirth and perinatal death*, Polytechnic of the South Bank Sociology Department Occasional Paper 4.

Lovell, H, Bokoul, AC, Shoba, M & Speight, N, (1986), 'Mothers' reactions to a Perinatal Death', *Nursing Times*, November 12, Vol. 82, No. 46, pp. 40-42.

Lugton, J, (1989), *Communicating with Dying People and their Relatives*, Austen Cornish & Lisa Sainsbury Foundation, London.

Lumley, J, (1990), 'Through a glass darkly: Ultrasound and prenatal bonding', *Birth*, Vol. 17, No. 4, Dec, pp. 214-7.

MacIntyre, S, (1975), *Decision-making processes following premarital conception*, Unpublished PhD Thesis, University of Glasgow.

MacIntyre, S, (1977), *Single and Pregnant*, Croom Helm, London.

MacLeod Clark, J & Bridge, W, (1981), 'Postscript Ch 10', in Bridge, W & MacLeod Clark, J, *Communication in Nursing Care*, HM&M, London.

Mallinson, G, (1989), 'Life Crises; When a Baby Dies', *Nursing Times* March 1, 85:9, pp. 31-4.

Mander, R, (1992a), 'Research Report: Midwives' care of the relinquishing mother', *The Iolanthe Trust*, London.

Mander, R, (1992b), 'Seeking approval for Research Access: The gate-keepers' role in facilitating a study of the care of the relinquishing mother', *Journal of Advanced Nursing*, December, Vol. 17, No. 12, pp. 1460-64.

Mander, R, (1992c), 'See how they Learn: Experience as the basis of Practice', *Nurse Education Today*, February, Vol. 12, pp. 11-18.

Mander, R, (1993a), "Who chooses the choices?" *Modern Midwife* January/February, Vol. 3, No. 1, pp. 23-25.

Mander, R, (1993b), 'Autonomy in midwifery and maternity care', *Midwives Chronicle*, October, Vol. 106, No. 1269, pp. 369-74.

Mander, R, (1994), *Loss and Bereavement in Childbearing*, Blackwell Scientific, Oxford.

Marck, PB, (1994), 'Unexpected Pregnancy: The uncharted land of women's experience Chapter 3', in Field, PA & Marck, PB, *Uncertain Motherhood: Negotiating the Risks of the Childbearing Years*, Sage, London.

Marck, PB, Field, PA & Bergum, V, (1994), 'A Search for Understanding Chapter 8', in Field, PA & Marck, PB, *Uncertain Motherhood: Negotiating the Risks of the Childbearing Years*, Sage, London.

Marris, P, (1986), *Loss and Change*, Routledge Kegan Paul, London.

Marsh, MJW, (1993), 'An Open Letter to a Diocesan Priest', *Reproductive Health Matters*, No. 2, November, pp. 87-91.

Marshall, C & Rossman, GB, (1989), *Designing Qualitative Research*, Sage, Newbury Park.

Martin, DH, (1985), 'Fathers and Adolescents', in Hanson, SMH & Bezett, FW, *Dimensions of Fatherhood*, Sage, Beverly Hills

McCorkle R, (1974), 'Effects of Touch on Seriously Ill Patients', *Nursing Research*, Vol. 23, No. 2, March-April, pp. 125-32.

McCubbin, HI, (1979), 'Integrating coping behaviour in family stress theory', *Jnl of Marriage and the Family*, Vol. 41, no. 3, pp. 237-44.

McCubbin, HI & Patterson, JM, (1983), 'The Family Stress Process', in McCubbin, HI, Sussman, MB & Patterson, JM, *Social Stress and the Family*, Haworth, New York.

McHaffie, HE, (1991), *A Study of Support for Families with a VLBW Baby*, University of Edinburgh Nursing Research Unit.

McKeown, B, (1988), *Methodology*, Sage Publications, London.

McLaughlan, SD, Manninen, DL & Winges, LD (1987), *The Consequences of the Adoption Decision*, Battelle Human Affairs Research Centre, Seattle.

McNeil, JN, (1986), 'Communicating with Surviving Children', in Rando, T, *Parental Loss of a Child*, Champaign Ill, Research Press.

Mech, EV, (1986), 'Pregnant Adolescents: Communicating the Adoption Option', *Child Welfare*, Vol. 65, No. 6, pp. 555-67.

Melia, KM, (1981), 'Student Nurses' Accounts of their Work and Training: A Qualitative Analysis', *Scottish Home and Health Department Report*, Edinburgh.

Melia, KM, (1988), 'Everyday Ethics for Nurses: To tell or not to tell', *Nursing Times*, July 27, Vol. 84, No. 30, pp. 37-39.

Menzies, IEP, (1969), 'The functioning of social systems as a defence against anxiety', in MacQuire, J, *Threshold to Nursing*, Bell, London.

Midirs, (1988), *Literature Search*, Personal Communication.

Moore, D, (1988), 'Confidentiality: All sewn up', *Senior Nurse*, Vol. 8, No. 6, June, pp. 6-7.

Morrin, H, (1983), 'As Great a Loss..', *Nursing Mirror*, Vol. 156, No. 7, 16 Feb, p. 33.

Morrin, H, (1989), *Personal Communication.*

Morse, JM, Bottorff, J, Anderson, G, O'Brien, B & Solberg, S (1992), 'Beyond Empathy: Expanding Expressions of Caring', Journal of Advanced Nursing, Vol. 17, pp. 809-21.

Munhall, P & Oiler, CJ, (1986), *Nursing Research - A Qualitative Perspective*, Norwalk, Connecticut, Appleton-Century-Crofts.

Munhall, PL, (1989), 'Institutional Review of Qualitative Research Proposals: A task of no small consequence', in Morse, JM, *Qualitative Nursing Research: A Contemporary Dialogue*, Aspen, Rockville.

Mussen, PH, Janeway, J, Kagan, J & Huston, AC, (1990), *Child Personality and Development*, Harper & Row, New York.

Myles, M, (1993), *Myles Textbook for Midwives*, 12th Edition, Eds Bennett, VR & Brown, LK, Churchill Livingstone, Edinburgh.

Nachmias, C & Nachmias, D (1981), *Research Methods in the Social Sciences*, Arnold, London.

Nicholson, J, (1968), *Mother and Baby Homes: A Survey of Homes for Unmarried Mothers*, Allen & Unwin, London.

Oakley, A, (1979), *Becoming a Mother*, Martin Robertson, Oxford.

Oglethorpe, RJL, (1989), 'Parenting after Perinatal Bereavement - A Review of the Literature', *Journal of Reproductive and Infant Psychology*, Vol. 7, No. 4, pp. 227-44.

Oppenheim, AN, (1992), *Questionnaire Design, Interviewing and Attitude Measurement*, Pinter, London.

Osterweis, M, Solomon, F & Green, M, (1984), *Bereavement: reactions Consequences and Care*, National Academy Press, Committee for the Study of the Health Consquences the Stress of Bereavement Washington DC.

Pannor, R, Baran, A & Sorosky, AD (1978), 'Birth Parents who Relinquished Babies for Adoption Revisited', *Family Process*, Vol. 17, No. 3, September, pp. 329-37.

Parkes, CM, (1986), *Bereavement: Studies of Grief in Adult Life*, 2nd Edn, Tavistock, London.

Parry, G, (1990), *Coping with Crises*, BPS & Routledge, Leicester.

Parse, RR, Coyne, AB & Smith, MJ, (1985), *Nursing Research: Qualitative Methods*, Brady Communications, Bowie, Maryland.

Patton, MQ (1980), *Qualitative evaluation methods*, Sage Publications, Beverley Hills.

Penson, JM, (1990), *Bereavement: A Guide for Nurses*, Harper & Row, London.

Peterman, F & Bode, U, (1986), 'Five Coping Styles in Families of Children with Cancer', *Paediatric Haematology and Oncology*, Vol. 3, pp. 299-309.

Quinton, A, (1994), 'Permission to Mourn', *Nursing Times*, March 23, Vol. 90, No. 12, p 31-3.

Rando, TA, (1984), *Grief, Dying and Death: Clinical Interventions for Caregivers*, 'Champaign Ill.', Research Press.

Rando, TA, (1986), 'Individual and Couples Treatment Following the Death of a Child', in Rando, T, *Parental Loss of a Child*, 'Champaign Ill.', Research Press.

Rando, TA, (1986), *Parental Loss of Child*, 'Champaign Ill.', Research Press.

Raphael-Leff, J, (1980), 'Psychotherapy with Pregnant Women', in Blum, BL (Ed), *Psychological Aspects of Pregnancy*, Human Sciences, New York.

Raphael-Leff, J, (1991), *Psychological Processes of Childbearing*, Chapman & Hall, London.

Rappoport, C, (1981), 'Helping Parents When their Newborn Infants Die: Social Work Implications', *Social Work in Health Care*, Spring, Vol. 6, No. 3, pp. 57-67.

Reading, AE, (1989), 'The Measurement of Fetal Attachment over the Course of Pregnancy', in van Hall, EV & Everaerd, W, *The Free Woman: Women's Health in the 1990s*, Parthenon, Carnforth.

Remez, L, (1992), 'Adoption vs. Parenting: Differences in Short Term Effects on Young Mothers', *Family Planning Perspectives*, Vol. 24, No. 5, Sept/Oct, pp. 238-9.

Richards, K, (1970), 'When Biological Mothers meet Adopters', *Child Adoption*, Vol. 60, pp. 27-30.

Richards, MPM, (1982), 'Commentary: The Trouble with 'Choice' in Childbirth', *Birth*, Vol. 9, No. 4, pp. 253-60.

Richmond, JB, (1957), 'Some Psychological Considerations in Adoption Practice', *Pediatrics*, No. 20, pp. 377-82.

Ritchie, CW, (1989), 'The Adoption Option', *American Journal of Nursing*, Vol. 52, no. 7, pp. 1156-7.

Roberts, RW, (1966), *The Unwed Mother*, Harper & Row, New York.

Roll, S., Millen, L & Backlund, B, (1986), 'Solomon's Mothers: Mourning in Mothers who relinquish their Children for Adoption', in Rando, T *Parental Loss of a Child*, Champaign Ill., Research Press.

Rose, X (1990), *Widow's Journey: A Return to Living*, Souvenir Press, London.

Rubin, R, (1970), 'Cognitive style in pregnancy', *American Journal of Nursing*, Vol. 70, p. 502.

Rukholm, EE & Viverais, GA, (1993), 'A Multifactorial Study of Test Anxiety and Coping responses during a Challenge Examination', *Nurse Education Today', Vol. 13, No. 3, April, pp. 91-99.*

Rynearson, EK, (1982), 'Relinquishment and its Maternal Complications: A preliminary study', American Jnl of Psychiatry, Vol. 139, No. 3, March, pp. 338-40.

Sachdev, P, (1984), 'Adoption Outlook: Projection for the Future', in Sachdev, P, (Ed), *Adoption: Current Issues and Trends*, Butterworths, Toronto.

Sachdev, P, (1992), 'Adoption Reunion and After: A Study of the Search Process and experience of Adoptees', *Child Welfare*, Vol LXXI, No. 1, Jan-Feb, pp. 53-68.

Sshaffer, R, (1977), *Mothering: The Developing Child*, Fontana, Glasgow.

Schofield, M, (1972), *The Sexual Behaviour of Young People*, Penguin, Harmondsworth.

Shaw, GB, (1947), *The Doctor's Dilemma: Getting married and the shewing up of Blanco Posnet*, Constable, London.

Shawyer, J, (1979), *Death by Adoption*, Cicada, Auckland.

Silverman, P, (1980), 'The Grief of the Birthmother Chapter 4', in *Helping Women to Cope with Grief: Sage Human Service Guide No. 25*, University Of Michigan School of Social Work.

Silverman, P, (1994), 'Spoiled Idendities Chapter 14', in Corless, IB, Germinobb & Pittman, M, *Dying Death and Bereavement: Theoretical Perspectives and Other Ways of Knowing*, Jones & Bartlett, London.

Simchak, M, (1990), 'Some Girls', *Birth*, Vol. 17, No. 4, December, pp. 242.

Simkin, P & Reinke, C, (1980), *Planning Your Baby's Birth*, Pennypress, Seattle.

Simpson, JA & Weiner, ESC, (1989), *The Oxford English Dictionary 2nd Edn*, Clarendon, Oxford.

Skelton, R, (1994), 'Nursing and Empowerment: Concepts and Strategies', *Journal of Advanced Nursing*, Vol. 19, pp. 415-23.

Skynner, R, (1976), *One Flesh: Separate Persons', Constable, London.*

Sluckin, W., Herbert, M & Slucken, A, (1983), Maternal Bonding, Blackwell, Oxford.

Sorosky, AD., Baran, A & Pannor, R, (1984), *The Adoption Triangle*, Anchor, New York.

Stainton, MC, (1990), 'Parents' Awareness of Their Unborn Infant in the Third Trimester', *Birth*, 17:2, June, pp. 92-6.

Stephenson, J, (1986), 'Grief of Siblings', in Rando, T, *Parental Loss of a Child*, Champaign Ill., Research Press.

Stern, PN, (1980), 'Grounded Theory Methodology: Its Uses and Processes', *Image*, February, Vol. 12, No. 1, pp. 20-23.

Stray-Pedersen, B & Stray-Pedersen, S, (1984), 'Etiologic Factors and subsequent reproductive performance in 195 Couples with a prior history of habitual abortion', *American Journal of Obstetrics and Gynaecology*, Vol. 148, No. 2, pp. 140-6.

Strindberg, A, (1960), *Fadren*, Tr Paulsen, A, ('The Father' in 'Seven Plays'), Bantam, New York.

Stroebe, W & Stroebe, MS, (1987), *Bereavement and Health: The Psychological and Physical Consequences of Partner Loss*, University Press, Cambridge.

Swanson, K, (1991), 'Empirical Development of a Middle Range Theory of Caring', *Nursing Research*, Vol. 40, pp. 161-66.

Sweet, B, (1992), *Bailliere's Midwives' Dictionary*, 8th Edn London, Bailliere Tindall.

Swinnerton, T, (1990), 'The Best Laid Plans ...', *Nursing Times*, June 6, Vol. 86, No. 23, pp. 70-71.

Teasdale, K, (1989), 'The Concept of Reassurance in Nursing', *Journal of Advanced Nursing*, Vol. 14, pp. 444-50.

Tennyson, MA, (1988), 'Experiences of a Woman who Intended to Relinquish her Child for Adoption', *Maternal and Child Nursing Journal*, Vol. 17, No. 3, pp. 139-45.

Thompson, JE & Thompson, HO, (1985), *Bioethical Decision Making for Nurses*, Appleton-Century-Crofts, Connecticut.

Thompson, J, (1993), 'Supporting Young Mothers', *Nursing Times*, Dec 22/9, Vol. 89, No. 51, pp. 64-7.

Triseliotis, JP, (1970), *Evaluation of Adoption Policy and Practice*, University of Edinburgh.

Triseliotis, JP, (1985), 'Adoption with Contact', *Adoption and Fostering*, Vol. 9, No. 4.

Triseliotis, JP, (1988), *Personal Communication*.

Triseliotis, JP, (1989), 'Some Moral and Practical Issues in Adoption Work', *Adoption and Fostering*, Vol. 13, No. 2, pp. 21-6.

Troseliotis, JP, (1991), *Adoption Services in Scotland: Recent Research Findings and their Implications*, Scottish Office Central Research Unit Papers, Edinburgh.

Van Maanen, J, (1982), 'Introduction', in Van Maanen, J, Dabb, S & Faulkner, *Varieties of Qualitative Research*, Sage, Beverley Hills.

Veatch, RM, (1989), *Medical Ethics*, Jones & Bartlett, Boston.

von Bertalanffy, L, (1969), *General Systems Theory: Foundations, Developments, Application*, Brazillier, New York.

Wallston, KA & Wallston, BS, (1981), 'Health locus of control scales', in Leefcourt, HM, *Research with the locus of control construct*, Academic Press, New York.

Whyte, DA, (1989), *The Experience of Families caring for a Child with Cystic Fibrosis: A Nursing Response*, Unpublished PhD Thesis University of Edinburgh.

Whyte, DA, (1994), *Family Nursing: The Case of Cystic Fibrosis*, Avebury, Aldershot.

Wilson, H, (1985), *Research in Nursing*, Addison Wesley, California.

Wilson-Barnett, J (1991), 'Gaining access to the Research Site.', in *The Research Process in Nursing', 2nd Edn. Ed Cormack, D, Blackwell Scientific, Oxford.*

Winkler, R & Van Keppel, M, (1984), Relinquishing Mothers in Adoption, Institute of Family Studies Monograph No. 3, Melbourne.

Worden, JW, (1992), *Grief Counselling and Grief Therapy: A Handbook for the Mental Health Practitioner 2nd Edition*, Routledge, London.

Wright, SG, (1990), *My Patient, My Nurse: Primary Nursing in Practice*, Scutari, London.

Yellowly, MA, (1965), 'Factors Relating to the Adoption Decision by the Mothers of Illegitimate Infants', *Sociological Review*, Vol. 13, No. 1, pp. 5-13.

Young, L, (1954), *Out of Wedlock*, McGraw Hill, New York.

Zeanah, CH., Carr, S & Wolk, S, (1990), 'Fetal Movements and the Imagined Baby of Pregnancy: Are They Related?', *Journal of Reproductive and Infant Psychology*, Vol. 8, No. 1, pp. 23-36.

Author index

Subject index